Cognitive Development: A Life-Span View

Life-Span Human Development Series
Series Editors: Freda Rebelsky, Boston University, and Lynn Dorman

Cognitive Development: A Life-Span View

George E. Forman

University of Massachusetts

Irving E. Sigel

Educational Testing Service

BROOKS/COLE PUBLISHING COMPANY
MONTEREY, CALIFORNIA
A Division of Wadsworth, Inc.

Printed in the United States of America

10 9 8 7 6 5 4 3 2 1

Library of Congress Cataloging in Publication Data

Forman, George E   1942–
    Cognitive development.

    Bibliography: p. 191
    Includes index.
    1. Cognition. 2. Developmental psychology.
I. Sigel, Irving E., joint author. II. Title.
BF311.F64   153.4   78-31176
ISBN 0-8185-0275-4

Acquisition Editor: *Todd Lueders*
Production Editor: *Fiorella Ljunggren*
Series Design: *Linda Marcetti*
Cover Illustration: *Jim Pinckney*
Interior Illustrations: *Ann Geiger*
Typesetting: *Typesetting Services of California, Pleasant Hill, California*

Series Foreword

What are the changes we see over the life span? How can we explain them? And how do we account for individual differences? The Life-Span Human Development Series provides a new way to look at these questions. It approaches human development from three major perspectives: (1) a focus on basic issues related to the study of life-span developmental psychology, such as methodology and research design, cross-cultural and longitudinal studies, age-stage phenomena, and stability and change; (2) a focus on age divisions—infancy, early childhood, middle childhood, adolescence, young and middle adulthood, and late adulthood; and (3) a focus on developmental areas such as physiology, cognition, language, perception, sex roles, and personality.

There is some overlap in the content of these volumes. We believe that it will be stimulating to the reader to think the same idea through from the viewpoints of different authors or from the viewpoints of different areas of development. For example, language development is the subject of one volume and is also discussed in the volume on cross-cultural development, among others.

Instructors and students may use the entire series for a thorough survey of life-span developmental psychology or, since each volume can be used independently, may choose selected volumes to cover specific concept areas or age ranges. Volumes that focus on basic issues can be used to introduce the student to the life-span concept.

No single author could adequately cover the entire field as we have defined it. Our authors found it exciting to focus on their areas of specialization within a limited space while, at the same time, expanding their thinking to encompass the entire life span. It can be beneficial to both author and student to attempt a new integration of familiar material. Since we think it also benefits students to see ideas in development, we encouraged the authors not only to review the relevant literature but also to use what they now know to point up possible new areas of study. As a result, the student will learn to think about human development rather than just learn the facts of development.

Freda Rebelsky

Lynn Dorman

Preface

As its title indicates, our book covers more than just cognition and less than all aspects of human development. We have written about cognitive development, not just cognition; in fact, the book attempts to cover cognitive development across the entire life span. And we have written about cognitive development, not about all aspects of human development, such as physical, social, esthetic, and language development. Our goal was to achieve a balance between breadth and depth.

All of us think, and we sometimes think about how we think. When we reflect on how we think, we can make some interesting discoveries. For one, we find that our thinking has definite patterns. This book outlines some of these patterns and describes their changes across the life span—how thinking becomes more abstract and more complex and how the individual becomes increasingly better able to discern reality. When we understand these patterns and their changes, we come to understand the "how" of human thought.

Our book devotes many pages to the comparison of different theoretical views of cognitive development. Any theory addresses only certain questions and not others. Some theories are concerned with the experiences that facilitate cognitive development. Others are concerned with a precise description of the nature of cognitive development from one stage to another. Our purpose in offering a broad variety of views is to give you, the reader, the greatest possible choice in deciding which is most useful for you.

This book maintains that cognitive development is a general term that cannot—and should not—be separated arbitrarily from other aspects of human development. Nearly every form of development involves thinking. It seems obvious, for example, that social development requires a parallel development in general cognition. When we see a young child share her toys with her playmates, we know that her advance in social behavior is necessarily accompanied by a parallel advance in the cognitive ability to think about another person's point of view. These parallels are discussed in detail in the chapter on social cognition.

The book also relates research findings to practical problems of education and human services and highlights the everyday significance of such findings. The research on aging provides a helpful tool for expanding our understanding of the elderly and our empathy for them. Most importantly, such research helps us reevaluate our views about old age. An example, which we cite often, is research suggesting that certain responses on the part of the elderly may be due not to regression in their cognitive abilities but to poorly designed assessment procedures.

Our discussion progresses from broad questions to specific topics. We begin by asking why one should study cognitive development in the first place. Then we look at six theories of cognitive development, and, in order to make our discussion as useful as possible, we use one common illustrative task to contrast the different approaches of these theories. Then we discuss, in turn, cognitive processes (memory and attention), cognitive structures (classification, proportionality, correlation, and conservation), basic-knowledge concepts (space, time, and causality), and, finally, cognition as it applies to social objects (social cognition). In other words, our discussion examines and tries to answer the simple but essential questions of how cognition works, what it "looks like," and what it produces.

This book is intended for upper-level undergraduate courses and introductory graduate courses for students in psychology, education, human development, and human services. Because of its life-span perspective, multitheoretical approach, and focus on integration of social and cognitive development, the book can be used in several ways. It can be used as a supplement to a basic life-span or human-development text to emphasize cognitive-developmental issues. It is also appropriate as a basic text for more advanced courses in cognitive and social development in departments of psychology, human development, and education.

Any book is the result of the combined efforts of many individuals. Their respective contributions are both unique and essential. To ensure consistency of style, the text was written by the first author, but the two authors shared equally in the choice of topics, the organization, and the striving for technical accuracy and currency of research. We gratefully acknowledge the invaluable help we received from the series editors, Freda Rebelsky and Lynn Dorman. Our reviewer, Gisela Labouvie-Vief of the Institute of Gerontology, Wayne State University, offered thoughtful and constructive criticism with regard to both specific topics and the book's overall organization and scope. We also thank Jan Thibodeau for her assistance in abstracting research on the elderly. Through his unfailing support, Todd Lueders, Associate Editor at Brooks/Cole, gave us incentive and confidence. Our greatest thanks go, without a doubt, to Fiorella Ljunggren, our production editor, who would not compromise on the meaning of a single sentence, being the consummate professional and friend that she is.

George E. Forman
Irving E. Sigel

Contents

Chapter One

The Study of Cognitive Development

This chapter is designed to introduce you to and—we hope—entice you into the study of cognitive development. The introduction is done by answering three questions; the enticement, by posing the same three questions and challenging you to think about them before they are answered. What is cognition? How does cognition change and develop over a person's life span? Why might the study of cognitive development be important to you?

What Is Cognition?

Common Thoughts about Thinking

Why define the relatively uncommon word *cognition* when defining the common word *thinking* would seem to do the job? Mainly because what people commonly think of thinking leads to an imprecise definition and understanding of a process that is more inclusively defined and better understood by using the term *cognition*. Following are three common attempts at defining thinking that lead us nowhere.

Thinking is a place. "Thinking is what goes on in the brain" is a common (and useless) definition. True, thinking does occur in the brain, but locating the activity tells us very little about the activity itself. That definition eliminates certain other activities, like riding bicycles and digesting food, for these do not occur in the brain. But what about things such as blood circulation, hallucinations, phobias, and pain? Certainly these activities, perceptions, and sensations do go on in the brain. Thus a definition of thinking based on where thinking occurs is an insufficient—worse, a useless—definition.

Thinking is ———— (some other term of similar meaning). "Thinking is reasoning—like reasoning out a problem" is another common attempt to define the term. Of what use is this definition? One word has been substituted for another, and we know no more than we did when we began. This practice of substituting one word for another—a form of circular reasoning—seems clearly a pointless exercise, yet it is used by even the most serious scholars. For example, shortly after Darwin published his work on biological evolution, scientists equated thinking with adaptive behavior. Thus, when a child showed adaptation to his or her environment, that child was said to be thinking. *Thinking* became *adaptation*. But, unless we know what distinguishes adaptive behavior from maladaptive behavior, how can we distinguish thinking from nonthinking? Back to square one.

Thinking is a quantity. "Thinking is something one can measure the effects of, as in the case of solving a problem" is yet another common and idle attempt at a definition. For one thing, it raises the question "What do we measure—increased heartbeat? cortical activity? perspiration? eye movement? the time it takes to solve the problem?"

Actually all of these measures have been tried. And, if one posits that thinking is some kind of measurable quantity, one measure is no better or worse than another as long as what is measured correlates to what we believe good thinkers can do, such as succeed in school. As you might surmise, and as Sigel (1963) has explained, these measures (achieved through so-called "intelligence tests") tell us very little about the working nature of thinking itself. Knowing that one child can solve a problem faster or generates more electricity than another child doesn't help us understand the nature of the thought processes in either child.

Now that we have dispensed with some common attempts at defining thinking, we will shift to the more inclusive term *cognition* in a search for greater precision. Let's begin by postulating that cognition refers to a complex mental process, a process that needs to be defined as an operating system of events.

Toward a Working Definition of Cognition

Since not all psychologists use the same definition of cognition, we will not attempt a polished, formal definition; rather, we will try to formulate a tentative "working definition" in order to keep open minds. As cognition is discussed in the chapters that follow, we will add to and subtract from this definition as needed. To begin with, we will compile a list of characteristics of cognition—the first step along the path of definition.

Cognition is an unobservable event. As implied above, we have good reasons to assume that we know *where* cognition occurs but we don't know—at least in any direct sense—*how* cognition operates. Thus we can observe the behavior of a person, but we can only make inferences about the mental processes that seem necessary to account for that behavior.

Let's say that I ask you to memorize ten feminine and masculine names given in random order with regard to sex. If you recite them giving first all the masculine names and then all the feminine names, I will infer that you have mentally rearranged the names from their random distribution. I cannot "see" your mind clustering the names before the recitation, but it is safe to assume that your ordered recall was deliberate. Since the order was not the same order I gave you, I conclude that you must have used a clustering process during cognition. In other words, what I observe is not cognition itself but, rather, the effects of cognition—in this case the adding of a structure to material presented without such structure.

Cognition is an organized system. A single thought—even a long list of thoughts—does not constitute cognition. Cognition refers to an organized system, a system in which thoughts relate to other thoughts in particular ways. These relationships of thoughts can be seen as rules or instructions that the mind itself uses to get from thought to thought. For example, when a child sees a white cow turn gray as the cow walks into a shadow, the child relates that information to previously known facts about light, shade, movement, and objects. The relationships among these facts help the child understand that the cow is not now permanently gray.

But watch it! Don't treat these mental rules or instructions as the cause of cognition. Cognition *is* the set of mental rules. There is no cell-sized Mr. Mind that directs the flow of information in the brain. At least for this part of our working definition, cognition is no more than the rules that an observer assumes a person is using when the observer sees organized behavior. Again, in describing these rules, we must resist the temptation to treat them as causes of cognition. The rules might define the functioning brain (cognition), but they no more cause cognition than the words on this page caused me to think them.

Cognition doesn't necessarily imply consciousness. An infant who adroitly removes the lid from a jar must be relating thoughts to one another, but it is doubtful that she is giving herself subvocal instructions such as "First grasp, then twist, then pull." Although the infant is not conscious of her own cognition, to assume that the organized scheme of actions in the event described was not deliberate is implausible. Some sort of cognition served to constrain the infant's actions and to limit her movements to only those few needed to remove the lid. The rules that limited or constrained the actions, albeit unknown to the infant, are indeed early forms of cognition.

Although increased consciousness of one's own methods of thinking is one form of cognitive development, it would be overly stringent to exclude unconscious rules of thought from the general domain of cognition.

(Later we will discuss the role of conscious thinking as we chart the development of cognition.)

To this point, then, we can state our working definition of cognition as follows: *cognition is an unobservable system of mental rules inferred from behavior suggesting that information has been organized in some manner that may or may not be consciously known.*

As suggested above, the mental rules that an infant uses to process information are quite different from those that older children use and also different from those that adults use. So far we have not talked about changes in cognitive processes across age, and that brings us to the second question we posed at the beginning of the chapter.

How Does Cognition Change during One's Life Span?

Change can be characterized in a variety of ways. A change can be specific, like a change of clothes, or general, like a change in fashion. Change can be continuous, like a promotion to a higher position, or discontinuous, like a change from one job to an entirely different job. Change can be unidirectional, like a continual improvement, or bidirectional, like a phase of improvement followed by a period of decline. These characteristics of change will be discussed, each in turn, as they are brought up in reference to cognition.

Specific Learning versus General Development

Every time we learn a new fact, something about our cognitive system changes. For example, if I learn that a student of mine was an abused child, my outlook on other information about that student changes, and I begin to relate this information in new ways. My thinking changes, and this change is a type of cognitive reorganization. The change is specific to those pieces of information that deal with the student, and specific cognitive change is called *learning*.

Cognitive development, on the other hand, is a general cognitive change. An example of general cognitive change may be seen in the different ways in which children of different ages remember something. A 4-year-old will remember who owns which toys by thinking in mental pictures, while a 7-year-old will mentally name each toy and memorize the list of such toys. The 7-year-old hasn't necessarily learned something specific about toys that the 4-year-old doesn't know. Rather, the 7-year-old has developed a general form of cognition.

Since cognitive development is more general than learning, it takes more time to see change. Learning can take place in a matter of hours, minutes, or even seconds. Cognitive development usually takes months or years. Most 9-year-olds can change from not knowing the names of any states in the Union to knowing the names of all 50 states in a matter of hours, but it will take several years before they can understand the difference between geographical boundaries (adjacent states) and, say, political boundaries (opposing parties). The change from knowing something with concrete referents to knowing something with only abstract referents is a more general change and takes more time.

Steps versus Stages

Given that cognitive development refers to general cognitive change over months or years, is this change continuous or discontinuous? To put it differently, how should we describe the relationship between successive periods of cognitive development? Some theorists describe the change by using the analogy of steps, each step higher than the previous one but not fundamentally different; that is, they see change as a continuous process. That analogy certainly applies to physical development, but does it hold for cognitive development?

If we are to do more than measure the relative amount of cognitive "stuff" taken in by children of different ages, the step analogy may break down. Once we begin to look at the processes by which children of different ages solve problems, we might discover fundamental differences between the periods of development indicating that the change is in fact discontinuous. There is evidence that the child may well pass from using one type of mental rule to using another type of mental rule. If so, such changes are perhaps best viewed as successive *stages* rather than successive *steps*. To recapitulate, the step-by-step analogy suggests that the child is simply getting better and better at one thing—that there is, for example, a quantitative increase in the number of items the growing child can keep in mind at once. The stage-by-stage analogy, instead, suggests that the mental activity of an older child in, say, keeping more items in mind at once is qualitatively different from the mental activity involved in recalling items at a younger age.

Note that both the step analogy and the stage analogy see the child as getting better and better at some mental activity. The difference between these views relates to the basic process by which improvement occurs. Step theories assume that the basic cognitive processes do not change across age; stage theories assume that the basic cognitive processes do change. As you will see in the next two chapters, this controversy, sometimes called the *continuity/discontinuity* controversy, is a key to categorizing existing theories of cognitive development.

Development versus Regression

However one decides on the continuity/discontinuity issue, one must still account for the direction of development; that is, one must view the change as unidirectional or bidirectional. Is cognitive development always upward toward greater ability, or does it sometimes appear to falter, to go downward? Although most theorists assume that older means better, a comprehensive theory of cognitive development across the life span has to face the issue of momentary versus permanent decline of cognitive functioning. Contemporary theories of cognitive development have difficulty accounting both for temporary regressions followed by further cognitive development and for permanent regression in the later years.

With regard to the difficulty of accounting for temporary regression, there is evidence to suggest that regression, as a temporary phase prior to a general advance, is a good thing, perhaps even a necessary thing (see Bovet, 1976). You've heard the expression "Things will get worse before they get better." As this expression suggests, an individual may regress before he or she improves; he or she may momentarily fall back on more elementary mental rules when faced with a challenging problem before moving ahead to solve it. Such a falling back on the more elementary rules might be necessary to assure that the ultimate advance, when made, includes an understanding of why the old rules don't work. Metaphorically speaking then, the "regression" is essentially backing up to get a running start in order to hurdle a higher challenge.

With regard to the second difficulty—permanent regression as a result of age—there may be no problem at all, since the regression may be illusory. The fact that young adults score better on cognitive tests than do elderly people may have little to do with any regression of cognitive functions. True, the test scores of young adults are better than those of older adults, but this may be the result of the fact that older adults never learned how to take certain types of tests in the first place. Because older adults belong to a generation with different educational experiences, the tests may not be valid, and to say that the older person has *regressed* is perhaps to confuse a difference between generations with differences observed over a person's life span. Thus, in order to truly know whether an individual has regressed in cognitive functions, one must test that same person at different times during his or her life using essentially the same type of test. The fallacy of treating test-score differences between *generations* (known as *cohorts*) as if they were differences within an *individual* will be referred to repeatedly in the chapters that follow.

In sum, cognitive development usually refers to a general change in cognitive functioning rather than to a specific change (which is more commonly called *learning*). Theorists disagree with regard to the question whether cognitive development is continuous or discontinuous. Some say that the basic cognitive processes remain the same albeit increase in efficiency, while others see change in the basic processes themselves. Finally, existing theories of cognitive development have difficulty accounting for a change in the direction of development—that is, regression. Regression in the young is seen by some as a temporary phase before further advance that is not just useful but necessary. Cognitive regression in the old is deemed by some theorists as illusory.

Now let's address the final question in the chapter: why should you bother to study cognitive development?

Why Study Cognitive Development?

As a field of study, cognitive development can be subsumed under the more general study of human development. Human development includes all aspects of what it means to be human, such as art, music, politics, and economics—all things that bear on the improvement of the quality of life. The impetus behind the study of human development is the need to both understand and improve life. The same impetus underlies the study of cognitive development.

Cognition is a tool, and we study it to improve our ability to solve problems. To increase the usefulness of this tool, we need to understand its complexity. For example, judgment is a result of cognitive functions. If we err in our judgment, we may be suffering from a number of cognitive "weaknesses" including poor attention, lapse of memory, fallacious reasoning, or incomplete information. Hence, as in this example, the study of cognition offers us a set of factors we should consider as we seek to improve the process by which we make judgments.

We also study cognition to improve our ability to communicate with others. As we have suggested, cognition changes with age. Therefore, to improve our skills of communication with people both older and younger than ourselves, we must understand some of the general ways in which this change takes place. As an example, a preschool teacher who assumes that all learning problems among his or her students result from inattention fails to appreciate that cognition itself may change with age, that children of different ages may "pay attention" in different ways.

The study of cognitive development can also serve to improve social interactions among people. Cognitive development is inseparable from general social development. Thus, in order to get along with others, we need to understand their modes of thought as well as our own. For instance, studying cognitive development can help us understand that people are not categorically stupid or crazy. What we call stupidity is a variation on normal cognitive development; what we call insanity is a variation on normal psychology, and both are explainable in the same terms. Thus the ostensibly pathological person can be understood best as a person with a different set of rules for processing information. Social interaction also requires that we understand the source of our attitudes about ourselves and others. Our sad times, happy times, neurotic times, healthy times share the essential element that it is always we ourselves who do the thinking. And this thinking has a definite structure and a definite course of development. Only if we gain this understanding are we able to make reasonable conclusions from the information at hand and can we avoid misjudging ourselves and others because we are ignorant of the cognitive activity that governs much of our behavior and that of others.

Chapter Two

Theories of Cognitive Development: The Piagetian Approach

Why a Theory

This and the next chapter are devoted to the discussion of six theories of cognitive development. Some of you may wonder why we should spend so much time talking about theory. Why not just present the facts? You may find the answer in your own response to the list of "facts" that follows:

1. At the age of 2, children respond to the words "Don't push" by pushing even harder if they have already begun the action.
2. At the age of 3, children have difficulty learning concepts about objects that are not physically present.
3. At the age of 4, children can follow the instruction "Make the mommy doll feed the baby doll" but do the opposite of what they are told when instructed to "Make the baby doll feed the mommy doll."

It is likely that, as you read each of the three statements above, you said "Tell me why." Perhaps you were also curious about the interrelation among these three pieces of factual information. Most readers want more than lists of facts. Facts become truly meaningful only when they are presented in the context of an organized whole, of a theory. Thus, explanation and organization of facts are two functions of theory. Snelbecker (1974) mentions two more. Let's examine each in detail.

Theories help systematize findings. Theory makes the difference between a list and a system, between a zip-code directory and a city map. Theory tells us not only what is there but also how to get there. Theory gives meaning to otherwise meaningless, isolated facts. Linking the ocean's tides to the phases of the moon would be impossible without a theory of gravitation. Using fossil remains as evidence about evolution would be quite senseless without a theory that assumes anatomical structure changes across long periods of time. Theory helps us relate and organize facts. Indeed, as Kaplan (1964, p. 302) states, data are themselves miniature theories. What we choose to call data is determined by what we are trying to prove—that is, what theory we are trying to substantiate.

A familiar illustration will make our point even clearer. A sighted deaf man and a blind hearing man "experience" a raging elephant about a thousand feet away. "What was that?" they think in unison. The sighted deaf man concludes that what he saw was a huge gray object—something like a boulder or a ship. The blind hearing man concludes that what he heard was a deep rumble—something like the sound of an amplifier or a crowd. Not only do the two men organize the "facts" differently; they also work with different "facts." The facts are what they individually sense as the basic units of experience, but what is basic is determined by the two men's individual limitations. A theory works in the same way; it limits what we choose to treat as facts. This is not to say that theories make us deaf and blind. Theories make us selective. And that can be an asset, as long as we are aware of the nature of this selectivity and don't get involved in futile arguments over whether the "fact" is a boulder or an amplifier. It is both.

Theories provide explanations. Theories explain phenomena by offering some general principles to which new, specific facts can be related and thus understood. This is true of theories of cognitive development as well. If we are going to talk about cognitive development, we need to speculate about what it is that is developing. Simply outlining an age-related sequence of behavioral changes would be most unsatisfying, as you probably realized when you read the list of data at the beginning of the chapter. Cognitive development is best understood as a change in the efficiency of something—more specifically, as a change in some general style or strategy of thinking. Theory tells us what these general styles or strategies are, thus providing an explanation for the development. This is not to say that these assumed general cognitive functions should be treated as causes of development. Causation is but one form of explanation. These general strategies may help us understand development, without necessarily telling us what physically causes development.

Theories generate hypotheses. A good theory can save scientists a great deal of time by helping them formulate hypotheses. In turn, the hypothesis suggests likely places in which to look for data. For example, a current theory maintains that dinosaurs were warm-blooded mammals rather than cold-blooded reptiles. This theory suggests the hypothesis that dinosaurs did not undergo extinction as reptiles but, instead, that they evolved into flying mammals. This hypothesis permits the paleontologist to return to those dust-covered fossil remains of dinosaurs and take a new look at them, searching for "facts" that will give substance to the hypothesis or prove it wrong. Under a high-powered microscope our paleontologist makes the remarkable discovery that the fossilized bones are fringed with traces of feathers! The theory generated the hypothesis, and the hypothesis guided the search. The fact that the discovery did validate, rather than refute, the hypothesis is immaterial. The value of theory as a source of hypothesis is not affected by the validity or invalidity of the hypothesis itself.

Theories make predictions possible. The fact that theories are organized systems makes predictions possible. The organized system indicates what events are likely to follow from what particular conditions. For example, a current theory of conflict resolution holds that, when a person is faced with two equally desired but mutually exclusive goals (an approach-approach condition), that person will quickly choose one of the two goals and forget the other. The theory also predicts that, when a person is faced with two mutually exclusive goals, both of which, however, have approach and avoidance values (approach-avoidance condition), that person will vacillate between the two goals for a long time. The theory rank-orders the degree of conflict for different conditions. Once a psychologist who knows this theory identifies the type of conflict condition at hand, he or she can make a prediction regarding the intensity of the conflict that will follow. A good theory provides the means to make educated guesses about what will happen in the presence of particular conditions.

Not all theories are effective in making predictions. Many theories don't give a clear definition of the conditions under which the predictions hold true. In the above example it might be impossible to measure a person's tendency to approach and avoid the same goal. Then it would also be impossible to make any accurate predictions about the intensity of the attempts to resolve the conflict. Accurate predictions depend on an accurate identification of what conditions are present.

An Overview of Six Theoretical Approaches

The distinctions we made in Chapter One between learning and development and between steps and stages can be used to compare and contrast theories of development. We have selected for our discussion six theories that incorporate in various measures these contrasting concepts.

The goal of our discussion is to make our basically Piagetian position more understandable. By becoming aware of what is and what is not Piagetian, you can decide which questions can be answered from a Piagetian perspective and which cannot. Too often we argue over which theory is "correct." Theories are seldom correct or incorrect; they are more or less useful as answers to particular questions. For example, proving that dreams occur with greater frequency after eating rich food does not invalidate the theory that dreams are an expression of repressed sexual desires. What causes an increase in dream rate is one question; what a dream means is quite a different question. A theory of dream rate cannot invalidate a theory of dream content any more than a theory of developmental rate cannot invalidate a theory of developmental content. These are separate questions and involve separate methods of research. Which theory you prefer to adhere to is determined by which set of questions you assume to be important.

The cognitive theories of Jean Piaget, Jerome Bruner, and Heinz Werner address such questions as "How does the average 4-year-old solve problems?" "How can we best describe the differences in the way the average 4-year-old and the average 7-year-old think?" "Is it necessary to assume that cognitive development is more than the result of learning?" Although all three psychologists pose similar questions, each of them offers different sets of answers.

The questions that Robert Gagné asks us to consider are different: "Which cognitive skills does a person need in order to solve a particular task?" and "Which cognitive skills are more complicated than others?" His theory focuses more on the nature of the task than on the nature of the thinker and is related to developmental theory only indirectly—that is, from the point of view that the simpler aspects of a task are learned at an earlier age than the more complicated ones.

Sidney Bijou and Donald Baer ask questions concerning what determines the rate of development and what determines the direction of development. Both address these and similar issues in order to explain an individual's development rather than to describe the general competence of an average x-year-old. David Klahr and J. G. Wallace, like Gagné, are interested in the particular cognitive skills needed to solve specific problems but, unlike Gagné, have also turned their attention to the actual thinking processes of a student in action. They give us a sort of "thinking-out-loud" picture of the procedures a student follows in solving difficult problems.

In sum, it is whether one is interested in issues concerning age-related competence (Piaget, Werner, and Bruner), the cognitive demands of specific tasks (Gagné and Klahr and Wallace), or the environmental determinants of individual development (Bijou and Baer) that will determine one's preferences for a particular theory or group of theories. This and the next chapter are devoted to a discussion of these various approaches, beginning with Piaget's.

Jean Piaget

Piaget's theory of cognitive development has been summarized in several excellent reviews (Flavell, 1963; Furth, 1972; Ginsburg & Opper, 1969; Piaget, 1970; Piaget & Inhelder, 1969). Our discussion of Piaget's approach draws most heavily from the last two sources.

The basis of Piaget's theory is biological. He sees cognitive development as a biological process and stresses the fact that the child brings a large supply of reflexes and other biological equipment to any new learning situation. This equipment includes not only anatomical structures like the opposable thumb, which makes grasping possible, or the big toe, which makes upright balance possible, but also certain cognitive processes, such as the infant's tendency to repeat interesting events simply because they are interesting. Biological structures, together with cognitive tendencies, are in constant interaction with the environment and thereby cause the child to develop an understanding of more and more complex perceptual inputs. Piaget sees the shape of our body as exquisitely compatible with the environment in which we exist. The opposable thumb of the human fetus would indicate to a visiting anthropologist from outer space that Earth must contain small, movable objects. The fetus' feet would tell this professor from Astro University that humans spend most of their time in a world that exerts a force (gravity) on bodies that move in an upright position. These structures are no accident. They are the result of the evolution of a species that has lived for thousands of years in the same general environment. It stands to reason that our brain, too, is biologically preadapted to the environment into which we are born.

The nature of this preadaptation is not as specific as early psychological theory held it to be. We don't have a built-in instinct to suck our thumb, for example, but we do have a built-in tendency and a cognitive ability to recreate interesting and pleasant situations once they have occurred. Piaget notes that the thumb stimulates the mouth, thus setting off a sucking reflex, but that afterward anything that touches the mouth has the same effect. It just so happens that the thumb is especially convenient for sucking, that it is used for that purpose by the child while still in the womb, and that it can come under the voluntary control of the baby. The biological marvel is that what occurs at first by happy accident eventually comes under the deliberate control of the infant.

Because of our brain structure we can "piece together" the spatial and temporal relations necessary to make a pleasant event happen again. Piaget's theory can, in part, be defined as a theory of the increasing awareness of what-causes-what and of what operations lead to what states. We will see that the sophistication of this increasing awareness gradually extends to events that are symbolic and logical rather than merely physical.

Assimilation and Accommodation

The fact that children grow in their ability to adapt to new experiences—that is, to change their reactions to the environment—is part of Piaget's biological focus. Both assimilation and accommodation relate to how one copes with the environment.

Assimilation is the process of integrating the external environment into one's own internal cognitive structure—in other words, changing the environment to fit the person. *Accommodation* is the process of changing one's own cognitive structure to fit the environment. These two processes work in a coordinated fashion to make adaptation to the environment possible. Assimilation and accommodation are not seen by Piaget as specific reactions, like the sucking reflex, but as overall *changes* in behavior, attitude, emotion, and cognition. Assimilation is any process of adaptation that takes some external object—such as a particle of food or a page of printed words—and modifies it to fit the person's current needs and attitudes. The food is broken into pieces, the written passage is interpreted. Accommodation is any adaptive process in which the perceiver himself changes to fit the external object—for example, by opening the mouth wider or by adding new words to his vocabulary. The adaptation of the child results from an interplay between changing, physically or mentally, the external inputs and changing the internal dispositions.

Both processes are always involved in cognitive functioning, from the development of gross motor skills and memory skills to logical thinking. Suppose, for example, that a baby has had several weeks of experience grasping a wooden ring that hangs from her crib. Then the ring is replaced with a wooden square. As the child moves her hand toward the new object that hangs above her, she is telling us that she has assimilated the hanging object into her memory: "This is something to grasp." Her fingers open as she approaches the wooden square. Until now she has not noticed that this object is different and that, unlike the ring, it has sharp corners. It is at the moment of contact with the square, particularly if she grasps it by a corner, that the infant discovers that this object is different.

The child now accommodates to the unique features of this new object by shifting her grasp to a more comfortable position. With more experience with the new object the child does more than merely accommodate (change her reaction) on a particular occasion. She also approaches the wooden square from an angle that permits her to avoid the object's sharp corners—something she didn't have to do with the wooden ring, which had no corners. This means that the child is now changing her behavior *before* coming into contact with the object. In turn, this indicates that she has changed her memory of what this particular object *means* in regard to the act of grasping. The child now has a two-object vocabulary: round things (grasp anywhere) and square things (grasp only on the side). These, of course, are not geometric concepts like knowing that a square has four equal sides. They are motor schemes that indicate to the observer what the child knows about the shape/grasp relation.

What the above example tells us is that the child knows more than the fact that a sharp corner hurts the palm of the hand. The child engages in a whole series of organized behaviors to grasp an object. The orchestrated organization of the tiny movements involved in grasping, and even the very fact that she attempts a grasp, indicates that the child knows a lot more than the simple shape/grasp relation. Piaget calls this practical knowledge *sensorimotor intelligence.*

One of the remarkable features of Piaget's theory is that it doesn't take any of these subtle elements for granted. For example, what are the implications of the searching behavior of a child who removes the handkerchief covering his favorite rattle and then grasps the rattle? The act itself is simple; it is no more than any other grasp. But its significance is immense. A child younger than 6 months will not attempt to remove the handkerchief, no matter how much he wants the rattle. He just sits there and frets. For Piaget, this behavior indicates that the child doesn't know that the rattle is still there, in a place concealed from view. But when, later in life, the baby removes the handkerchief to get at his rattle, he is telling us that he knows that objects have an existence independent of one's own visual contact with them. The baby has discovered object permanence.

This concept manifests itself in countless ways, all indicating the same thing. For example, the child knows that space has various planes. He knows that there is a self and also an object that is independent of his own perception. And he knows how to reestablish an interesting sight. The child who has discovered object permanence has learned more than *when* to do something; he has learned *what* space is. He has developed a system of spatial and temporal relations that, in any subsequent occasion and no matter what the shield or the hidden object, allows him to retrieve the object.

The essential characteristic of this type of knowledge is that it is not the result of having learned some unique physical feature of an object—say, a black monogram on a handkerchief. Seeing a black monogram on one handkerchief may cue the child to remove the handkerchief if that same monogrammed handkerchief is used over and over again as a shield for the rattle. But the monogram, or any other specific cue, couldn't help the child cope with other situations in which the rattle is hidden under entirely different shields, like a cardboard box. The distinction between object out-of-sight behind something and object out-of-existence altogether can be made only by the coordination of actions into a coherent system of movements and positions. The child *constructs* this system of interrelations gradually, through everyday experiences, by moving objects and by moving himself.

For Piaget, cognitive development is an interaction between the biological processes that make inferences possible and the child's activity in the physical environment. Through the dual process of assimilation and accommodation, events are spontaneously organized by the mind. This process of organization continues through several increasingly complex stages of development. Each stage is qualitatively different from each previous stage, yet each stage incorporates the gains of each previous stage.

According to Piaget, the child goes through four stages of development: the sensorimotor stage (birth to 2 years), the preoperational stage (2 to 7 years), the concrete-operational stage (7 to 11 years), and the formal-operational stage (beyond the 11th year).*

The Sensorimotor Stage

During the first stage of development, from birth to the onset of the use of symbols (language and gestures), children deal with real objects at the perceptual level and in a very egocentric manner. They do not yet use an object as a representation, or symbol, for another object. The plastic spoon is something to be put in the mouth; it is not a "pretend" piece of candy. In this stage objects have meaning according to what can be done with them. The round block can be rolled, and the square block can be slid; but the round block is not treated symbolically as if it were a choo-choo train. (This comes later, during the preoperational stage of development.) During the sensorimotor stage objects are associated with actions and events but objects do not stand for actions and events. The sound of running water signals that someone is in the kitchen. The child goes to the kitchen to see. The sound causes the child in this stage to remember past events that have actually happened.

Piaget has made us aware of the complex nature of the "simple" task of remembering where something is. This task is much more than associating some particular sight, like a toybox, with the desired object (the toy inside the box). This task involves an awareness of the permanence of objects—of the fact that objects don't cease to exist when they are out of sight. In other words, in order to remember where an object is, the child must first understand that the object, although no longer in sight, still exists. This, in turn, means that the child must relate the movement of the object with the position of the place where the object is hidden; that is, the toy goes *behind* the walls of the toybox. If a child didn't understand that the toy still exists somewhere in space even though she cannot see it, she would not commit to memory the toybox as the signal to the toy's whereabouts. It is the concept of object permanence that gives the child a reason to make an association between two objects, which in itself is a rather simple task.

During the sensorimotor stage the child progresses in his ability to deal with several displacement situations—movements of an object or of himself. The child develops the mental wherewithal to organize the path that an object takes, even though some segments of the path may not actually be seen, as in the case of a ball that rolls under a piece of furniture (see Bower, 1974). Let's look in detail at several ways in which the sensori-

*The following sections on the sensorimotor, preoperational, and concrete-operational stages are from *The Child's Construction of Knowledge: Piaget for Teaching Children,* by G. E. Forman and D. S. Kuschner. Copyright © 1977 by Wadsworth, Inc. Reprinted by permission of the publisher, Brooks/Cole Publishing Company, Monterey, California.

motor child organizes object movement—what Piaget (1970) calls the *group of translations*.

Learning to negotiate *detours* is one such way. An object that can be reached by making a direct crawl from here to there can also be reached by going in many other and less direct paths from here to there. During this first step of development children show less and less difficulty with detour problems. In fact, they can even turn their backs on the desired destination for a moment while executing the detour. All of the segments of movement become organized into a closed system (what Piaget calls *the group*), which is no less than the space in which all these paths exist. All these paths lead to the same end point; that is, the segment from point *A* to point *B* plus the segment from point *B* to point *D* is one path (Figure 2-1a); the segment from point *A* to point *C* plus the segment from point *C* to point *D* is a variation of that path but still ends at *D* (Figure 2-1b). In practical terms (but, of course, not in mathematical terms) $AB + BD = AC + CD$. The child can get to his chair either by crossing the carpet or, if that way is blocked, by going around the obstacle—in this case, the package.

The 1-year-old is capable of using *negation* in displacement situations. Piaget defines negation as the undoing of a transformation by the most direct means. If a child goes from *A* to *B* and then back to *A,* she has actually negated her advance by reversing her direction. This situation can be expressed with the formula $AB + BA = 0$. The child in the sensorimotor stage can also deal with displacement by using *reciprocity*. Reciprocity is an indirect means to undo a transformation. If a child rolls a toy on a string away from himself (movement *A* to *B*), he can then undo that movement by either a direct or an indirect reversal. The direct reversal (negation) would be pulling the toy back to its original place—a movement from *B* back to *A*. The indirect reversal (reciprocity) would be walking toward the toy—a movement from *A* to *B*. In both cases the separation between *A* and *B* is "undone." Figure 2-2 shows both forms of reversal.

None of the displacement situations we have just discussed involved hidden movements, even though the desired object may have been temporarily hidden from sight (in the detour situation, for example, the chair was hidden by the package). But, as children approach the end of the sensorimotor stage, they learn to handle situations that do involve invisible displacement. These situations require children to mentally fill in (extrapolate) something they actually didn't see but that they assume exists. When children begin to deal successfully with invisible displacement, they demonstrate that they are beginning to use symbols—mental representations of the hidden movement. Here is an example.

Keith puts a small doll into his pull wagon and pulls the wagon around the room, watching his toy over his shoulder. For a brief moment the wagon is hidden from the child's view by an ottoman. After pulling the wagon a few more yards, Keith stoops over to lift out the doll. But the doll

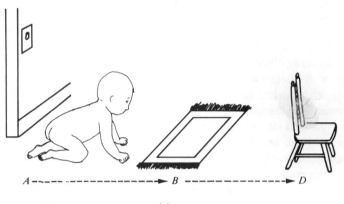

(a)

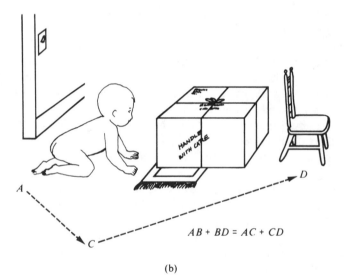

$$AB + BD = AC + CD$$

(b)

Figure 2-1.

is not there in the depths of the wagon. Keith instantly checks behind the ottoman. Even though he didn't see the doll bounce out of the wagon behind the ottoman, he assumes that it must be there. He has more than a mental image of the doll; he has a mental image of the doll bouncing out of the wagon. When children are 2 years old, they can mentally represent translations (object movements); they can mentally coordinate movement, position,

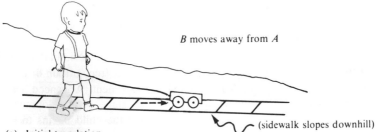

(a) Initial translation

B moves away from *A*

(sidewalk slopes downhill)

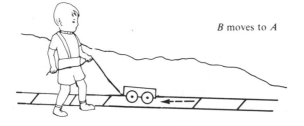

B moves to *A*

(b) Reversal by negation

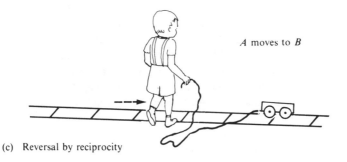

A moves to *B*

(c) Reversal by reciprocity

Figure 2-2.

and object and come up with the mental image of the translation. This is a much more elaborate task than recognition, which involves a fairly automatic affair—that is, the mental image of the particular missing object. This higher degree of complexity explains why it takes about two years before the child can deal with invisible displacements of the type described above.

Invisible displacement involves an inference of sorts. If object *A* (the doll) is placed out of view in *B* (the wagon) and then object *B* moves behind object *C* (the ottoman), object *A* could be either in *B* or behind *C*—if not *B,* then *C.* Solving the problem presented by invisible displacement is an early form (a precursor) of the *transitive relation* in logic. In a transitive relation the child knows that if *A* is larger than *B* and *B* is larger than *C,* then *A* is necessarily larger than *C.*

The mental representations of the sensorimotor period are limited to either the recall of the physical features of an object (recognition of form) or the construction of an individual, invisible displacement. Advanced levels of representation mark the beginning of the next stage of development, the preoperational stage. In the preoperational stage the child begins to under-stand how one displacement affects another displacement. As we said be-fore, the mental structures the child builds in one stage make the mental structures of the following stage possible.

The Preoperational Stage

This stage begins around age 2, with the acquisition of symbolic thought—the use of mental images and words to represent actions and entire events that are not present. It is called preoperational because it precedes the onset of logical operations. Children begin to imitate in some detail objects or events that they have seen in the recent past. One morning a 2½-year-old sees a seal in the zoo. That afternoon she does something that she had never done before. She bumps her wrists together and belts out several loud arffs. The child is evidently acting out a mental image that she recalls at the mo-ment she imitates the seal, not presently in sight.

The child's new ability to represent the nonpresent event in gesture and in words helps her establish a relation between two events. In fact, the defining characteristic of preoperational thought is the child's ability to an-ticipate the effect of one action on another action. Piaget calls this type of relation a *function.* A function is a one-way relation between two events and can be direct or inverse. The rise of water in a glass is a function of the drop in the water level in the pitcher from which the water is poured. In this case we have an inverse function: as one level goes up, the other level goes down. Preoperational children understand at the practical level that more water in the glass means less water in the pitcher, just as they understand that throwing a ball down harder will make the ball bounce higher—an example of a direct function: the more of one action, the more of the other.

Preoperational children develop the mental competence to organize events into functional relations; they understand that a change in one factor causes a change in the other factor. This change can be an increase or a decrease; that is, it is a change *in a particular direction*—depending on the events involved. Children at this stage know not only that throwing a ball down harder will make the ball bounce higher but also that throwing the ball down with less force will make the ball bounce lower. The concept of func-tion represents more than the simple knowledge that *X* leads to *Y*—like the infant's knowledge that kicking leads to release from the blanket. The concept of function involves the coordination of two *changes,* not just of two actions. An increasing change here leads to a decreasing change there (inverse function). An increasing change here leads to an increasing change there (direct function).

What is it then that preoperational children do not yet understand? We defined the function as a one-way relation, and we said that preoperational children can anticipate functions. But what these children cannot understand is the implication behind the fact that a function can be carried out in two ways. They know that the water can be poured from the pitcher into the glass and from the glass into the pitcher, but they don't grasp the implication that those combined events carry for the concept of conservation. Preoperational children, therefore, could not answer the question "Do you have as much water now as you did before?" They can understand that more in *X* means less in *Y,* but they do not yet understand that the change in *X* is exactly compensated by a change in *Y.* They have reached the stage of understanding the *direction* of the change, but they don't understand the *quantity* of the change. Quantity in this instance does not refer to an absolute number of ccs but, rather, to the conservation of amount, since nothing was added or subtracted during the pouring of the liquid.

Children in the preoperational stage are deceived by appearance. You and we know that, if you push a blob of spinach into a compact heap, what the heap gains in height is exactly compensated by what the blob lost in circumference. In Piaget's terms, the quantity of substance is conserved despite changes in spatial distribution. When the 4-year-old looks down at the reduced circumference of her portion of spinach, she thinks that she has less to eat. (She may also think that she has more to eat, if she concentrates instead on the increased height of her portion of spinach.) Now this child may well understand that a decrease in circumference leads to an increase in height and vice versa. But she can think about these functions in one direction at a time only; she cannot integrate the two directions into a mental structure that has applications for conservation of quantity. Her failure to make this mental integration leaves her open to errors of perception, such as thinking that she has more (or less) spinach to swallow. This inability is not surprising when you think that the child has just learned the function, which involves the coordination of two changes. Conservation of quantity, which involves the coordination of two coordinated changes, is a far more complex operation, and we will discuss it in greater detail when we talk of concrete-operational thinking. Now let's go back to preoperational children and to what they can, rather than can't, do.

All functions are expressed by the general formula $A = f(B)$. This is read "A change in A is a function of a change in B." By "change" we mean a directional difference—that is, an increase or decrease. As you read the following discussion, look at Figure 2-3, and keep in mind that the point

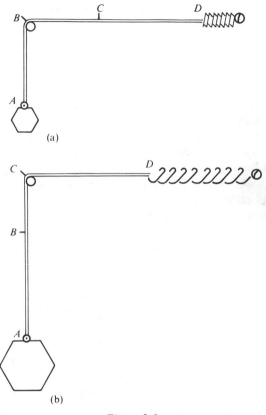

Figure 2-3.

of the discussion is to show that the group of translations of the sensorimotor stage is used by the child to understand functions in the preoperational stage. In Figure 2-3a a string is drawn over a nail hammered into the wall. End *D* of the string is attached to a light spring, which is itself anchored to the wall. A small weight is attached to the other end *(A)* of the string. The more weight is added to end *A*, the longer the vertical segment *AB* becomes: *AB* changes to *AC* (Figure 2-3b). At the same time, the horizontal segment *BD* becomes shorter: that is, *BD* becomes *CD*. The preoperational child knows that the length of the vertical segment changes as a function of the length of the horizontal segment: $V = f(H)$.

How have the translation problems of the sensorimotor stage helped the preoperational child to understand the function we have just discussed? Go back to Figure 2-1, which shows the infant solving the detour problem. In terms of practical action the infant knows that $AB + BD = AC + CD$; that is, both of these paths are variations of the same path from *A* to *D*. In Figures 2-3a and 2-3b the child understands that both situations (3a and 3b) are variations of the same span of string *AD*. The reason why *V* gets shorter as *H* gets longer is that *V* takes its length from *H*. It is all one piece of string. Even though the preoperational child does not yet understand that the gain in *V* is exactly compensated by the loss in *H,* he knows where the additional length in *V* comes from. He knows that the change from *AB* to *AC* (a gain) is correlated with the change from *BD* to *CD* (a loss). But he does not yet understand that *AB* + *BD* equals *AC* + *CD*. In sum, the translation problems that the child solved in the sensorimotor stage help him relate the changes in the vertical and the horizontal spans as parts of one continuous space, but he has to go through the activities involved in preoperational thought before he can handle conservation of length. Right now he is perfectly willing to conclude that the string in Figure 2-3b is longer than the string in Figure 2-3a.

When asked the conservation question "Is the length of the string in Figure 2-3a the same as the length of the string in Figure 2-3b?" the preoperational child looks at segment *AC* as we see it in Figure 2-3b and mentally compares it with his memory of *AB*, the vertical segment in its initial state as we see it in Figure 2-3a. Since *AC* is longer than *AB*, the child concludes that the length of the string has increased. He has used the final product of the translation—the way segment *AC* appears—but has not integrated this final product *AC* into a total system of translations that includes the change of *BD* as well. This concern with final products, the way things look, is called by Piaget *figurative knowledge*. During the next stage of development (the stage of concrete operations) the child begins to include in his thinking the very nature of translations and other transformations in general. The shift from thinking about static states to thinking about transformations plus static states characterizes what Piaget terms *operational knowledge*.

The Concrete-Operational Stage

What is concrete about this stage, and what is operational about it? Somewhere around the age of 6 or 7, children make a shift in their ability to deal with change. The word *concrete* refers to the fact that children at this stage are still dealing with concrete objects; when they deal with change, they deal with changing objects, not with change in the abstract. It should be clear that here the word *concrete* does not refer to concepts—more specifically, concrete versus abstract concepts. Concrete-operational children are quite capable of dealing with abstract concepts, although they deal with them in a concrete manner. As we shall see, they can, for example, integrate both directions of a function and conclude that quantity has been conserved. The word *operational* refers to the fact that children at this stage of development do indeed create logical structures (mental operations) that allow them to conserve, albeit the data they use to build these mental structures are concrete events. They don't deal with hypothetical assumptions, but they do go beyond the figurative aspects of things—the way things look at one particular time. We could say that the term *operational* denotes the outer reaches of this stage and the term *concrete* denotes its limits. Children in concrete operations can integrate (mentally combine) functions that pertain to concrete objects, but they cannot yet integrate two or more mental operations—an ability that they acquire in the next stage.

Let's use the problem of conservation of length illustrated in Figures 2-1 and 2-3 to see what the child in the concrete-operational stage can and cannot do. The sensorimotor understanding of the $AB + BD = AC + CD$ translation (Figure 2-1) helped the child learn that moving from A to C, instead of moving from A to B, can still lead to D (Figure 2-1). Piaget maintains that development builds on and includes the previous stage. How do translation and function combine to help the child understand conservation of length? In Figure 2-3a string AD bends in a right angle at point B. In Figure 2-3b string AD bends in a right angle at point C. In essence, the conservation question ("Is the total length of the string the same in Figures 2-3a and 2-3b?") asks the child to reason that $AB + BD$ (Figure 2-3a) is equal to $AC + CD$ (Figure 2-3b). Does this formula look familiar to you? Implicitly the child must understand that the imaginary segment BC in Figure 2-3a is the same as the equally imaginary segment BC in Figure 2-3b. In other words, segment BC has been displaced from the horizontal segment H to the vertical segment V—displaced, not added. The portion that the horizontal segment loses (BC) is the same portion that the vertical segment gains (again, BC). This means that BC is contained within the total distance AD, just as the crawl AB was contained in the total crawl AD in Figure 2-1. The conservation problem is no doubt more difficult, but it does contain, embedded in the thought required for its solution, problems that have been solved in previous stages.

So why can't the sensorimotor-stage child or the preoperational child solve the conservation problem? The sensorimotor child could understand in some absolute sense that the two strings in Figures 2-3a and 2-3b are one and the same string. He knows that a change in the position of the string does not change the existence or the absolute identity of the string. He may even be able to learn how to make the vertical segment longer. But he wouldn't be able to relate the increasing length of V with the decreasing length of H. The preoperational child, on the other hand, would be able to relate the increase with the decrease but couldn't go beyond that. In order to understand conservation, the child must be able to realize that segment BC is *at the same time* a part of the vertical segment AC and a part of the total length AD.

But how can something be a part of two different things? Can my nose be at the same time a part of my face and a part of your face? That's just the kind of question the preoperational child would ask. He knows that in the world of physical objects and actions one object cannot be in two places at once. What he fails to realize is that the conservation question does not ask about the position of an object but, rather, about the relation between segments, a relation independent of position. The concrete-operational child understands the distinction between a logical relation and a physical position. (In terms of logic, segment *BC* can be both a subsegment of the vertical span and a subsegment of the entire string.) He can also understand other relations—for example, that 2 can, at the same time, be larger than 1 and smaller than 3. This relation is not confused by the concrete-operational child with a physical change, such as an actual change in size. In sum, the concrete-operational child has gone beyond the way things look at a particular moment in time (figurative knowledge) and has begun to understand how things relate (operative knowledge).

In the concrete-operational stage the "facts" are always a set of concrete objects or activities rather than a set of hypothetical assumptions. It is not until the final stage, which begins around age 11 or 12, that the child can deal with purely hypothetical propositions—that is, is capable of truly abstract thinking. For example, we can say that in Figure 2-3 the concrete-operational child can conserve length because segment *BC*, a concrete object, is simultaneously a logical "member" of the vertical segment and of the total string, both also concrete objects. What she cannot do is make a verbal description of the relations between these classes and perform some mental manipulation of such relations. In the same way, the concrete-operational child could not perform in her head a multiplication of a multiplication—like $3 \times 4 = 12$, $12 \times 4 = 48$. The product 12 cannot be "seen"; it is the mere result of a mental operation (multiplication). If the child is then asked to perform a mental operation on a mental operation— that is, 12×4—she cannot do it or, if she can, she doesn't realize that 12 is simultaneously a product and a multiplicand.

In Figure 2-4 we have summarized the basic differences among the first three stages of development to help you remember the main points of our discussion. In the sensorimotor stage (0 to 2 years) children learn to associate one action with another action: a pull *(X)* on a string leads to a

a. Sensorimotor stage (0–2 years): Motor schemes
   $X \longrightarrow Y$: Action associated with action
b. Preoperational stage (2–6 years): Functional relations
   $X \longrightarrow X' \Longrightarrow Y \longrightarrow Y'$: Change correlated with change
c. Concrete-operational stage (6–11 years): Logical relations

$$\left. \begin{cases} X \longrightarrow X' \Longrightarrow Y \longrightarrow Y' \\ X' \longrightarrow X \Longrightarrow Y' \longrightarrow Y \end{cases} \right\}: \text{Function integrated with function}$$

Figure 2-4. Basic differences among the first three stages of development. (The sign $\longrightarrow$ means "associates"; the sign $\Longrightarrow$ means "correlates"; and the double sign $\{\ \}$ means "integrates.")

movement *(Y)* of the object tied to the string (Figure 2-4a). In the preoperational stage (2 to 6 or 7 years) children learn to correlate two changes. This is called a *function:* as X changes to X', Y changes to Y' (Figure 2-4b). Children at this stage can relate the direction of change in one action to the direction of change in another action. However, they cannot yet understand the implication behind the fact that the correlation can run in both directions; for example, they cannot deduce the concept of conservation from the fact of physical reversibility. They know that changing the weight from X to X' will change the vertical span from Y to Y', but they cannot integrate the initial state with the final state to prove that length has remained the same. In the concrete-operational stage (age 6 or 7 years to 11 or 12 years) children can integrate the correlations in both directions (Figure 2-4c) to prove that length has remained the same. The concrete-operational child would say "I know that the string is the same length because, after all, you can put it back just as it was." This child can now see the implication behind the physical reversal, because he or she has the mental ability to think about the two functions as variations of each other.

The Formal-Operational Stage

Formal-operational thought begins around age 12 or 13. Whereas concrete operations deal with the logical organization of movements and with classifications of real objects, formal-operational thinking deals with purely verbal propositions and is, therefore, truly abstract thinking. It involves, for example, the ability to perform operations on other operations, such as a multiplication of a multiplication.

The adolescent in the formal-operational stage can also predict what is possible, even though it may never exist in actuality. Let's say, for example, that a young biology student knows that there are three types of birds and three primary colors. This means that there is a total of nine *possible* combinations. The student thinks first about how to generate all combinations. She thinks of a matrix of three rows (the three colors) and three columns per row (the three birds). Using this 3×3 matrix, she can discover that there is a category called *blue cardinal*. This student has never seen a blue cardinal. In her problem solving she didn't even think of looking for one. But, because she approached the problem formally, she discovered a possible case she had never seen. She used a matrix to organize the pairs of color/bird combinations. In other words, the student knew how to relate (organize) the relations (pairs) to each other.

Here is another example of the adolescent's ability to relate relations. Given a snail on a movable board (Figure 2-5), does the child understand that there are two ways of canceling the forward movement of the snail? One is to move the snail forward from the middle of the board *(M)* to the right end C while, at the same time, moving the board backward until end C is at point X on the ground. The snail's move forward is directionally

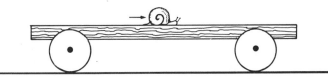

Figure 2-5.

the opposite of the backward movement of the board; that is, it is an *inverse function*. Moving both board and snail back to their original positions is another inverse function. If the adolescent can *integrate* these two functions, he understands that the snail's advance beyond point X on the ground has been canceled.

There is another way of canceling the forward movement of the snail—moving the snail backward to end A of the board while, at the same time, moving the board forward until A is at point X. To understand that these two *relations* (relation A and relation B in Figure 2-6) are equivalent—in other words, that there are two forms of cancellation—requires placing all four functions into a system of relations that form a closed group. Piaget calls it a *closed group* because each function has implications for the other three. Since a detailed discussion of a closed group of relations (what Piaget calls the *INRC group*) would be beyond the scope of this book, we confine ourselves to simply saying that it is an example of relating relations or of performing operations on operations. Figure 2-6, which uses the same scheme presented in Figure 2-4, highlights the structure of this formal operation.

In brief, Piaget's theory describes four stages of cognitive development. In the first stage (sensorimotor) children can think about the relations of themselves to other objects, both social and physical. They become aware of object permanence, be the object a hidden toy or a nurturing adult out of sight. Development then proceeds through the second stage (preoperational), when children understand how changes in one object effect changes in another object (functions). At the third stage (concrete operational) children begin to grasp logical relations between and among objects (classification and conservation); and at the last stage (formal operational), adolescents are capable of constructing a system that provides rules for relating relations stated in verbal propositions (matrix and closed group of relations).

Beyond Formal Operations

Does Piaget's theory carry implications for cognitive development beyond adolescence? Arlin (1975) presents some preliminary data that suggest a fifth stage, a stage she terms *problem-finding stage*. If formal operations is the problem-solving stage, it makes good sense to see in problem finding a

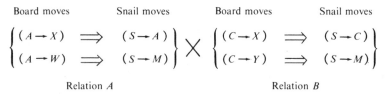

Relation *A*   Relation *B*

The board's movement
forward is canceled
by the snail's
movement backward.

The board's movement
backward is canceled
by the snail's
movement foreward.

In formal-operatonal thinking, the child
"multiplies" these two relations by placing
all four functions in a closed group, which
implies that there are two ways of canceling
the advance of the snail.

Figure 2-6. Diagram of formal-operational thinking as applied to
the example (illustrated in Figure 2-5) of a snail (*S*) in the middle
(*M*) of board *AC*. (The sign ⟶ means "associates"; for example, *A* moves to point *X*. The sign ⟹ means "correlates";
for example, when *A* moves to point *X*, *S* moves to end *A*. The
sign { } means "integrates"; for example, one correlated set
of moves cancels out the other. The sign × means "closed
group"—the two relations *A* and *B* are understood as mirror
images of each other.)

still higher phase, since finding a problem is more difficult than solving a problem that has been clearly defined by the experimenter. Kennedy (1974)
makes a similar point when he envisages a stage beyond formal operations,
which he calls the *metatheoretical stage.* He claims that people in formal
operations fail certain tasks because they fail to question the question. At the
metatheoretical stage, the adult judges the wording of the problem in order
to decide if it is empirically solvable.

An example may clarify the point. How would you go about determining whether the following statement is correct or not?

The inhabitants of Nepal are good mountain climbers because of their skill
in reaching high altitudes.

The truth of the matter is that there is no way of testing the statement,
because it doesn't relate to a "fact" that can be confirmed or denied by
empirical investigation, no matter how systematic the analysis. You are confronted with a circular statement, since the "skill in reaching high altitudes"
is none other than a descriptor of a good mountain climber.

The person in formal operations, says Kennedy, may not necessarily have the metatheoretical perspective that is required to find the real prob-

lem. Yet, others maintain, the difference between problem solving (formal operations) and problem finding (metatheoretical) may not be a difference in developmental stages. The supposed fifth stage may be only a difference in content rather than a difference in the cognitive operations required to solve the problem (see Fakouri, 1976). This interesting debate will no doubt draw others to look for stages beyond formal operations.

Is Piagetian theory relevant for middle and late adulthood? Many researchers doubt it. In the chapters that follow we will refer to cases in which attempts have been made to relate Piaget's theory to the aging process. We pointed out in Chapter One that, when we deal with the process of aging, we must account for what seems to be a regression. Most researchers explain changes in cognitive functioning beyond middle age in terms of motivational variables—such as willingness to be tested, distractibility, and practice—rather than in Piagetian terms of mental structure. We shall return to this point in Chapter Four.

Chapter Three

Theories of Cognitive Development: Other Approaches

Heinz Werner

In this chapter we discuss other key figures among the cognitive theorists. We begin with Heinz Werner, who, like Piaget, looks at cognitive development as part of a total process of biological evolution. Both theorists emphasize that any change in the development of an individual is the result of an interaction between the environmental history of that individual and the biological history of our species.

Werner was well read in embryology and neurology, as well as anthropology, pathology, and aesthetics (Baldwin, 1967). Each of these interests influenced the construction of his theory of mental development.[1] Unlike Piaget, Werner studied development in a wide range of settings. He studied cognition as it changes across age levels, across cultures, and across the spectrum from pathological to normal thinking. He examined any shift in development that would indicate change from a more primitive, elementary mode to a more advanced, organized mode. But his greatest talent lay in his ability to discern general patterns of development across a wide variety of situations.

To Werner, any organic system—be it a cell, a person, or a culture—develops through a process he calls *orthogenesis*. Whenever development occurs, it proceeds from a state of relative globality and lack of differentiation to a state of increasing differentiation and organization. Thus, development is always governed by a specific sequence of changes. The developing fetus, for example, grows by a complex process of differentiation and specialization, in which the specialized cells develop into four groups of primary tissue: epithelial, connective, muscular, and neural. All

---

[1]Excellent reviews of Werner's theory can be found in Baldwin (1967) and Langer (1970).

the organs of the body result from combinations of these tissues. Body systems, which are combinations of organs working together in an integrated manner, represent the highest level of differentiation and integration. The organization of the body functions is hierarchic, which means that several functions at one level combine to support a function at a higher level. In turn, the higher function combines with other functions at that level to support still higher functions, and so on.

Werner identifies three stages of mental development: (1) sensorimotor, (2) perceptual, and (3) contemplative. The terms *global, differentiation,* and *hierarchical integration* are the key words he uses to describe development in general.

The Sensorimotor Stage

This is the stage at which the development of actions and emotions takes place. The first actions of the infant are rather global, random, everywhere-at-once movements. When an object appears in sight, the infant's arms jerk now and again as if the muscles of the arm were all operating at once (a movement that Bruner [1969] calls *ballistic*). Later this global reaction to objects begins to become differentiated into small, goal-directed movements. Only the arm closer to the object moves, and it moves in the direction of the object rather than at random. While moving his arm toward an object, the infant can also elevate his shoulders for better leverage and turn his head for a better view. The separate component movements are integrated to serve a single goal. To put it in Werner's terms, the component acts are subordinated to the common goal. It is this common goal—in our example, reaching for the object—that gives more importance and more attention to some component acts than to others. The integration of the movements is hierarchical.

Emotions, too, are at first rather global and diffused. The infant can express diffuse rage or pleasure but does not differentiate between fear and anger or between joy and surprise. These emotions become differentiated across age and then become integrated into a melody of changes that indicate specific moods and transitions between moods.

Like Piaget, Werner sees the differentiation of self from object as an important developmental landmark. The body must be taken into account as an object in space that does not "disappear" simply because the infant's attention has shifted to other things. The child who, in the process of placing one block on top of another with her right hand, gets her left hand sandwiched between the two blocks fails to differentiate her own left hand from the block resting on the table. Eventually the child will learn to think about the position of her hand as differentiated from the position of an object. She will adjust the hand-to-object relation in order to accomplish an object-to-object relation. In our example, removing the left hand will become subordinated to and hierarchically integrated with placing one block on top of another with the right hand.

The Perceptual Stage

Whereas the sensorimotor stage involves the differentiation and integration of actions and emotions, the perceptual stage involves the differentiation and integration of representations of objects, such as drawing and imitating rhythms and sounds. Representation of objects is one step removed from direct action on objects and is, therefore, more difficult. Thus, the shift from practical knowledge to representational knowledge is emphasized by both Werner and Piaget.

Representation, too, goes through an orthogenic process. At first, the act of representation is undifferentiated (Werner calls it *syncresis*). In her first attempts to represent what she sees, the child will mix (thereby the term *syncresis*) what an object means to her as an object in action with what that object looks like because of its static qualities, like size and shape. Werner himself (1948) reports that one child, when asked to draw a triangle, took the pencil and began to puncture the paper with the pencil point. The act of representing the static form of a triangle was confused by the child with the action of the object to be represented—a pointed triangle that physically punctures paper. As time goes by, the actions used to represent an object become differentiated from those used in the actual handling of the object, following the same sequence of changes as the physical actions of the previous stage.

Instances of syncresis (nondifferentiation) occur throughout the perceptual stage. Young children have difficulty constructing a mental picture of a familiar terrain independent of the paths they use to walk to various places within the terrain. Here, too, action on the real object interferes with the representation of the static arrangement of the elements within the object. Consider the following example (Werner, 1948, p. 329), illustrated in Figure 3-1.

Peter, a 5-year-old, is going swimming with his older sister, Martha. From the hay barn *(H)* the two children walk to the grove of trees *(G)* and then to the pond *(P)*. After swimming, Peter and his sister leave the pond, walk behind the small hill *(T)*, and come across a tree laden with apples *(A)*. After eating some apples, they return to the hay barn for a nap by way of the bridge *(B)*. Dreams of the apples left behind make the boy leave his sleeping sister and set out in search of the apple tree.

To Peter the delicious reward lies at the end of the path $H \rightarrow G \rightarrow P \rightarrow T \rightarrow A$. These points are not present in the child's mind in a coordinated frame of reference that would lead him to reach the tree by crossing the bridge. The location of the tree is inextricably tied to the action of walking and, therefore, to the original path he followed to get to it. So he leaves the barn, directed toward the grove and the pond and the hill.

Figure 3-1.

Martha awakens, discovers that Peter is gone, recalls his complaints about leaving the apples behind, and strikes out across the bridge, getting to the tree five minutes before her brother—who will surely be convinced of his older sibling's divinity. To the older child the tree is "between the bridge and the hill," not "after the hill," as it was when she first saw it while walking. These spatial relations exist as a mental map that can be "navigated" in a variety of paths, many of which can lead to the same point. The landmarks, in Werner's terms, are differentiated from one another and then integrated again into a network of relations.

The Contemplative Stage

The contemplative act is the act of making inferences from general principles about objects. Language is an important part of this process. The word, as a symbol bearing no physical resemblance to the idea it represents, helps the child think about the relations themselves rather than about the physical objects alone. Part of making correct inferences is the ability to abandon "thingness"—what Werner calls the *progressive transparency* of concepts (Langer, 1970, p. 767).

Take, for example, the word *inside*. This word refers to a relation between two objects. The concept of "insideness" does not change with a change in the two objects that are one inside the other. The concept is transparent in the sense that the particular objects are "invisible"—that is, unimportant to the meaning of the concept. In other words, the concept is general, not specific to particular objects.

Once words begin to lose their "thingness" and acquire general meaning, the child can use language as a tool to make correct inferences. At first this is difficult. Werner (1948, p. 329) cites the following illustrative case. A 10-year-old boy had had a teacher who was quite tall and very kind and another teacher who was short and tended to be cross. One day the child met a new teacher, who was short, and greeted him with the comment "I'm afraid you'll make a cross teacher." The boy was reasoning from one

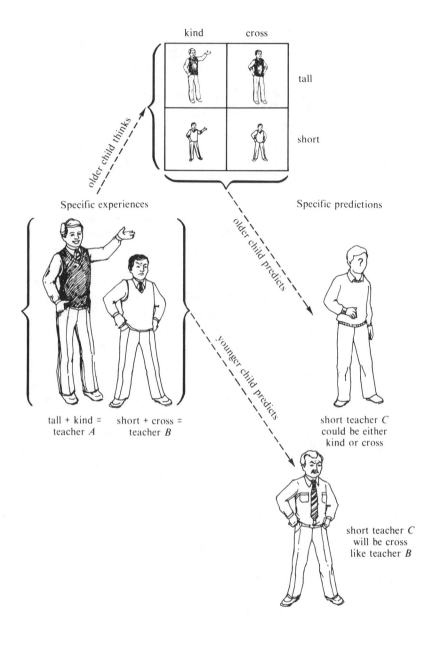

Possible relations

kind   cross

tall

short

older child thinks

Specific experiences

Specific predictions

older child predicts

younger child predicts

tall + kind =   short + cross =
teacher *A*   teacher *B*

short teacher *C*
could be either
kind or cross

short teacher *C*
will be cross
like teacher *B*

Figure 3-2. Older children make predictions after considering all four possible combinations. Younger children predict directly from their personal experiences.

specific situation (his first short teacher) to another specific situation (his new short teacher)—short teacher, therefore cross teacher. He was not reasoning from one specific situation to a general form of relationship between height and temperament, independent of the particular situations he had experienced. Thought independent of experience would have led the boy to consider the possibility that short and kind could coexist, as could tall and cross.

Figure 3-2 illustrates the different thinking processes of younger and older children. The younger child reasons from specific experiences to specific predictions. The older child reasons from specific experiences to possible relations and then to specific predictions. The fact that he has never had a short and kind teacher does not prevent the older child from considering that possibility, since he has the ability to think about relations independently of actual experiences.

The example above also illustrates the progression from globality to differentiation in contemplative acts—the same orthogenesis we saw at work in sensorimotor and representational acts. The younger child holds the idea that short teachers are cross as true in all cases. The older child, instead, differentiates physical stature from temperament. Once differentiated, these dimensions are organized by the older child into a matrix, as shown at top of Figure 3-2. The process of differentiation and integration applies to contemplative acts just as it does to sensorimotor and representational acts.

This is how Langer (1970, p. 749) describes in words and diagram the relationship among Werner's three stages of mental development.

> The orthogenetic relationship of the three major stages of mental construction is such that the most advanced contemplative systems hierarchically integrate the more primitive sensori-motor and intuitive systems, when all three systems have developed in an organism. It is highly unlikely, for example, that adult humans ever construct a pristine percept that is untinged by any contemplative operation. This means, however, that perceptual or intuitive representation is not only a stage of development but one of three parallel systems of action that may develop into the most mature (differentiated and hierarchically integrated) organization possible. Consequently, development may be schematized, according to Werner, as a three-branched tree.

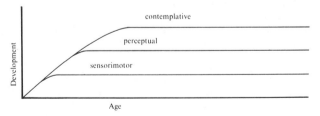

Figure 3-3. Werner's three stages of mental development. (From ''Werner's Comparative Organismic Theory,'' by J. Langer. In P. H. Mussen (Ed.), *Carmichael's Manual of Child Psychology* (3rd ed., Vol. 1). Copyright 1970 by John Wiley & Sons, Inc. Reprinted by permission.)

Jerome Bruner

Jerome Bruner is an American psychologist and the past director of the Center for Cognitive Studies at Harvard University. Of his numerous publications two books on cognitive development are the primary sources for this section—*Beyond the Information Given* (Bruner, 1973) and *Studies in Cognitive Growth* (Bruner, Olver, & Greenfield, 1966).

Bruner's theory shows similarities with both Piaget's and Werner's. Like Piaget, Bruner chooses to describe cognitive development as a process that goes through qualitatively different stages. Like Werner, Bruner emphasizes the importance of the child's representational acts. It is, however, the use of representation to discover and keep track of regularity in the environment that is the focus of Bruner's attention. His use of the word *regularity* is similar to Piaget's use of the term *conservation*—what remains invariant in spite of other, irrelevant changes. For Bruner, development is the process of learning to think about regularities that are more and more complex. For example, the fact that the picture of the smiling clown, even when turned upside down, is still a picture of a smiling clown is a much simpler type of regularity than the regularity involved in conservation of length or weight. Only if children develop new ways of representing objects and changes in objects can they deal with the more complicated regularities. Bruner has identified three modes of representing objects and events: enactive, ikonic, and symbolic.

Enactive Representation

The first mode is representation by action. In what sense are actions representative? For Bruner, the representativeness of an action is the action's "habitual" pattern. A particular action pattern, such as grasp-and-lift an object, is so well practiced during the first year of life that it takes on the role of a unit that can be combined with other motor units. It can even "substitute" for other motor units, like grasp-and-push, when the habitual unit does not cause the desired result. It is the self-contained nature of motor units, as well as the child's ability to combine, recombine, rearrange, and invent new motor "sentences" composed of these same motor units, that causes Bruner to treat action as an early "language"—as a mode of representation.

Enactive representation is what we generally call know-how. A child first knows a knot because she knows how to actually tie the knot. The knowledge is represented by the motor units used to tie the knot. Later the child may be able to represent in a drawing the successive actions required to tie a knot (ikonic representation) or to tell someone over the ship-to-land phone how to tie it (symbolic representation).

Ikonic Representation

This second mode refers to representation in the form of images. Images are spatial wholes, like a map or a picture. The mental image (ikon) is more than a remembered sequence of actions, even though, during the first year of life, the formation of mental images may be aided by recalling how an object feels when one handles it (Witkin, Dyk, Faterson, Goodenough, & Karp, 1962).

How do we know which type of representation a child is using? Bruner cites this example:

> We ask him to tell us the fifty states of the Union. If he "reads out" in this order "Maine, New Hampshire, Vermont . . . ," we can guess that the supporting representation for his recital is spatial. If the order is "Alabama, Alaska, Arizona, Arkansas, California . . . ," the support is inferred to be more list-like, ordered by an alphabetical rule [Bruner et al., 1966, p. 7].

In Bruner's example the first recitation indicates that the child was using an ikonic representation (mental image) to guide his answer. The second recitation indicates that the child was using a symbolic mode of representation—the next mode we discuss.

Symbolic Representation

This type of representation involves the use of some conventional code, usually language, to represent objects and ideas. The symbol, unlike the ikon, does not bear any physical resemblance to the object it represents. For example, the word *alligator* when spoken does not sound like the hiss of the animal to which it refers. When written, the word does not make a spatial configuration that looks like the scaly beast. Since children cannot see the relationship between the symbol and its referent, they must learn such relationship from parents, friends, and older siblings—that is, from their culture.

The natural spoken language, the sign language of the deaf, the Morse code, and mathematical symbols are all examples of codes (symbols) that have been conventionalized so that many people can use them to communicate with one another. Children learn symbolic representation primarily because it is the best mode for communicating with others.

Representation and Cognitive Development

How do these three modes of representation relate to cognitive development? By the age of 3, most children are using all three modes of representation. They wave bye-bye (enactive), draw a face (ikonic), and speak a language (symbolic). It is how a child uses these modes of representation to solve problems that defines the child's level of cognitive development.

Let's say that a child is presented with two shoe trees. They are both for a left shoe, although the child doesn't know it. The child is asked whether the two shoes are identical or not. Which mode of representation does the child use to figure out his answer? He may make hand gestures representing the shapes of the two shoe trees as he tries to figure out whether they match. This enactive mode indicates an elementary level of development. If the child is slightly more advanced, he may try to create a mental match or mismatch by imagining one of the two shoe trees in a different position. If he does that, he is using an ikonic mode of representation. The more advanced child may say to himself "The hump on the right side of this one matches the hump on the right side of the other one." He looks for features that he can verbally label and then reasons on the basis of such labels—a symbolic mode of representation.

These modes of representation can work in combination with one another. Words can help the juggler to keep his Indian clubs in the air if he says to himself "Lead with the right." We can use actions to improve our memory of words by acting out the meaning of a new word—for example, *slide* or *contrite*. Images can facilitate the learning of new actions and new words, as the old proverb about pictures and words has told us for a long time.

The different representational modes can also aid cognition by coming in conflict with one another. It is through his work on such conflict that Bruner has made his special contribution to our understanding of cognitive development. When conflict occurs—that is, when the child's expectations are violated—the child has an opportunity to rethink his or her approach to objects and events and grow intellectually. Conflict causes the child to experience a mental dissonance. That dissonance goads development, because the child seeks to reduce the dissonance and, in so doing, progresses intellectually. The following is an example of how cognitive development results from the conflict between two modes of representation.

Children younger than 5 or 6 tend to judge the quantity of liquid in a glass by looking only at the liquid's level—at its appearance, so to speak. Pouring water from a short wide glass into a tall narrow glass can create the illusion that the second glass contains more water than the first glass. In a study conducted by Bruner, Olver, and Greenfield (1966, p. 192), children between the ages of 4 and 7 were shown two glasses: one, long and thin, was half filled with water; the other one, wide and short, was empty. A shield was placed in front of the empty glass, so that only its top was visible. Next, the experimenter poured all the water out of the tall glass into the wide glass and asked the children to guess the water level in the wide glass and to mark it on the shield.

The children guessed that the level of the water in the wide glass was the same as it had been in the narrow glass, because "you just poured the same water from here to there." They were quite surprised when the shield was removed and they could see that the water level was lower in the wide glass. After several such experiences the children were given the standard conservation task; that is, the water was poured from the narrow into the broad glass, and the children were asked whether the *amount* of water was or was not the same as before. Many of the children who had failed this task before practicing with the shielded glass now understood that the amount only "appeared" different (different levels) but in "reality" was the same, because "it is just the same water poured from here to there."

Bruner concludes that the shielding caused the ikonic representation (the mental image of the water level behind the shield) to conflict with the symbolic representation (the verbal statement that it was the same water). The conflict caused the children to think more clearly about what was happening and helped them depend less on the ikonic features of the task. This, however, was true of the older children only. The younger children did not experience the conflict. But those who did sense the conflict went on to understand that the amount was conserved.

Robert Gagné

Robert Gagné sees cognitive development as cumulative learning; that is, complex forms of learning represent the accumulation of simpler forms of learning. A person's ability to compute the area of a triangle, for example, is contingent on the person's having previously learned the simpler concept of triangle. The concept of triangle itself is learned after one has learned to discriminate straight lines from curved lines. And so forth. In other words, once the person has acquired the simpler skills, the acquisition of new and more complex skills is mostly a matter of combining and ordering the simpler ones. If one analyzes any intellectual skill, one can easily recognize the hierarchical order in which the various levels of skill are organized. Each level represents the prerequisite for the next one and is, in turn, based on even simpler, prerequisite skills.

Unlike Piaget, Gagné does not describe cognitive development in terms of general mental stages. Gagné's emphasis is on the specific skills that are required to solve a particular problem. For example, if a child fails to conserve length, Gagné does not presume the absence of some general cognitive operation, like Piaget's reversibility or closed group. He prefers to identify the specific rules, concepts, discriminations, and associations that the child needs in order to be able to conserve length (see Gagné, 1970, p. 296).

Gagné has identified eight types of learning. The first four will be mentioned only in passing, because they are quite elementary. In *signal learning,* the person learns that a particular stimulus usually signals the occurrence of a certain event; for example, footsteps signal the imminent appearance of someone. In *stimulus-response learning,* the person, after having learned the signal, learns what response to make when the signal occurs. Such response usually affects the occurrence of the event announced by the signal. The person, for example, locks the door at the sound of footsteps, thereby avoiding the "occurrence" of the stranger.

The next two types of learning, *motor chaining* and *verbal association,* are sequences of stimulus-response associations. The hustle, a one-time craze of discotheques, is a sequence (a chain) of motor responses. The sentence "Let's do the hustle" is a sequence of words (verbal association)—that is, words chained together. Learning a verbal chain is far simpler than understanding the meaning of the verbal chain and is, therefore, a lower form of learning. The 4-year-old may be able to repeat the sentence "Let's do the hustle" as a verbal chain, without having the slightest idea of what the sentence means.

The child who does understand the meaning of the verbal chain exhibits still higher forms of learning. These other, and higher, forms of learning are much more complex than the four we have just mentioned and require a more detailed discussion.

Discrimination Learning

This form of learning may be defined as the ability to distinguish between similar stimuli and, consequently, make different responses to different stimuli. Gradually the child learns that rabbits and hamsters are different animals, that *p* and *b* are different sounds, and that a circle and an ellipse are different shapes.

Discrimination learning is not simply a matter of learning the verbal label of an object. Discrimination learning is an active process by which the child learns to distinguish different things that initially appear the same. Most frequently the child learns to search for some distinctive feature in each of two similar objects that will help to keep the objects distinct. The long ears of the rabbit, the explosive breath of the *p,* the flatness of the ellipse are all physical cues that the child may use to discriminate these stimuli from similar ones.

Gagné admits that giving names to objects—that is, using verbal labels—does make discrimination easier (Norcross & Spiker, 1958); however, the verbal label is not necessary for discrimination learning. Even little chicks can be taught to discriminate the circle from the ellipse.

Concept Learning

Unlike discrimination learning, concept learning does not depend on the presence of specific physical distinctive features. It is a more general and more abstract type of learning. Take as an example the concept of "middle." Learning this concept involves establishing a relation among various objects. In the sequence *XOX,* the letter *O* is the middle object. In the sequence *OXO,* the letter *X* is the middle object, as it is in the sequence *WXY.* What is learned is more general than the mere recognition of a particular letter; it is a relation among several objects. The relation itself is not a distinctive feature that can be pointed to and is, therefore, a higher type of learning than discrimination learning.

Children of different ages use different forms of learning to approach the same task. Kendler and Kendler (1959) found that children younger than 7 approach certain two-choice learning tasks as a search for distinctive features (discrimination learning), while children older than 7 approach the same tasks as a search for the relevant concept (concept learning).

In the Kendler and Kendler study, the children were presented with two food-wells covered with squares of different sizes and colors (two small and two large red squares and two small and two large white squares altogether). One food-well contained some candy, and the other one was empty. The children were to discover in which food-well the candy was hidden on each presentation—that is, on each trial. On half of the trials the candy was always under the *large* red square and never under the adjacent small white square. On the other half of the trials the candy was always under the *large* white square and never under the adjacent small red square. The sequence of the trials was random. After about 60 to 80 trials the children had learned to identify without error the food-well containing the candy.

But what had the children learned? Had they learned that they should choose the well covered by the square with a tiny chipped corner (which happened to be the large red square) or, on other trials, the well covered by the square with roughly cut edges (which happened to be the large white square)? Or had they, instead, learned that they should choose the well covered by the large-*sized* square? In other words, were the children using discrimination learning or concept learning?

To find out which type of learning the children were using, Kendler and Kendler shifted the candy's hiding place, without, of course, telling their subjects. Now the candy was placed on half of the trials under the *small* white square and never under the adjacent large red square. On the other half of the trials the candy was hidden under the *small* red square and never under the adjacent large white square. From an adult point of view this shift remains within the same dimension, *size;* that is, size remains the relevant aspect of the stimulus (see Figure 3-4). For the adult the candy has been under a large stimulus in all previous trials and is under a small stimulus in all present trials.

This type of shift would present little problem for the child who had responded to the initial learning task on the basis of concept learning—that

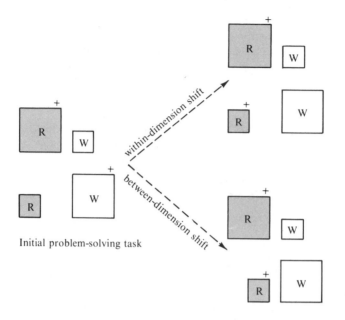

Figure 3-4. Diagram for within-dimension and between-dimension shifts. (The sign + indicates which square covers the candy.)

is, to the child who had learned to respond to size and ignore color. But, for the child who had used discrimination learning, the shift presents greater problems, since he or she has more to unlearn. The cues he or she used in the initial learning task (chipped corner or rough edges) are no longer helpful, and new ones must be found. This child, however, would be in a much better position should the experimenter shift to the large *red* square on some trials and to the small *red* square on the other trials (see Figure 3-4)—that is, should the experimenter shift from the dimension of size to the dimension of color. If the large red square is the one with a chipped corner and if it is still the square that hides the candy, the only stimulus the child has to unlearn is the rough edges. Conversely, the child who had used the concept of size would find this shift from size to color (between-dimension shift) quite difficult, because he or she would have not only to unlearn to respond to size but also to unlearn to ignore color.

By this ingenious method, Kendler and Kendler (1959) discovered that children younger than 7 find the between-dimension shift (which they called *nonreversal* shift) easier and that children older than 7 find the within-dimension shift (*reversal* shift) easier. These researchers saw in their experiment a clear example of children's development from discrimination learning to concept learning.

Rule Learning

Like concept learning, rule learning is more than connecting a particular response to a particular stimulus. In fact, rule learning involves the organization of several concepts. If a child learns the rule (a verbal statement) that "liquids turn into gas when heated," she has learned a relation among at least three concepts: liquids, gas, and heat. The concept of liquids, for example, does not refer to a particular liquid, such as Henry's glass of cola. Rather, it refers to a whole class of substances that share certain properties. The rule learned in this example instructs the child on how to order the concepts—first liquid, then heat, then gas, which is the consequence of the previous two. Not all rules tell the student what to do, but they do relate concepts. Take, for example, the rule "A nation consists of many states." Here the relation among concepts gives the definition of a nation by describing a part/whole relation.

The essence of rule learning is in understanding the meaning of the rule, not in memorizing it. If the child understands the meaning, she can then use the rule to make predictions in the real world and to explain unfamiliar events. If the child cannot generalize the rule to predict or explain novel events, she has not learned a rule but only a verbal chain.

Problem Solving

The eighth, and most complex, level in Gagné's hierarchy is problem solving. Problem solving involves combining, sequencing, and organizing rules. It also requires the person to combine rules in novel ways to fit a particular situation.

The combination of rules may need to be changed as the nature of the problem changes. Consider this problem: "Does a 2-inch square (Figure 3-5a) still have an area of 4 square inches when the top of the square is pressed over slightly (Figure 3-5b)?" Some students say yes and justify their answer by saying that what is lost on the left is gained on the right, thus the

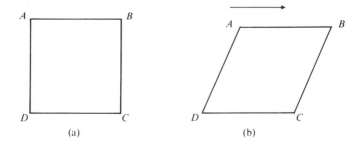

(a)   (b)

Figure 3-5. Square *ABCD* (a) is pressed down slightly (b). The student is asked whether the area in (a) is the same as the area in (b).

area remains the same. This answer, based on the principle of rearranging parts, is wrong. All you have to do to convince yourself is press the square further, so that it is completely flattened. If you do this, the "square" has virtually no area at all.

To find the right answer, another set of rules must be applied. The fact is that, by pressing the top of the square, we have changed it into a parallelogram (Figure 3-5b). Since the area of a parallelogram is obtained by multiplying width by altitude and since the altitude of the square is different from the altitude of the parallelogram, the areas of the two figures are also different. The question here is one of deciding which set of rules should apply—rules of rearranging parts or rules of changing altitude.

The Specific Nature of Cognitive Development

Unlike Piaget, Werner, and Bruner, Gagné assumes that the development of general cognitive abilities is no more than the result of learning specific tasks. To Gagné, there is no general age-related stage of concrete operations or a stage at which children are able to use only discrimination learning. If a 4-year-old is not using conceptual learning on a certain task, it is because she has not had sufficient experience and feedback on that particular task. If the child cannot solve conservation-of-length problems, she should be taught the component skills involved, such as compensation, identity, and straight line. In fact, studies using the approach of teaching component skills rather than the approach of repeated drill on the more complex tasks have reported some success (Bearison, 1969; Kingsley & Hall, 1967).

It is not clear from Gagné's work just how far he thinks teaching can take a child. After all, even after a child has learned the component skills of a task, he still has to organize them on his own. The teacher cannot lead the child step by step through all the relations. Take the transitive relation as an example. The transitive relation requires an inference: if stick A is longer than stick B and stick B is longer than stick C, the inference can be made that stick A is longer than stick C. The teacher can give the child the AB/BC relation, but the child must reach the AC relation by inference. If the child asks the teacher for information about AC, he has not yet learned transitivity. By its very nature transitivity depends on the child's sensing the implications of a set of facts; it is not itself just another fact. According to Inhelder, Sinclair, and Bovet (1974), this type of knowledge—knowledge based on logical necessity—cannot result from the cumulation of specific concepts alone. The child must construct the relation between A and C by deduction in order to sense its logical necessity.

Perhaps the main point here is not whether children abruptly reach a stage at which they can use mental operations like transitivity (previous example) in many situations but whether a specific experience can ever lead a child, even gradually, to make the necessary inference. Whereas Gagné suggests that specific experience is sufficient, Piaget would insist that experience, while necessary, is not sufficient. Experience must be combined with the biological capabilities of our species that make it possible for us to organize specific experiences into a closed group (see section on Piaget in Chapter Two). But Piaget's theory does not carry too many implications for how a particular concept should be taught. Piaget was more interested in determining the necessary biological capabilities, which is a somewhat more academic question than Gagné's interest in instruction.

Gagné's concern for the specific skills needed to solve a given problem makes his work relevant to teachers who are trying to improve their instruction methods. Gagné's analysis of the component skills needed to master, say, map reading offers teachers definite guidelines on how to increase students' attention and motivation to learn map reading.

Let's take the example of map reading to see how the three forms of learning operate in concert.

> *Discrimination learning:* A star indicates the capital city; an airplane indicates an airport.
>
> *Concept learning:* A red numeral next to a black roadline indicates the mileage between the two cities on either side of the numeral along the roadline.
>
> *Rule learning:* On a topographic map, the brown lines represent a difference in elevation; the numeral on each brown line indicates feet above sea level. If the numerals on successive brown lines are getting smaller and smaller as one reads from east to west, a stream (indicated by a blue line) cutting that terrain would flow from the east to the west.

The task analysis—that is, the breakdown of the task into the forms of learning it requires—tells the teacher that the discrimination of individual symbols should be taught before concepts, since concepts involve relations among symbols. It also tells the teacher that concepts should be taught before rules, since they are easier to learn. In the early lessons on map reading, the teacher directs the students' attention to the symbols, comments on the symbols' distinctive features, and plays games that make learning such symbols fun. Gagné's focus on the specific skills of classroom learning makes it possible for him to specify how distinctive features can be highlighted (for example, by underlining and using different colors) and motivation can be increased (for example, by teaching to read a map that leads to a small treasure somewhere on the school grounds).

Gagné is perhaps better known among educational psychologists than among developmental psychologists. His primary interest is in learning and instruction rather than in development. But the fact that he has proposed a hierarchy of types of learning makes his work relevant to the issue of age-related changes in the child's ability to learn. We have presented his work because of its precision and because many of the concepts he uses will be referred to elsewhere in the book to discuss cognitive development. You will recognize, in the last section of this chapter, Gagné's influence on the work of Klahr and Wallace.

Sidney Bijou and Donald Baer

Bijou and Baer (1961, 1965) are more interested in the observable, environmental events that determine behavior than in the unobservable, complex mental operations. These two behaviorists see psychological development as the "progressive changes in the way an organism's behavior interacts with the environment" (Bijou & Baer, 1961, p. 1). Behavior, for Baer and Bijou, is a function of stimulus events. This is why this approach to the environment/person interaction is called the *functional analysis* of behavior.

Bijou (1975) is quick to point out that, just as stimuli influence responses, responses influence stimuli. For example, the nipple of the milk bottle elicits the infant's sucking. But, in turn, the act of sucking changes the stimulus properties of the nipple. The round nipple becomes oblong, and, because of the effect of the baby's saliva, its taste changes. The path of effect is a two-way path.

Environmental events fall into two broad categories: reinforcers and discriminative stimuli. Those stimulus events that come after a response and increase the likelihood of the response are called *reinforcers*. If I chuck the baby under her chin each time she smiles at me and if I notice that she begins to smile more often as I continue to chuck her each time she smiles, I can be fairly confident that chucking is reinforcing. *Discriminative stimuli* are those stimulus events that occur before a response and signal an opportunity for reinforcement—that is, they signal the time to make a particular response in order to bring about a particular consequence. To the baby the sound of her mother's footsteps signals the best time to cry in order to be gently rocked. Crying at other times doesn't lead as quickly to the same consequence. The footsteps don't reinforce crying; they signal when to cry.

What if crying doesn't affect the mother's behavior? What if crying is not followed by rocking with any greater frequency than other things the baby does? In other words, what happens when the stimulus event (rocking) is not contingent on the infant's response (crying)? Then the crying response is not an *operant;* it does not operate on the environment to cause particular events. Not all responses are operants. Those that don't increase the probability of the occurrence of some event generally disappear in the course of time.

Responses can also disappear because they *do* lead to particular consequences. If, every time Spencer shoves Trina, the teacher puts Spencer in the corner, we may notice that Spencer's shoving disappears across time.

Shoving is an operant that leads, with relentless regularity, to sitting in the corner. Conversely, not shoving is an operant that leads to freedom from the corner. In sum, an operant is a response that changes in its frequency because of its consequences. The change may be either an increase or a decrease of the measured response.

How does functional analysis explain the changes in the child's behavior across broad age spans? For example, how does it account for the differences between a child in Piaget's sensorimotor stage and that same child, years later, in the concrete-operational stage?

Stages of Development

In their two small books Bijou and Baer (1961, 1965) treat development as a continuous process. The basic principles of learning remain the same across age. In each stage of development the child is faced with the task of learning which stimuli signal the occasions when a particular response will yield a reinforcer. What *does* change with age is the nature of the reinforcement and the complexity of what can serve as a discriminative stimulus.

During the first 18 months of life—which Bijou and Baer call the *universal stage*—children learn to coordinate their hands to grasp and manipulate objects. They also learn to coordinate their bodies and to acquire the necessary balance to walk upright. Those movements that perform their function successfully increase in probability; those that lead to failure decrease.

Development during the next four or five years of life—called the *basic stage* (Bijou, 1975)—centers on learning certain social responses to other people. Verbal and gestural responses are reinforced when they lead to desired consequences, like mother's attention, control of a peer, or mastery of some task at hand. During the basic stage children develop social responses that influence, or even determine, their general personality types for years to come. Children who receive approval for small portions of their bids for acceptance will develop personality types quite different from those of children who are consistently reinforced for almost every bid. Development is a function of the reinforcement history of each individual child. Bijou and Baer have not given us details of development beyond those early years. But we assume that they would apply the same principles of learning to late-childhood, adolescent, and adult development.

At the end of the preceding section we asked how functional analysis explains the changes in the child's behavior across broad age spans. Functional analysis sees these changes as no more than changes brought about by stimulus events that are discriminative and reinforcing. In infancy stimulus events that directly affect the body—like cold, sweetness, brightness, and so on—increase responses that are also defined by reference to the body—like reaching, drinking, and talking. In early childhood stimulus events are more symbolic—for example, social approval rather than actual stroking. But the effect is the same.

We may distinguish here between theories that account for what environmental events are common to a particular age and those that account for what mental events are common to a particular age. The theories of the four psychologists discussed earlier (Piaget, Werner, Bruner, and Gagné) belong in the latter group. Functional analysis belongs in the former. Let's take the number-conservation task to contrast the two kinds of approaches.

Most 4-year-olds fail to understand that two rows of five marbles each contain the same number of marbles regardless of the fact that in one row the marbles are spread out and in the other they are close together. Bijou and Baer would account for this difficulty by looking at the reinforcement history of 4-year-olds in general. They might reason that a 4-year-old, because of the reinforcement history of the average 4-year-old, considers all longer things as "being more" than shorter things. For example, the child may remember that a longer bar of candy offered more to chew than a short one.

Piaget, Werner, Bruner, and Gagné would be interested in another aspect of the question. These theorists, particularly Piaget and Werner, would not be satisfied with the answer that five single objects are confused with a single long object. Since they believe that stimuli are complex mental constructions, they would want to know how children think about the five marbles spread out and how such a form of thinking leads them into error. They might reason that 4-year-olds fail to understand that the increase in the length of one row is compensated by an equal decrease in the proximity of the marbles in the other row.

In sum, Bijou and Baer explain an error as a case of making the wrong response because one stimulus was assumed to be another. Piaget, Werner, and, to a certain extent, Bruner and Gagné do not so quickly dismiss error as a case of misidentification of stimuli. For them, the stimulus itself, as a mental event, becomes the issue to be addressed. To say that a row of five objects is confused with a single long object is to ignore the mental events that make the child treat five objects as if they were one long object. Bijou and Baer accept the confusion between stimuli without question and proceed to look for the reinforcement history of the *assumed* stimulus. Piaget and the others try to explain the confusion.

David Klahr and J. G. Wallace

Klahr and Wallace (1976) see cognitive development as information processing (IP). Their model of cognition reflects the moment-to-moment decisions that an individual makes when solving problems. The individual's thoughts are represented as an ordered series of self-instructions regarding what to do when certain conditions are present. These instructions to the self are called *productions*. The network of productions relevant to any one type of problem is called a *production system*. For example, solving the problem of a ceiling light that doesn't work could be represented in terms of the IP model as follows:

Condition	Action
Light doesn't work	check fusebox.
If fuse is blown	replace; try light switch.
If light works	stop.
If fuse is not blown	replace light bulb; try switch.
If light works	stop.
If light doesn't work	replace switch; try switch.
If light works	stop.
If light doesn't work	call electrician.

The information-processing approach has been used for many years, primarily to explain adult cognitive processes. For Klahr and Wallace (1976), the value of IP is that it permits us to make nonambiguous statements about cognitive development. They feel that Piaget's discussions of cognitive development are not precise enough to avoid ambiguity. The more detailed language of production systems, they argue, can help us reach a clearer understanding of what the child is developing from and what the child is developing toward. It also allows for a clearer statement regarding what the child gains in the transition from one stage to the next.

A description of cognition in terms of productions (self-instructions) must take into account the limits of short-term memory (STM) and the manner in which children deploy their attention. Short-term memory contains those six or seven elements that we can keep active in memory without external prompting, like a phone number that can be remembered without looking at the phone directory. Without external prompting, these six or seven elements in STM will soon decay or be replaced by newer elements as we continue to take in more information in the next few seconds. From the time we look in the phone book to the time we dial the last digit, we are taking in new information, such as the house address of the person we are calling, and this new information then crowds out the complete number from STM before we finish dialing. Furthermore, what enters STM is determined by our intentions—that is, what we choose to seek. The interaction between memory and attention is fundamental to Klahr and Wallace's approach, while it is less explicit in Piaget's work.

Perhaps a look at one type of problem, conservation of quantity, will make the IP approach to cognitive development easier to understand.

According to Klahr and Wallace (1976), conservation of quantity is no less than a production system that "knows" when one can correctly estimate the number of objects in a set without counting them. For example, if we know (because we counted them) that a set contains 12 objects and then these 12 objects are spread apart, we don't need to recount them. We know that their number has not changed in the process of the objects' becoming spread out. The transformation of "spreading out" the objects is a perceptual transformation (T_p), not a quantity-changing transformation such as adding (T_+) or subtracting (T_-). A production system that can conserve number can discriminate T_p from $T_\pm$ and knows that it is not necessary to recount when the transformation is of the class T_p.

The discrimination of T_p from $T_\pm$ begins with an elementary form of judging numbers called *subitizing* (Q_s). When the set of objects is small, say three or four, the child can usually judge, just by looking, whether new elements have been added or subtracted. If the question is "Do you have the same number as before?" the child can say yes or no without ever counting the elements in the first place. This is an elementary form of quantification that even some animals possess. By using Q_s, a 3- or 4-year-old child can discriminate quantity-changing transformations, like receiving a new marble from a playmate, from quantity-preserving transformations, like changing the spatial distribution of the three or four marbles. Not only can the child apply Q_s to one collection that undergoes transformation, but he or she can also learn to apply Q_s to make judgments about the equality and inequality of two sets. Knowing that the quantity of one set remains the same after a T_p is called *identity conservation (IC)*. Knowing that the initial equality between two sets does not change with a T_p of either set is called *equality conservation (EC)*.

Development in conservation occurs when Q_s is generalized to larger and larger sets. When the child is confronted with 10 or 12 objects, he or she cannot use Q_s alone, since the span of subitizing (that is, judging numbers without counting) is around 3 or 4 elements only. If the child understands that the act of counting 1, 2, 3, and so on (Q_c) is a form of quantification, just like Q_s is a form of quantification, then Q_c will be used in those cases in which Q_s is too difficult. After all, counting (Q_c) and subitizing (Q_s) can both be used when the set of objects is small. When the set exceeds 3 or 4, then the child needs to count the objects individually.

Both the Q_s production system and the Q_c production system can be activated when the setting condition contains discrete, discontinuous, countable objects. But what about the generalization of Q_s and Q_c to conditions in which we are no longer dealing with countable objects but with continuous media, such as clay or water? This kind of conservation of quantity represents a much more difficult task. For one thing, the types of transformation possible with continuous media are more diverse than those with discontinuous media. For another, with continuous media the perceived appearance can be quite deceptive. For example, pouring the water contained in a short tumbler into a tall and skinny cylinder may lead the young child to conclude that the thinner glass contains more water than did the short glass. The opposite operation (pouring the water from the tall, thin container into the short, broad glass) would lead the child to conclude that the water is now less. The reason is simply that it *looks* more or less depending on the container. So, how does the child deal with conservation of continuous media?

According to Klahr and Wallace (1976), the child learns to make estimates of how much stuff is there by using some arbitrary units. In the case of, say, a rectangular piece of pie dough, the child figures that it is about the size of six postage stamps. If the dough is "transformed" by rotating it 90 degrees, the child will be able to say that its quantity is still the same, because it still looks about six postage-stamps big. The application of these quantification estimates (Q_e) helps the child discriminate quantity-preserving transformations (T_p) from quantity-changing transformations $(T_\pm)$ in continuous media.

The reason why Q_e develops later in life than Q_s and Q_c is contained in the formal description of just what Q_e is, and here is the power of the IP model. When Q_e is written out in the form of a production system, it actually contains as subcomponents the systems of Q_s and Q_c. That is, Q_s and Q_c must develop first as independent production systems before Q_e can develop, since Q_e uses both Q_s and Q_c. The precision of this formal description makes quite clear why the ability to conserve continuous media develops later in life than the ability to conserve discontinuous media. In order to conclude that quantity of continuous substance has not changed, the child must first subitize the mass of matter into imaginary discrete units and then count these units as if they were physically discrete. After numerous such experiences, the child generalizes that many of the transformations that do not change quantity with discontinuous material also do not change quantity with continuous material.

Attention plays a particularly important role in the Q_e production system. If the child attends to only one dimension of the transformation, he or she will make a false judgment regarding conservation. In the example of the conservation of liquid, the child needs to notice not only that the water gains height when poured into a skinnier jar but that it also loses width. The gain in height is compensated by the loss in width. Once "pouring the same liquid into a new jar" has been classified as a T_p, the child need not use Q_e again. He or she knows that the amount has remained the same, because T_p doesn't change quantity.

The advantage of the IP system is that it can specify why tasks that seem to be similar are not performed equally well by children of different age groups. The IP approach takes the instructions of the task and the stimuli that are present and represents them explicitly as part of the problem to be solved. If children at a particular age tend to ignore certain types of information, the production system describing that age group's performance will show that this critical information did not enter STM (short-term memory). The rest of the production system will be determined by the absence of this one piece of information.

If children at a particular age have not yet learned particular rules, such as the rule that addition is commutative, then the production system for those children will show an absence of that rule in LTM (long-term memory). For such children the production of certain arithmetical problems is therefore impossible, since the critical rule is not present in their repertoire of relevant rules. Klahr and Wallace have approached the study of cognitive development by asking what rules are in LTM, what rules are learned first, what do children select to place in STM in particular task situations, and what sort of interrelations can children at different ages establish among various production systems that they possess. This last characteristic of cognitive development—establishing relations among various mental operations—is easily handled in the language of production systems. Production systems are just that: sets of instructions that specify how various conditions and actions are to be interrelated in a total system that yields task solution.

According to Klahr and Wallace (1976), there are several factors that "drive" cognitive development forward. One is the cognitive system's need to be economical. As life progresses, the demands on cognition increase. Any way in which the system can reduce the load on information processing is most adaptive. The shift from recounting a set of objects to applying a conservation rule is a shift toward less mental effort. If the transformation is recognized as a T_p, then the system bypasses counting the objects again. Another factor that "drives" cognitive development is the system's need to be consistent. If counting leads to one conclusion and estimating leads to a different conclusion, the system will make attempts to reduce this discrepancy. For example, a set of six long matches may be judged to contain more matches than a set of seven short matches if Q_e is used; but the opposite judgment is reached if Q_c is used. This kind of conflict perplexes children and causes them to rethink the assumptions they are making about the concept of numbers. In fact, these conflicts can be used deliberately as a teaching device, as we shall see in Chapter Five.

The IP model has much to offer to the study of cognitive development across the life span, even though Klahr and Wallace have not yet applied their system beyond concrete operations. Developmental changes in memory and attention, so prevalent after the age of 60, can be adequately represented in IP language. Unlike Piaget's model of cognition, the IP model can, for example, handle reaction-time differences. And these differences are a frequent research finding; the elderly take longer to answer complex questions than do young adults. In information-processing terms, the longer reaction time in elderly subjects could be the result of the faster decay of items in STM, or poorer retrieval from LTM, or of nonsystematic search through an array of stimuli. These mental characteristics can be represented in the production systems of IP but cannot be represented in the more static structural descriptions that Piaget has been currently using. In the chapters that follow, particularly Chapter Four, the value of representing the task requirements (Piaget) as well as the ongoing, second-by-second information processing (Klahr and Wallace) should become quite apparent.

The Six Theories Look at Conservation

Now that we have discussed the basic approaches to cognitive development of these six theories, let's see them in operation by taking one problem and discussing how each theory would handle it. We have chosen conservation of volume as such a problem.

Figure 3-6 illustrates the problem as presented to children, say, from 5 to 8 years of age. The glasses are rectangular containers, so we can easily refer to the three dimensions of length (L), height (H), and width (W).

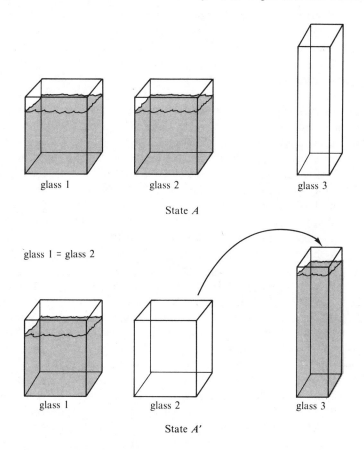

Figure 3-6. Test for conservation of nonmetric volume.

In state A, glasses 1 and 2 are identically shaped and contain the same amount of water. In state A', all the water of glass 2 has been poured into glass 3. Note that glass 3 is smaller in width and depth and is taller than glasses 1 and 2. The children are asked "Does glass 3 contain the same amount of water as glass 1?" The children don't have to compute the actual quantity. All they have to do is consider whether the two quantities are the same. Since no units of measure are necessary, we call this task _conservation of nonmetric volume_.

We will use each of the six theories discussed above to account for the children's cognitive development indicated by a shift from nonconserving to conserving answers. A nonconserving answer would be something like "No, glass 3 has more water, because you can see that it [the height of the water level] is more." The conserving answer would be something like "Yes, it is still the same, because glass 3 is taller but is also skinnier." In order not to labor this comparative analysis, we limit our discussion of each theory to a general idea or two.

Piaget explains the younger children's inability to conserve as follows. The 5-year-old can understand that glass 2 has been emptied into glass 3 and that no water has been added or subtracted. What the child cannot grasp is the reversibility of the act of water pouring. The child does not understand that the water can be poured back from glass 3 into glass 2 in order to reestablish the evidence that the amount of the water being poured is the same as the amount of the water contained in glass 1. The 5-year-old cannot integrate these two actions simultaneously (A changes to A', and A' changes back to A). What this inability indicates is that the 5-year-old doesn't sense the _logical implications_ of the reversibility of an action.

The 7- or 8-year-old, instead, understands that the effect of the initial pouring of the water can be undone (reversed) by pouring the water back from glass 3 into glass 2. Also, and even more importantly, the older child senses the possibility of this reverse action and sees it as the reason for his or her conservation answer. Cognitive development, to Piaget, is the increasing ability to relate facts, to relate relations, and to sense the logical necessity of certain conclusions—in this case, conservation.

Werner would probably see the 5-year-old's performance as a manifestation of differentiation without integration. The 5-year-old has reached the stage at which he or she can differentiate a glass with a high water level from a glass with a low water level and can make the association between height and amount. A 2- or 3-year-old is likely to be in a more global stage—a stage at which the glasses are just containers of water, with no salient differences. At this age the child doesn't make the association between water level and amount that will become automatic in later years.

The 8-year-old, on the other hand, not only can differentiate water levels but can also integrate the change in water level with other changes. There are two cases in which water level changes. In one case only the water level changes; the width and depth of the container remain the same. This means that the volume of the water has changed. In the other case the water level changes along with changes in the width and depth of the container. This means that the volume has not changed. The 8-year-old has done more than differentiate levels of water. He or she has organized these changes into a hierarchy that leads to conclusions regarding conservation.

Bruner would focus on the child's mode of representing state A and state A'. A 5-year-old is most likely to use an ikonic mode, perhaps a mental picture. He or she sees the two states A and A' as two separate and unrelated conditions. The ikonic mode allows the child to think about the physical difference in water level, which is something that can be represented in a mental picture. But the fact that the new glass holds the same water cannot be represented ikonically.

The 8-year-old uses the symbolic mode to solve the problem. He says to himself "Well, after all it's the same water in both cases." The fact that in both state A and state A' the water quantity is the same cannot be brought to bear on the conservation question if the child has only ikonic representation at his disposal. To Bruner, cognitive development is a case of learning to use the more advanced modes of representation that the culture has to offer. Whereas the ikonic mode, by relying on images, orients the child toward the differences in the two states, the symbolic mode helps the child ignore these apparent differences in favor of similarities—in this case, the use of the same liquid at two different times. Since the similarities can be expressed only in language, it takes the symbolic mode of representation to think them through.

Bijou and Baer have not, to our knowledge, made attempts to explain conservation within the framework of the functional analysis of behavior. Our guess is that they would look at both kinds of responses—nonconserving and conserving—as they would at any other responses. In the everyday experiences of the 5-year-old, a glass with a higher level of water usually offers more to drink. When given the choice between a half-full and a nearly full glass of juice, the thirsty 5-year-old (or any-year-old, for that matter) would take the glass with the higher level. If the 5-year-old says "There is more there" (pointing to glass 3), it is because she is using water level as the discriminative stimulus that usually signals that the reward of more-to-drink will follow. She has not learned that the stimulus event of pouring from glass 2 to glass 3 without spilling any water is itself a signal that glass 3 will not lead to more-to-drink in comparison to the original amount in glass 2. With experience, the child learns that pouring-without-spilling is a better discriminative stimulus, since it does a better job of signaling the amount of reward. To Bijou and Baer, cognitive development is a matter of learning which discriminative stimuli make the best prediction about the consequences of a response. The 8-year-old learns when to say "They have the same amount." He says it in the presence of the discriminative stimulus pouring-without-spilling but doesn't say it in the presence of pouring-with-spilling.

Gagné maps out the various concepts and rules that are all part of a full-blown conservation answer. Before the child can understand that the amount of liquid is the same in glass 1 and glass 3, the child must be able to master, among other things, discriminations, concepts, and rules. Examples of discrimination are "The water level in glass 3 is different from the water level in glass 1" and "The width of glass 3 is different from the width of glass 1." An example of concept is "The liquid in glass 3 is the same liquid that used to be in glass 2." Examples of rules are "Volume equals length $\times$ width $\times$ height" and, even more complicated, "If length increases without a change in width and depth, volume has increased." The 5-year-old may have learned some of the discriminations and concepts and even some of the rules, but her failure to give the correct answer indicates that she has not learned all of the rules. To Gagné, cognitive development represents the cumulative learning of the specific discriminations, concepts, and rules that are necessary to solve a specific cognitive task (see Gagné, 1968). Gagné emphasizes the role of learning the relevant concepts and rules, while Piaget emphasizes the types of learning that are not available to children in the early stages of development.

Klahr and Wallace, like Gagné, map out the various concepts and rules implicit in the law of conservation. But they add another element—the decision-making sequence as it might occur second by second. A 5-year-old might have at his disposal certain rules and concepts, but, to solve the conservation problem, he has to know which rules to retrieve from LTM (long-term memory) and which stimulus events to notice and place into STM (short-term memory). Klahr and Wallace do more than make an ordered list of the rules and concepts that the child must have in LTM (which is Gagne's almost exclusive concern). They also add the interplay between LTM and STM as the child tries to make up his mind about which is the correct answer. They add a set of self-instructions to Gagné's discrimination, concepts, and rules. This is how, in abbreviated form, these self-instructions would sound.

> Look at level of water in glass 3; store in STM.
> Look at level of water in glass 1.
> Retrieve level in glass 3 from STM and compare to level in glass 1.
> If levels are different, retrieve T (transformation) from LTM.
> If T was of the class T_p (quantity-preserving transformation), conclude that the amount has not changed.
> If T was of the class $T_{\pm}$ (quantity changing), conclude that the amount has changed.
> If levels in glass 3 and glass 1 are the same, look at width of glass 3; store in STM.
> Look at width of glass 1, . . . and so on.

The 5-year-old might have difficulty at any number of places in this information-processing program. If the task makes too many demands on her STM, performance will suffer. If she doesn't have the requisite concepts and rules stored in LTM, performance will suffer. If the child directs STM to irrelevant events, such as the empty glass 2, or directs STM to relevant stimuli but at the wrong point in the information-processing program, performance will also suffer. To Klahr and Wallace, cognitive development is a matter of using STM (attention) and LTM (memory) in the most economical and consistent way in order to solve problems. Of the six theories presented, Klahr and Wallace's offers the most specific description of what happens during the problem-solving process.

Summary

We hope that our examination of how the six theories would approach the same problem will make the following summary discussion clearer. All six theories are attempts to answer broad questions regarding cognitive development. Piaget's theory seeks to understand universal patterns of thinking—patterns that are not dependent on particular experiences, even though they result from experience in general. Throughout his work, Piaget has attempted to impress on the scientific world that cognitive development involves certain biological laws of organization. In order to give a complete account of development, these biological laws must be taken into consideration together with the child's experience. Piaget's interest in the emergence of new modes of thinking, such as sensing the logical necessity of conservation, makes him useful to those interested in the basic nature of cognition but, perhaps, not as useful to those interested in how to design a specific program of instruction. Gagné and Klahr and Wallace have more to offer to those interested in curriculum design because of their specificity and emphasis on motivation and attention.

Bruner and Werner are both interested in the development of representation of objects and events, and both see the ability to create a hierarchical integration as dependent on an advanced symbol system. Words give us the power to relate objects symbolically in ways that are not possible physically. Unlike Piaget, Bruner does not relate development to biological laws of organization. Rather, he studies the organization contained in the tools of culture, particularly language. Children learn the language of their culture and, in so doing, learn what is conserved and what changes.

Bijou and Baer make no commitment to either biological or cultural laws of organization. They ask what signals behavior to occur and what reinforces it so it occurs again. There is a definite practicality to their approach. Teachers who are seeking means to increase student motivation find the functional analysis of behavior most helpful. However, this approach almost completely ignores the question of how to determine the difficulty of a task, short of actually trying to teach the task. The task-analysis approach of Gagné and of Klahr and Wallace would be quite helpful from this point of view.

The difference between Gagné and Klahr and Wallace can be described as the difference between a list and a set of instructions. Gagné is most helpful to teachers who want to prepare a sequence of lessons that gradually increase in difficulty. Klahr and Wallace are most helpful in teaching teachers how to observe their students in action, as they try to solve problems. In fact, the information-processing program can be seen as a verbatim transcript of a student in action thinking out loud. Such programs would, in effect, enable the teacher to compare the student's real pattern of thinking with the ideal program that describes the correct pattern. (Note that the production systems designed by Klahr and Wallace have an essential structure but can actually play themselves out in numerous sequences, all correct.)

Like the blind hearing man and the sighted deaf man, each theory "experiences" the same elephant, but each seeks out evidence from a perspective that is determined by its own purpose. Similarly, consumers of theory—that is, the practitioners—can choose to study whichever perspective is most suitable to their purpose. There is no need to engage in pseudocontroversies among theories designed to perform different functions.

Unfortunately none of these six theoretical approaches helps to organize the facts of cognitive development across the entire life span. Piaget's theory, at least as it now stands, ceases to distinguish developmental changes beyond the age of 16 or so. Bruner and Gagné stop making critical distinctions at about the same age level.

Bijou and Baer have not yet offered a functional analysis of behavior in the elderly years, but this would prove interesting, as would the application of information-processing models to adult and elderly cognition. Yet these latter two approaches are not, in a strict sense, theories of development. Rather, they are methods of studying behavior and cognition. Bijou and Baer make few general statements about why some reinforcers lose their effectiveness and others gain it across the life span; they are more concerned with the direct objective of identifying those reinforcers.

Klahr and Wallace's theory, a relatively new approach on the scene, has potential but has not yet been tried. The change in the memory and attention capacities of the elderly (see Chapter Four) could well be described in IP models. These models of cognition in old age could then be compared with IP models of cognition in the younger years. This comparison might give us clues regarding the nature of the change, even if the change was regressive rather than progressive.

For the present we have no comprehensive theories to account for both development and regression. The theories that we now have explain development in terms of each step building on each previous step. Development is explained by those cognitive processes that are added across time.

How does one account for regression? Some think that regression is simply the subtraction, in reverse order, of those cognitive processes that were added during development. But why is a cognitive process lost? It doesn't seem reasonable to assume that something like logical necessity is "unlearned." As you will see, regression in old age, if it exists at all, is attributed to factors "outside" strictly cognitive processes—for example, to changes in social contacts and changes in brain cells.

These determinants of regression inhibit cognition but are not themselves part of cognition. That the elderly are out of practice because of social isolation is a statement that tells us very little about changes in cognition. It tells us about their level of performance but not about their basic competence after a refresher course in logic or whatever. As this book will try to show, a true case of regression of cognitive competence is hard to find and, if found, is hard to explain in terms of some reverse process of development. To date comprehensive theory has not proved helpful in understanding the immense differences in the cognitive processes of middle and older adults.

Chapter Four

The Development
of Information Processes

This chapter discusses the development of memory and attention across the life span. Over time, both of these information processes come increasingly under the control of the individual's general intelligence and knowledge. Children become more clever in how they set about remembering material; they reorganize it, rehearse it, and make funny associations that help them recall the material later.

Also, as children become more knowledgeable about the world at large, they realize that certain things are not possible. This general knowledge about the world helps children to reduce the number of possibilities concerning some past event, thereby reducing the number of things they must consider when they have difficulty recalling some aspect of that event. For example, a child might forget what type of fish she caught in her uncle's pond, but at least she knows that it was not a whale. Children also become more aware of the level of difficulty of certain tasks and of the limitations of their own memory and attention. This awareness is especially important, because it is a governing factor in the amount of effort that the child will put into the task.

Of the theories that we reviewed in the preceding chapter, one is particularly relevant to a discussion of the development of memory and attention. Klahr and Wallace use an information-processing (IP) model that clearly includes memory and attention. These theorists, who are interested in the second-by-second course of thinking, discuss the ways in which information is stored and retrieved and the ways in which children selectively attend to what is currently happening.

As we mentioned in Chapter Three, the IP approach does not identify general developmental stages, as do the theories of Piaget, Werner, and Bruner. The IP approach usually treats cognitive development as the accumulation of fairly "task-specific" mental procedures, such as subitizing and estimating (Klahr & Wallace, 1976). For convenience, we shall present an IP model in the section on memory, even though the model includes aspects of attention. We shall return to those aspects when we discuss attention.

Memory

A General Model of Memory

The IP models presented in Chapter Three dealt with particular problems such as conservation tasks. Here, instead, we outline a more general IP model, which can be used to understand most any task that makes demands on a person's memory. Take, for example, the relatively simple task of remembering someone's name. Within that task, several things can happen that will either improve or hamper success.

Say I meet Ms. Dial for the first time on November 11 at a party. One week later, I see her again in a different setting—the grocery store instead of the home of a friend. I cannot recall her name. Why? First of all, I could have been distracted at the time her name was first mentioned and didn't hear it at all. Or I did hear her name *then* but cannot recall it *now*, because I have confused Ms. Dial's name with that of someone else I know who looks like her. In other words, the information has made it to the first step but not to the second. This idea that information has a ''flow'' from one point to another is basic to the model presented in Figure 4-1. The figure diagrams the flow of information from the first detection of a sensory input to the later attempts to retrieve that input. The boxes in the figure identify the sequence of steps in which the information is received, transformed, and retrieved.

For the first step, *detection,* to occur, a clear sensory input is required. An inaudible whisper or a garbled mumble may not be detected by the listener. Nothing can be stored—that is, committed to memory— if first it is not detected. The detection of stimulus events is governed by the physical properties of the event (loudness, size, proximity, and so on) and by the momentary state of the person (direction of gaze, sleepiness or alertness, and so forth). We shall have more to say about detection in the section on attention.

Information that is clearly detected can be sidetracked, so to speak, by *distractions*. It is possible that on November 11 I did detect Ms. Dial's name but was immediately distracted by a hail-fellow slap on the back from another person in the conversation circle. In other words, I heard the name clearly, but the name did not register in my immediate memory, which is called *short-term memory* (STM). Short-term memory is a temporary store of information—temporary because it can hold the information for a very short while only. Inputs are registered or not registered in STM, depending on what happens immediately after detection.

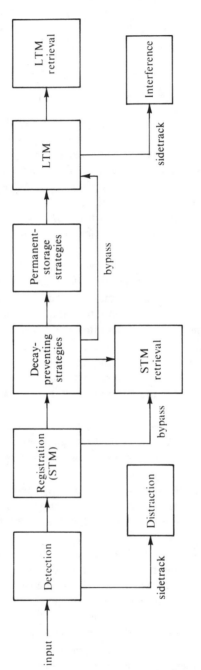

Figure 4-1. A model of memory.

It should be noted that *registration* is a memory process, not a simple case of seeing or hearing something, and refers to the active process of committing an item to short-term memory. As we said earlier, distraction can prevent registration. In our example, this would have happened if I hadn't been able to repeat Ms. Dial's name even a few seconds after I clearly heard it. We are all familiar with the embarrassing situation of having to say "Glad to meet you Ms. . . . err" (gulp). With increased effort, we can concentrate and eliminate distractions in order to register new information in STM.

Once information is registered in STM, it cannot rest secure there. The items stored in STM have a tendency to "decay" very rapidly (Melton, 1963). However, there are strategies we can adopt to keep the STM stores from decaying. These are called *decay-preventing strategies* (see Figure 4-1). If we know that we are going to need to call Ms. Dial by name, say, at the end of a short conversation, we can repeat her name silently a few times. Silently rehearsing the new information prevents the decay of the item registered in STM.

If, instead, we know that we'll have to use information some hours or days in the future, we must do more than prevent the decay of the memory trace in STM; we must convert the item from a short-term store to a long-term store. This brings us to the next box in Figure 4-1, which depicts *permanent-storage strategies*. Here the information is converted by an active process from STM to LTM (long-term memory). These strategies improve the chances of our retrieving the information at some time in the future.

Permanent-storage strategies are, in large measure, the basic strategies of learning. For example, if I am trying to remember Ms. Dial's name for some later occasion, I may make the following association: Ms. Dial has a smooth complexion, her name is Dial, and perhaps she uses Dial soap to keep her complexion smooth. These memory tricks are strategies to ensure permanent storage. Later in the chapter, we will discuss strategies of permanent storage that make recall easier by reorganizing the information.

Now a word about both decay-preventing strategies and permanent-storage strategies. Not all age groups use spontaneously these strategies to either prolong STM or convert STM to LTM. Young children do not. In Figure 4-1, a "bypass" line indicates that these strategies are not always used. The first bypass goes straight from STM to STM retrieval without going through decay-preventing strategies. The second bypass goes straight from decay-preventing strategies to LTM without going through permanent-storage strategies. It should be mentioned that people who take these bypasses are less likely to make effective STM or LTM retrieval.

Not even the best permanent-storage strategy can preclude failure in the heat of retrieval. Now it is November 18, I am in the grocery store, and this familiar-looking woman is approaching me with a friendly smile. It is retrieval time in the aisle. I notice her smooth complexion again, recall my "soap" association, and greet her with the nonchalant approach of someone seeing an old friend: "Good morning, Ms. Camay." Her smile drops, and she and her complexion walk coolly by. I have confused my soaps. My downfall has been brought about by *interference*—two similar items competing for expression at the time of retrieval. Interference should not be confused with distraction, which, as we said earlier, takes place immediately before registration in STM. Both distraction and interference prevent correct retrieval, but the breakdown due to distraction occurs earlier in the flow of information.

What are the developmental trends of these memory processes? As we shall see, children do not spontaneously use active memory strategies, elderly people suffer from knowing too much, and, despite stereotypes to the contrary, memory itself is not likely to decline with the passing of the years.

In the sections that follow, each of the processes identified in Figure 4-1 will be discussed in turn. Think of the model in general terms rather than as a diagram of one specific task. This means that some memory tasks do not involve the complete model illustrated in Figure 4-1, while others involve combinations of several such models. For example, repeating an oath of office after someone doesn't really require the use of permanent-storage strategies.

In addition, memory is also affected by factors that are beyond the basic processes and strategies we are discussing. One is the role of general knowledge, which helps to reduce the amount that has to be recalled. Another is the individual's *metamemory*. This is the term used by Flavell (1977) to refer to the person's awareness of his or her own memory processes—his or her own skills and limitations in remembering different types of information—which influences the ultimate success of remembering.

Registration

At what age does the infant show the first evidence of having registered information in STM? The act of sucking the nipple when the lips are stimulated could be a reflex action, which does not necessarily indicate that some memory has been stored. The fact is that in this situation no memory is required. Since the tickle to the lips (stimulus) continues after the sucking response has begun, there is no time interval between stimulus and response. Consequently, no memory trace is required to span the interval.

A clearer indication of memory is represented by anticipatory sucking on the part of the infant; that is, the baby starts sucking at the sight of the nipple even before her lips touch the bottle. Babies are not born with a reflex to suck upon seeing a nipple! The infant remembers that this round brown object is associated with a pleasant taste. In the course of her experience with this object, the baby registers its sight in STM long enough to think about it while sucking the milk (remember that most babies keep their eyes closed while sucking and, therefore, don't look at the nipple). The fact that the infant can recognize the nipple, as shown by anticipatory sucking, suggests that the information has gone through the IP model at least as far as STM retrieval.

Note that we are speaking here of *recognition,* a simple form of retrieval that requires only that the infant attribute some meaning to a stimulus presented by someone else. The infant doesn't have to recall the nipple as I had to recall Ms. Dial's name. *Recall,* a more advanced form of retrieval than recognition, requires that the child mentally provide the stimulus when the stimulus is not present. Had the child searched under her blanket for her bottle, while at the same time sucking vigorously, we might have assumed that she was recalling the bottle, which was itself not present. Recall seems to develop later in infancy than does simple recognition (Munsinger, 1970; Piaget, 1952b).

Despite the relative simplicity of recognition, the very young infant has difficulty with it if the time interval between the last sight of the nipple and the opportunity to suck is too long. The longer the interval is, the longer the memory trace (STM) must endure. If the memory trace of the round brown object has decayed beyond a point, there is nothing left to be associated with sucking. In other words, seeing the nipple does not produce a mental association with sucking for milk. The problem of STM decay seems to be significant in the first month of life, even with delay intervals under one second (J. S. Watson, 1967). Beyond this age, the infant matures neurologically and learns to apply more active and more efficient methods of registration.

Some memory tasks require a rapid registration of information. If I recited a phone number very quickly, you would have to hear and register each digit just as quickly in order to recite the whole number back to me. The speed of registration—that is, the speed at which items are placed in STM—does not seem to degenerate with age (Belmont, 1973; Botwinick & Storandt, 1974). Now, here's a myth-busting finding. Does this mean that memory does not decline with age? Not exactly. The elderly do have difficulty with rapid-fire tasks (Canestrari, 1963), but their problem is not due to poor registration or to more rapid decay in STM. If the phone number were read more slowly, they would do fine (Kinsbourne, 1973).

What is the problem, then? Evidently each digit reaches STM, but each digit follows on the heels of another so closely that the person doesn't have time to use the strategies of permanent storage that assist recall. The items in STM actually interfere with one another (Arenberg, 1973; Talland, 1965). If the items were never registered or quickly decayed, they would not interfere with one another. These problems are greater for the elderly than for children and adolescents (Botwinick & Storandt, 1974).

The studies we have just mentioned suggest that memory decline in old age is not due to deterioration of the nerves. One can argue that an indication of faster STM decay in the elderly may mean that their nerves cannot register information very well, like overused recording tapes. Yet, research on memory decline in the elderly indicates that decay is not the problem. The problem seems to be in the failure to apply efficient memory strategies rather than in general neurological deterioration. In the next two sections we will discuss some of these memory strategies.

Decay-Preventing Strategies

There you are, on the phone, taking instructions on how to get to a friend's house. You don't have a pencil, and you must go search for one. What can you do to spare yourself the embarrassment of having to ask your friend to repeat the whole thing? Instead of having your friend repeat the instructions, you repeat them to yourself during your search for a pencil. You are trying to register these items in STM, and, at the same time, you are also trying to prevent their decay. This *rehearsal,* as it is called, has received some interesting attention in memory-development research.

Flavell, Beach, and Chinsky (1966) conducted a study to find out whether elementary-school children knew how to mentally rehearse material to be recalled. The study showed that first-graders didn't hit on the idea of using the rehearsal strategy. They would just sit there, let the delay interval (the time they had to wait before asked to recall) pass, and then try to duplicate the order in which the experimenter had pointed to the seven pictures they were asked to recall. Second- and fifth-graders, instead, showed a certain amount of lip movement and emitted nearly inaudible mutterings during the delay interval. Their recall was better than that of the first-graders. However, when the first-graders were asked to name the pictures out loud as the experimenter pointed to each of them in a given order, their recall improved. Apparently, naming the pictures while the experimenter pointed at them caused the children to mentally rehearse during the delay period before recall.

This study and the many that followed it have generally confirmed that children pass through three phases in their use of rehearsal strategies. In the early phase (preschool years), children don't use rehearsal, and instructions to do so don't improve recall. Even when rehearsal is attempted, it somehow doesn't mediate (span) the delay interval. This phase is called the *mediation-deficiency phase.*

Later (early elementary grades), as we saw in the Flavell, Beach, and Chinsky (1966) study, children reach a phase in which they don't spontaneously think of using rehearsal but can be taught to do so. For some reason, at this stage children do not spontaneously produce the strategy when it is needed but have no mediation deficiency. This is called the *production-deficiency phase,* since only the production is lacking.[1]

---

[1]Some researchers, like Reese (1976), divide this phase into an initial phase—in which instruction helps only partially—called *production-inefficiency phase,* and a later stage —in which instruction helps completely—called *production-deficiency phase.*

In the third phase (later elementary years), rehearsal strategies are spontaneously produced even without prompting or instruction from others. These older children know when to apply rehearsal strategies. Knowing what type of strategies are appropriate to a given situation is part of metamemory and will be discussed again in the final sections of this chapter.

Do older adults show a recurrence of production deficiency followed by mediation deficiency? The answer is yes and no. Production deficiency does reappear, but there is little evidence of mediation deficiency (Reese, 1976). The natural question, then, is: why don't elderly people use strategies that apparently they could use effectively? Reese (1976) cites several studies that interpret memory failure as a result of disuse. But these laboratory-type tests have very little relevance to the everyday life of the elderly. These tests involve episodic tasks, or tasks that require the recall of bits of unrelated information, which are common in the world of the college student but not in that of the older person. Memory of highly meaningful and interrelated material (semantic memory), such as a newspaper story, doesn't show a similar decline with age. Memory decline on episodic tasks is just one form of a general decline in what Horn (1970) calls *fluid intelligence,* defined as the ability to mentally manipulate new information quickly. Semantic memory—an example of what Horn calls *crystallized intelligence*—shows no decline with advancing age.

Grant for the moment that the elderly do use registration strategies less than they did when younger. We know that young children, too, fail to use these strategies. But does it necessarily follow that the reasons for this failure are the same for the child and for the elderly person? The child probably hasn't had enough experience with memory tasks to know when to use what type of strategy (metamemory). The elderly person has probably had a great deal of experience in the past but not recently. It may seem more likely, therefore, that production deficiency in old age is better explained as a case of motivation, or lack of it (disuse, lack of confidence, and so on), than as a problem of metamemory (awareness of strategies).

As Reese (1976) points out, the elderly are generally aware that they tend to forget things and may, therefore, need to use memory aids. But the strategies they do use sometimes don't work, because they use them ineffectively. So it might be more accurate to describe memory decline in the elderly as a case of "spontaneous inefficiency." This inefficiency makes memory failure all the more frustrating for the elderly. Their awareness that they used to do better and could still do better reduces their self-confidence even more than the inefficiency itself.

Permanent-Storage Strategies

The distinction between decay-preventing strategies and permanent-storage strategies is not always easy to apply to specific tasks. In general, decay-preventing strategies are deliberate attempts to arrest the decay of items in STM. Permanent-storage strategies are attempts to convert items from STM to LTM. The use of the latter strategies is necessary when the delay between registration and retrieval is long and beyond the limits of the decay-preventing strategies.

Two permanent-storage strategies have received research attention: clustering and chunking. Both are attempts to reorganize information in a form that is easier to remember. *Clustering* refers to reorganization based on conceptual categories. For example, if the child hears the teacher say "In the Okefenokee Swamp, you can see egrets, copperheads, mallards, lizards, alligators, and flamingos," the child does well to organize these six items into two clusters: egrets, mallards, and flamingos in one cluster and copperheads, lizards, and alligators in another cluster. If the student thinks "The teacher mentioned three birds and three reptiles," he is less likely to think that the teacher had mentioned roach or hornet, since neither of these animals is a bird or reptile. Grouping items according to certain conceptual categories—in our example, classes of animals—helps the person remember by providing an additional cue and by eliminating certain possibilities.

Chunking, another permanent-storage strategy, refers to a different kind of grouping. In clustering, the student groups by rearranging the order in which the items were presented. In chunking, which is generally used to recall items in a certain sequence, the student groups items by creating natural breaks in the series to be recalled, thus reducing the amount of material to be learned. For example, in order to try to learn the 39 U.S. presidents in chronological order, one could use the major wars as "breaks" in the series—the presidents who were in office between the Revolutionary War and the Civil War, those between the Civil War and World War I, those between World War I and World War II, and so on. The 39 individual items can thus be reduced to 6 or 7 chunks.

The data on the growth and decline of these two strategies during the life span point to a situation similar to that we encountered with regard to rehearsal. A phase of mediation deficiency is followed by a phase of production deficiency, in which first graders can be taught how to cluster (Cole, Frankel, & Sharp, 1971). A deliberate and spontaneous effort to cluster is not encountered until around the fifth grade (Appel, Cooper, McCarrell, Sims-Knight, Yussen, & Flavell, 1972). Prior to this age, children do try to concentrate harder but don't appear to use any special memory tricks like clustering or chunking. We see here a case in which metamemory is slightly ahead of memory skills per se. The fourth-grader may know that the task calls for special effort (this knowledge is a case of metamemory) but doesn't know what specifically to do. This awareness can be contrasted with the average preschooler's oblivion to which tasks require greater effort.

How about older people? As we said earlier, the elderly show some decline with regard to episodic (unrelated) material but very little decline, if any, with regard to semantic (interrelated) material (Botwinick & Storandt,

1974; Reese, 1976). The more the material lends itself to clustering, chunking, or other organizational strategies, the better the elderly perform. This obviously indicates that older people use organizational strategies very much. As we stated in the previous section, the slight memory decline on episodic tasks can be explained as a case of disuse. Even the memory decline that does exist for episodic tasks could be a case of poor retrieval rather than failure to apply permanent-storage strategies (Anders & Fozard, 1973).

Retrieval

Sometimes we cannot recall things that we know we know. This common "tip-of-the-tongue" problem is a retrieval problem. The title of a book or the name of a movie star is information that has many times reached STM and has more than likely been stored in LTM. The active processes that a person uses to remember stored information are called *retrieval*.[2]

As we mentioned earlier, retrieval includes both recognition and recall. If an individual fails to recognize someone, it could be that he did not, for the moment, retrieve the first meeting. Once reminded, he remembers quite clearly, thus indicating that the failure to recognize was not a case of forgetting (that is, decay) but a failure to retrieve information that was "there" in LTM. The same can be said about the failure to recall. The person may not be able for a moment to remember the message her husband asked her to relay to his friend, but after a while she remembers the message perfectly. The message was not forgotten; the woman was having temporary difficulty at retrieval.

As is true in other aspects of memory, the development of retrieval can be viewed as in increase in the conscious use of strategies. Yet, there are also developmental differences in the speed of retrieval with regard to tasks in which strategies are not so important. An experiment conducted by Anders and Fozard (1973) seems to indicate that older adults search through LTM at a slower pace than do young adults. In the experimental task, young and older adults were given a list of items to learn. A day later, they were given a single item and were asked whether that item was included in the list they had learned the day before. The experimenter measured the time it took the subjects to answer. The longer it took, the longer the time the subject was spending searching through LTM. The older adults took longer to answer but made no more errors than the younger adults.

This study doesn't tell us what the older adults would have done if pressured; it tells us only that they were asked to respond as quickly as possible. Studies that place greater demands on fast responding generally show that older subjects score less well than younger subjects (Hulicka &

---

[2]As indicated in Figure 4-1, retrieval can occur immediately after input (STM retrieval). Note that the research cited in this section refers to retrieval of information from LTM. STM retrieval was mentioned briefly in the section on decay-preventing strategies.

Weiss, 1965). These findings indicate that older people prefer to take more time at retrieval and show deficits when hurried. Slow retrieval time shouldn't be confused with poor learning. The older subjects in the Anders and Fozard study had learned and remembered the items as well as the younger subjects. The older were only more cautious.

Caution is almost a defining characteristic of aging adults. Caution pervades their approach to many areas of life, from making investments and changing residence to just taking a new route to visit their children (Neugarten, 1968). Their caution in answering a question on a memory task is probably part of this general caution toward novel situations, and it should not be interpreted negatively. After 60 or 70 years of life, a person is quite aware of the ill consequences of impulsive behavior. The caution of the older person is not the slowness of a dull mind but, more likely, the forethought of an experienced person.

The developmental shift from impulsiveness to caution seems to begin as early as the elementary-school years (Kagan, 1965) and continues throughout life. It is important to note that the impulsiveness of the first-grader is different from the quickness of the young adult. Children's impulsiveness causes them to make errors, while young adults' quickness is within the limits of their recognition skills. Certainly, the tempo at which people of different ages retrieve information has profound implications for educational practices. In the elementary grades, it is the child who needs to be slowed down; in adult education, it is the pace of instruction that needs to be slowed down. By improving the match between the tempo of the individual and the tempo of instruction, we are likely to find that all ages can retrieve information equally well.

So far we have not mentioned research on retrieval strategies—only on retrieval tempo. Research on retrieval strategies in children has just begun, and the research on the elderly is often anecdotal or based on self-reports. The general experimental setup tests the effects of making certain retrieval cues either available or unavailable and then checks the differences in memory scores. Here is an example of such a setup. I tell you that you should learn all the names of the people in my seminar class, because I will need to report attendance (an unlikely situation). You memorize the ten or twelve names and recite them to me after class without a single error. The next day, in the hall, I tell you that I misplaced my course roster (a more likely situation) and ask you to repeat the names as best as you can. You can remember only eight of the twelve names. So you hit upon the idea of returning to the classroom, figuring that the vacant chairs there will jog your retrieval system. And it works. The chairs serve as retrieval cues, and you now remember all the names.

When first-graders are provided retrieval cues, they don't profit from them, but third- and sixth-graders do (Kobasigawa, 1974). In the Kobasigawa experiment, when the first-, third-, and sixth-graders were told how to use the retrieval cues, they all performed at the same high level. This is another example of the transition from production deficiency to spontaneous and accomplished use of strategies across the elementary-school years. Hultsch (1974) provides data suggesting that older adults profit less when retrieval cues are present than do younger adults. The study does not provide a means to separate out the possibility of production deficiency from that of mediation deficiency.

How do we account for the decrease in the retrieval scores of older adults? Goulet (1973), after reviewing the then current research, concluded that the retrieval problems of the elderly were due to what has been called their *interference proneness*. The argument makes a distinction between forgetting by decay and failing to retrieve because of interference from other material. (See the sidetrack box labeled "Interference" in Figure 4-1.) The presence of retrieval cues may confuse an elderly person. When one of the cues is used, and then another, and then another, the cues themselves begin to interfere with one another. What the person had associated with one retrieval cue gets incorrectly transferred to another item in storage. For example, a conscientious elderly man wants to make sure that he will remember to do two things: pick up his wife and call the vet. So he ties a string on his finger and hangs the dog's collar on the door knob. When the time comes to do these two things, the man looks at the collar and string, *drives* to the vet, and *calls* his wife! The retrieval cues were there, but they interfered with each other. The frustrating aspect of this type of memory failure lies in knowing that the two tasks were clearly understood and that deliberate attempts were made to assist their recall.

There are more efficient methods that all of us, not just the elderly, can use to improve our chances of correctly recalling important information. For example, we can make educated guesses by eliminating certain possibilities, and we can use explicit retrieval cues, such as writing down self-instructions. These types of strategies involve both general knowledge about the world—a knowledge that eliminates improbable guesses—and specific knowledge about memory. Assuming that the retrieval problems of old age are the result of disuse—in other words, a production deficiency only— older people should profit from a refresher course on memory strategies. After all, older people have had a great deal of experience with their physical and social surroundings and a great familiarity with the strengths and limitations of their own memory functions. Once they start to practice these memory strategies, they can also bring into play their general knowledge of the world and metamemory.

Level of Learning and Rate of Forgetting

Do young children and elderly people fail to recall material because they didn't learn it well in the first place or because they forget faster than people in the midrange ages? The relationship among rate of learning, level of learning, and rate of forgetting has intrigued psychologists for the past 30 years (Underwood, 1949). When the rate at which information is presented to the subjects is controlled by the experimenter, the elderly do much more poorly than young adults. But when the older subjects can proceed through the task at their own rate, item by item, memory differences between old and young all but disappear (Hulicka & Weiss, 1965). This fact suggests that, even though it takes older people longer to learn material to be recalled, once they have learned it, they don't forget it more quickly than younger adults. Once learned, the item decays in memory at the same rate for older and for younger subjects. Evidently, older people prefer to take their time and do so even when they take a test with time limits. This means that, when the clock runs out, the elderly subject has learned less of the material and, consequently, will show poorer recall. The recall score is not, in this case, an index of forgetting; it is an index of lack of initial learning.

By the same token, when children show poor recall scores, the problem lies in a low level of learning rather than in a fast rate of forgetting. If preschool children and lower-elementary-school children are asked to study a set of pictures so that they will be able to remember the pictures' content later, they do poorly for several reasons. For one, they are characteristically impulsive and flit from feature to feature, without concentrating on any feature long enough to learn it. For another, if they do settle on some features long enough to learn them, they have a tendency to fixate on only one or two features to the exclusion of the others. Then, when the time comes to report what they "remember," they can't describe more than the one or two features on which they did center. In other words, children at this age are either impulsive and don't learn a single feature (Kagan, 1965) or are centered and respond to only one or two things (Piaget, 1969). When steps are taken to assure that the child attends to all features of a task, it seems that, at least from the age of 4 onward, the rate of forgetting is no greater in the younger years than it is in later years. Once 4-year-olds learn a task, they forget it no faster than older children (Arenberg, 1973; Belmont, 1967).

The learning level can be low because the material is presented too fast, but it can be low also because one doesn't know how to profit from practice. Repeated practice with a task can improve learning if the subjects are able to detect some pattern that they can use to direct their responses. It is much easier to memorize the sequence 2, 3, 4, 7, 10, 15, 20 if one can discover the progression rule behind it. It has been shown that young children and elderly people profit less from such implicit patterns than do subjects in the midrange ages (Furth & Milgram, 1973; Kamin, 1957). Practice, practice, practice is no guarantee that learning level will increase. In order to benefit from repeated practice, the learner must think about the material, discover cues, and understand the relationship between the general instructions and the specific material. That is to say, there is a difference between repeated exposure and repeated practice. The following example illustrates such a difference.

A 4-year-old was in the process of putting together a jigsaw puzzle. She had inserted 11 of the 12 pieces into the puzzle formboard and was trying in vain to insert the last piece. She was holding it the wrong way, and the piece wouldn't fit. The child was getting increasingly upset and kept jabbing the piece into the only remaining space again and again. Then, with a smile, she stopped her attempts, lifted the piece high with her left hand while, at the same time, tracing the contour of the piece with the extended finger of her right hand. (One of the authors later learned that the children had been exposed to contour tracing for the past week in classroom lessons.) After carefully tracing the contours of the jigsaw piece with her finger twice, the child immediately proceeded to jab the piece into the empty space exactly as she had done before (Forman, Laughlin, & Sweeney, 1971).

This child had received repeated exposure to an exercise (contour tracing), and, yet, she had not profited from it. Why? She remembered exactly what to do: lift, look, and trace. But she didn't know what information this exercise was meant to provide—that is, the shape of the piece as it related to the shape of the empty space. We often leave a great deal of the message of instruction unsaid; we don't tell the children just what the practice is meant to provide. Even so, there probably is a point beyond which the children themselves must establish the relationship between the instruction and the specific task demands. We, no doubt, commit the same sorts of errors when we try to teach or test the elderly. The 70- or 80-year-old has long since forgotten all the subtle rules of the funny games that research psychologists are prone to play.

In this first half of the chapter, we have discussed how past events are stored in memory and later retrieved. In the second half, we will discuss the way in which attention processes—what we look at, how completely we attend, and how well we integrate the different things we notice—change across age. You will also see how memory influences attention.

Attention

A General Model of Attention

Attention refers to mental processes that deal with stimuli in the immediate present. In order to relate the attentional processes to memory processes, let's compare Figures 4-1 and 4-2. Note that we have added a box called "Selection" between the raw detection of a stimulus and the storage (registration) in STM. This box highlights the fact that attention is an active process of selection, guided by both STM and LTM (thus, note the feedback circuits from STM and LTM to "Selection"). Also note that we have omitted any reference to LTM retrieval, since this is primarily a memory process

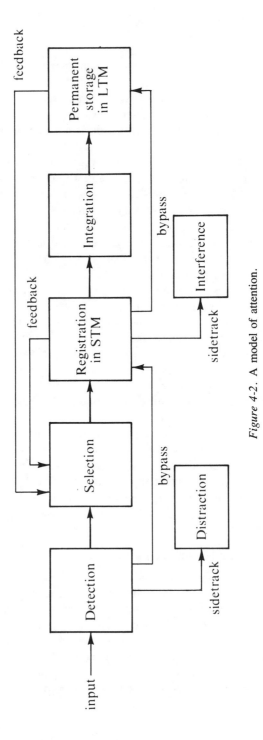

Figure 4-2. A model of attention.

and was discussed in the first half of this chapter. Of course, as we will explain in detail later, the feedback from STM and LTM is a type of retrieval from these stores, but with the specific purpose of improving ongoing attention to present stimuli. The arrow at the far right of Figure 4-2 indicates that the person has made an overt response, that he or she has said or done something that required use of attentional processes. Now let's follow the flow illustrated in Figure 4-2 from the beginning.

For information to enter the IP system, something must be detected. *Detection,* as we stated earlier, is a rather automatic registration of sensations, and sometimes these sensations enter short-term memory without the person's active and deliberate search. Thunder, gunshots, and screeching brakes are all heard without any need for the person to make active attempts to hear. *Selection* is a more active, more conscious, and more purposive process than mere detection. A ballistics expert selects qualities of sound in the gunshot that serve his purposes better than just random listening. Not all sensations that are detected are then selected for registration in STM. But some very loud or otherwise unavoidably obvious noises, like thunder, can reach STM without having to be selected. These very dominant sensations take the bypass that appears in our figure under the box labeled "Selection."

Since selection is a "guided search," we need to indicate in our diagram some of the sources of this guidance. That's why we have drawn arrows that lead back to "Selection," one from STM and one from LTM. These *feedback loops,* as they are called, represent those occasions in which prior experience guides selective attention. This guidance could come from events currently present (items in STM). For example, I see some spilled milk and look over toward the edge of the table to see whether the milk (now an STM item) has dripped onto the carpet. Or this guidance could come from items in permanent storage. For example, a man loses his wallet and then searches behind the cushion of his favorite chair. His knowledge that his wallet sometimes slips out when he is slouching on that chair (item in LTM) guides his search.

Feedback from LTM is also important for a particular type of selective attention called *discrimination.* Discrimination involves attention to the similarities and/or differences between two or more things (see the discussion on Gagné in Chapter Three) and calls for a judgment of similarity or difference. This is the judgment I make, for example, when I decide that this bicycle (item in STM) is my bicycle (item in LTM) and not my brother's bicycle (another item in LTM). My brother, no doubt, would discriminate differences where I had discriminated similarities.

Sometimes I can't see clearly enough to unambiguously identify an object—say, the face of a person I had previously met. Suppose that I see a woman's face through a beaded curtain. I can see only parts of her face through the gaps in the curtain. Have I ever seen this beaded lady before? (In other words, is the face an item in my LTM?) In order to identify that face, I must integrate the parts of the face that I can see. Then I compare this "reconstructed" face to some remembered whole face (item in LTM) in hopes that I can recall who she is. *Integration* refers to the piecing together of parts to identify the whole (item in LTM). Since not all perceptual tasks require integration, we have drawn a bypass loop that goes directly from "Registration in STM" to "Permanent storage in LTM." Note that this bypass loop and the arrow leaving the "Integration" box represent the conversion of STM into LTM. This conversion involves most of the memory strategies that we discussed in the first part of this chapter.

A discussion of distraction and interference will complete our explanation of Figure 4-2. *Distraction* occurs when one sensory event distracts attention from another sensory event. For example, when two people are talking at the same time, both their voices are detected but one voice never makes it to STM in order to become a message rather than just a noise. *Interference*, on the other hand, occurs when items that have reached STM interfere with one another. As a consequence, some never make it to LTM. That is, the distraction does not come from the environment at large but from the environment as selected and registered in STM. This happens when a person tries to attend to so many things that he or she becomes confused and ends up by learning very few of those things.

Distraction is more closely related to registration in STM (attention), and interference is more closely related to storage in LTM (learning). For example, we say "That stray tennis ball *distracted* her concentration" and "The similarity between the letter *b* and the letter *d interferes* with his spelling." Both boxes "Distraction" and "Interference" are drawn as dead-end sidetracks in Figure 4-2.

Detection and Selection

If the newborn infant shows a startled reaction to a dog's bark, we know that the baby has heard the noise; that is, the infant has detected the presence of the stimulus (the bark). Infants, in fact, can detect the presence of even quite mild stimuli, like odors and tastes (Lipsitt, 1966). Yet, the detection of smells, sounds, or tastes doesn't necessarily require the infant to select one stimulus instead of another. The studies above used procedures that made the registration in STM (attention) unavoidable. It is true that infants are born with the ability to detect many more stimuli than we had imagined, but the question is to what *degree* they are able to *direct* their attention. The matter of stimulus selection is the crux of attentional processes. It develops with age and becomes more and more sophisticated.

Attention is a selective process. The development of attention can, in part, be plotted by describing what the child selects at different ages. If I project the photograph of a line drawing of a triangle on the wall facing a baby's crib and the baby looks in the direction of the photograph, is the infant attending to the form of that stimulus (that is, to the triangle) or to the bright patch of light on the wall? How would I ever know, since I cannot ask the infant?

Research seems to indicate that, during the first two months of life, the infant is more likely to be looking in the direction of the projected photograph because of the change in illumination it produces on the wall (Munsinger, 1970). Beyond the second month of life, it seems that the infant is more attentive to the form of the stimulus. He will move his eyes so that the angles of the triangle are focused in the fovea, the most sensitive part of the retina (Salapatek & Kessen, 1966).

If the form is changed, the baby's eye movements change, too, which indicates that the infant perceives the shape before him. This is not to say that he can tell the difference between two kinds of triangles or that he recognizes a particular triangle as familiar. But he is at least able to direct his attention to the angles, which are the essential physical features of the triangle. This type of eye control is important for later, more complicated uses of visual attention. It would be an overstatement to say that the baby is looking *for* something, but, for some reason, the angles are particularly captivating, and we can say that he is looking *at* something. Looking for something develops later and is a search for some particular information, like the missing arm of a doll or the distinguishing feature between this and that. As we shall see in the next section, memory plays a greater role in these more sophisticated types of looking.

Discrimination of Differences

At what age does an infant experience two objects as distinct and different from each other? There are two procedures we can use to answer this question. If, when we show the infant two objects several times and in different positions, the infant always looks at one of them, it becomes obvious that she can see the difference between the two objects. It wouldn't be reasonable to say that the infant keeps looking at the same objects by accident. Fantz (1961), who studied the direction of infants' gaze, discovered that infants less than 1 month old do make choices.

The other procedure we can follow to answer our question is to present two objects, one at a time, to the baby, making sure that she observes both. Then, if the experimenter, by making something pleasant happen in the presence of only one of the two objects, can get the infant to react more to that one than to the other, we can say that the infant discriminates one object from the other. Suppose that, every time a clown's face appears, the infant turns her head; this activates a switch whereby the baby receives a nippleful of milk. When, instead, a checkerboard picture appears and the baby turns her head, nothing happens. The moment the infant starts turning her head only when the clown's face appears, she shows that she can discriminate the difference between two stimuli.

In both of the procedures above, the infant is selecting one thing and actively ignoring another. However, in the first procedure—in which the infant simply looks at one of two simultaneous stimuli—there is no evidence that the infant has *learned* to look. There could be biological reasons why one stimulus is more captivating than another, such as the fact that the human eye is more sensitive to the color yellow than to the color blue. In this case the "choice" of the yellow object is not so much a choice as it is a near reflex orientation to a dominant stimulus. That is, the infant may not be comparing two objects, even though she is selectively attending to one rather than to the other.

In the other procedure—in which the experimenter makes sure that the baby does observe both objects—it is clearer that at one point the infant has *learned* to detect features that discriminate the two objects. She has learned something about both stimuli. She moves her head when she sees the clown's face and inhibits moving her head when she sees the checkerboard pattern, but she is attending to both. That is, she studies the checkerboard pattern long enough to know that this is not the time to move her head. This type of discrimination involves memory more than the type of discrimination exhibited in the first procedure. That's probably why the capability to use this kind of discrimination develops somewhat later—around 3 months of age (Watson, 1967)—than the capability to show preference for one of two simultaneously present objects (Fantz, 1961), which occurs within the first month of life.

Age Changes in Stimulus Dominance

What people choose to attend to is determined, in part, by their intelligence and, in part, by their preferences. A college student may choose to watch the milling patterns of people in a football stadium, while her classmate may be more interested in the distribution of the peanut vendors. A first-grader would not have the intellectual skills to observe either pattern. But he may notice the erratic course of a rising balloon, while his twin brother may be watching a man tossing a cushion up to a friend.

Our discussion focuses more on general categories of stimuli, such as pattern versus object movement, since these categories tell us more about cognitive development across age. Specific preferences within these stimulus categories are a matter of individual differences. The dominance of general stimulus categories changes with age because (1) the child gradually develops the thinking competencies necessary to discern the more complex stimulus events and, once discerned, (2) these stimulus events play into the purposes and preferences of the individual.

It has been repeatedly reported that children in their first two years of life are more attentive to moving objects than are older children (Kagan & Lewis, 1965). Older children, even though they certainly notice moving objects, can at the same time attend to the shape and pattern of objects. These differences can be explained as follows. The older children are, the more actively they search for stimulus variation. Younger children are no less sensitive to stimulus variation, but the variation—that is, object movement—must be provided for them. Older children, instead, by scanning their eyes across a motionless pattern, can provide their own stimulus variation. Therefore, what is not obviously a "busy" stimulus to an infant can be so to the older child, who has developed more thorough and longer-lasting procedures for looking.

The controversy over the importance of touch and feel in early childhood is a long-standing one. The preschooler certainly spends a great deal of time touching and feeling objects. To what extent does the "hand train the eye"? Is there some type of "motor copy" that results from palpating objects? Furthermore, is a "motor copy" necessary before the child can recognize objects with her eyes alone? The importance of early manual explorations has been given a great deal of research attention by Russian psychologists (see Zaporozhets & Elkonin, 1971). White (1965) discusses the shift from the reliance on touch of the early years to the increasingly greater use of vision and hearing after age 5 or 6—a shift he describes as a shift from dependence on the "near receptors" to a greater dependence on the "distance receptors."

Several rather well-accepted findings come from this research. First, while it is true that touch and feel can improve the child's ability to recognize an object, touch and feel don't seem to be a prerequisite for visual recognition (Denner & Cashden, 1967). Second, learning from touch and feel takes longer and requires more mental effort than learning from looking (Jackson, 1973). Then, what is the role of manual explorations of objects? The answer may be easier if we ask the question differently. Why do young children look so closely at what they are manipulating and, as they grow older, not do so anymore?

White (1965) says that those events that occur "close at hand" have greater value for survival. Until children learn to manipulate objects smoothly, so they can avoid pain and grasp objects securely, their eyes will focus on events that occur at their fingertips. According to Werner (1948), as children mature, their attention decenters from events proximal to the self to distal events. This shift occurs because children (1) discover that they can get advanced information about things that are about to happen and (2) have acquired the cognitive wherewithal to make use of the more distant events.

Is there evidence that this shift from proximal to distal stimulation is age related? White (1965) cites several studies. Forman, Kuschner, and Dempsey (1975a) provide some additional and more recent data. In the

Forman et al. study, children were given two pieces of wood and asked to put them together. As Figure 4-3 shows, the children could create a form either by putting the two pieces together to form a square (that is, creating a form by the physical, touchable outline of the object) or by joining the two painted semicircles together to form a complete circle.

The younger children (3-year-olds) chose to complete the physical shape (Figure 4-3a); the older children (4½-year-olds) chose to complete the painted form (Figure 4-3b). The children in between these age groups showed a great deal of conflict, oscillating back and forth between the two options! The developmental trend is clear. The younger children were more attentive to the palpable features of the object—that is, the physical edges of the wood they held in their hands. The older children, instead, were more attentive to the painted form. Those in between these two age groups were in a phase of transition and couldn't make up their minds.

For the older children the wood was little more than a slate or background that carried the more important, painted form. Forman et al. (1975a) reasoned that, since our culture presses the child to use two-dimensional information, such as pictures, lotto boards, and printed material, the touchable cues provided by the physical outline of an object decrease in their dominance of attention as the child is socialized in preschool and elementary school.

Age Changes in Selection Strategies

In order for a child to detect the similarities and differences among objects, she needs to visually scan each object accurately. Her toy truck may look exactly like her friend's toy truck, except for a missing headlight. She may, in her haste to ride away, see only the similar color and shape, assume that it is her truck, and, when her friend yells, insist that it is *her* truck. As they mature, children discover the utility of thorough visual scanning and develop that facility to use it.

Child makes square
(a)

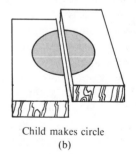

Child makes circle
(b)

Figure 4-3.

In an interesting study by Vurpillot (1968), children were asked to find in a set of 12 very similar pictures the two that were identical. In order to do so, the children frequently had to examine all 12 pictures. Vurpillot recorded the children's eye movements. The older the child was, the more systematic the visual scanning became and the longer the child scanned before reaching a conclusion.

It was obvious that the older children (elementary-school age) would first look at a feature in a picture and then look for the presence or absence of that feature in the other pictures. Since the pictures depicted houses, the older children would compare the houses pair by pair, focusing on all the details. If, for example, both houses had chimneys, the children would check some other feature, such as windows, to make sure they were identical.

The younger children would more often jump to the conclusion that the two pictures were identical, simply because both houses had chimneys. Furthermore, the scanning patterns of the preschool children didn't clearly reveal a feature-by-feature analysis. It was a random kind of scanning. The older children spent considerable time looking *for* particular features. The younger children, instead, looked *at* the pictures and in a rather unsystematic manner. This is what we meant when earlier we said that the development of the attentional processes reflects an increase in the use of memory to guide the act of looking. Systematic looking reduces the overload that results from too much information, helps to keep track of what has been checked, and prevents the observer from mistaking identities.

It should be kept in mind, however, that the more planful and systematic strategy of visual analysis that develops with age is only one aspect of cognitive development. As we pointed out in the section on Piaget in Chapter Two, advancing to the stage of concrete-operational thinking is more than learning to look at objects more closely and more completely. Even the child who notices detail and who sees the difference between a tall thin glass and a short broad glass can fail to understand that the water we pour from one into the other doesn't change in quantity because its level is different in the two glasses. This task requires the organization of details, not just the mere note of details. Of course, if the child has the wherewithal to construct the necessary relations but fails to notice the details of width and height, procedures that direct his attention to these details can improve the child's performance (Whiteman & Peisach, 1970).

Sometimes, however, these procedures can backfire, causing the child to change a correct judgment into an incorrect one. Wallach (1963) poured water from a drinking glass into a bathtub and asked 8-year-olds whether the amount of water in the tub was the same as the amount that had been in the glass. Many who had said yes when the difference between the two containers was less dramatic now said no. This answer would make one wonder whether the children had ever understood why the amount of water was conserved, since conservation, by definition, is not dependent on appearances.

Certain changes that occur in the visual-scanning behavior of people beyond middle adulthood indicate a decrease in efficiency. These age changes are not so much a matter of the elderly taking too little time to inspect critical features but, rather, a matter of the elderly requiring more time to decide what it is that they see. For example, as people age from 5 to 30, they get increasingly fast at identifying the odd one of three pictures. But then, from age 30 onward, people need increasingly more time on this task (Rajalakshmi & Reeves, 1963).

The decline in reaction time seems to be due not to poor eyesight but to the longer time needed to make a decision (Weston, 1948). This means, as we said earlier when we were discussing memory, that the elderly show poor performance scores on tasks that are timed. The elderly subject is more cautious, less willing to take a risk, than the college-age subject (Eisdorfer, 1965). The perceptual caution of the elderly can be seen as almost the opposite of the perceptual impulsiveness of the preschooler. Yet, the test scores of timed perceptual tasks for the preschooler and for the elderly could be identical. It behooves us to go beyond the poor score itself and try to understand the mechanisms by which the score was obtained.

Distraction and Interference

In this section, the discussion of these two terms focuses on attention rather than on retrieval. We are concerned here with the degree to which distraction prevents items from being registered in STM and with the degree to which redundant and irrelevant information that is registered in STM interferes with transfer to LTM. More specifically, we are concerned with the changes in distractibility that occur with age and with the elderly's greater susceptibility to interference when they are engaged in attention tasks.

Is distractibility as characteristic of old age as it is of early childhood? Infants cannot divide their attention when using two different senses, such as touch and vision. For example, babies cannot attend with their lips to the bottle nipple if an interesting sight catches their eyes (Bruner, 1969). Children younger than 7 also have difficulty, but only when the two attention channels are intrinsically similar—for example, if they try to do one thing with their left hand and something else with their right hand (Longobardi & Wolff, 1973). As far as older people are concerned, they have difficulty dividing their attention between two simultaneous conversations (Broadbent & Heron, 1962). Keeping track of two conversations, however, is a more demanding task than patting one's head while rubbing one's stomach. So, since these studies used different and harder measures with the elderly, it is difficult to conclude that the elderly are as distractible as young children. What we can say is that the task of following two simultaneous conversations is more difficult for the elderly than for young adults.

Older people are also more easily distracted if, in a learning task, they must perform some repetitive action (Heron, 1962). Adult-education instructors should be aware of the types of situations that are distracting for the elderly, without, at the same time, assuming that the attention of the elderly is indivisible in all situations. There is no evidence that a healthy 70-year-old has any trouble preparing a pie while talking on the telephone or knitting a sweater while watching a program on television.

How do various age groups fare when they must deal with an excess of information in STM—that is, with interference? Learning to ignore information that is not useful to the task at hand is one aspect of cognitive development. In other words, we learn to reduce the load of how much we must look at or listen to.

There are two types of information we can usefully ignore. One is information that tells us no more than some other information that we already have; that is, we can ignore information that is *redundant,* without loss in accuracy or performance. If I want to distinguish between lemons and limes, I can attend to their color. There may be other distinguishing features, like differences in taste, average size, and texture of skin. But, if all I want to do is simply distinguish a lemon from a lime, these extra features are redundant. Of course, any one of them would do as well, but, once I have found one way to make the distinction, there is no need to search for additional ways.

Some features may not be redundant but are actually *irrelevant* to my purpose. For example, I couldn't use the fact that squeezing a lemon produces juice as a means of distinguishing a lemon from a lime, just as I couldn't use the fact that the lemon can be peeled. I couldn't even use the fact that this particular lemon has mold on its skin and this lime does not to help me to make future discriminations, since in some future comparison the lime, too, may have mold. Information that is not correlated with the essence of what makes a lemon a lemon is irrelevant to my purposes, albeit I might not know this as a novice produce manager. Both redundant and irrelevant information can be distracting, and both should be ignored for more efficient discrimination.

How does the ability to ignore redundant and irrelevant information change with age? One might predict that the more ways I have of distinguishing between two objects, the better chances I have of making an accurate discrimination. The need to ignore redundant information does not apply in the case of accuracy measures. But, if I am told to make an identification as quickly as possible, attending to redundant information can slow me down. Older people tend to learn more than is necessary, either out of a fear of making errors or because they have trouble deciding what information is less important. Since redundant information does result in slower learning and since, when information is correlated to correct responding, the elderly have a tendency to attend to it, their efficiency is reduced (Rabbitt, 1965).

The presence of redundant information does not have the same slowing effect on children. In fact, children profit from redundancy (Bourne, 1966). Young children are impulsive rather than cautious. They are quick to make a guess, and redundancy increases the probability that their guesses will be correct. Unlike the elderly, young children don't spend additional time learning more than they have to learn. However, as we saw in the previous section on visual scanning, children's tendency to focus on only one stimulus dimension can lead them into error when two or more dimensions are needed to define a concept (Vurpillot, 1968).

The developmental trends regarding the distracting effects of irrelevant information are rather clear. The ability to ignore irrelevant information increases until young adulthood and then starts decreasing. In one study, preschoolers and elementary-school children were asked to close their eyes and follow with their fingers a row of small tacks stuck into a board. The younger children had great difficulty ignoring the larger tacks that were stuck near and around the row of smaller tacks (Corsini & Berg, 1973). The younger children were side-tacked, so to speak.

In another study, subjects ranging in age from 6 to 50 were asked to read aloud the word *green,* which was printed in red ink, and the word *orange,* which was printed in blue ink. The young children and older adults had great difficulty inhibiting a tendency to say the name of the ink color. College-age subjects performed the task better than any other age group. In a third study, elderly people had more difficulty than young adults in finding a particular figure embedded in an elaborate design, such as a diamond shape buried in a field of other geometric shapes (Basowitz & Korchin, 1957). These studies yield the conclusion that the ability to filter out irrelevant information increases until young adulthood and then gradually decreases as old age is approached.

Integrating Parts into Wholes

Sometimes we get only a glimpse of a scene; that is, we see only part of it. Riding in my car, I pass an archway that leads into a courtyard. As my position with regard to the arch changes, what I see inside the courtyard changes as well. First, I see a crowd of people and, then, a streamer of small flags. From my past experience, I piece these two parts together— crowd plus streamer of flags—and conclude that what I saw was a festival of some sort. So I drive around the block, return to the courtyard, and join the festival, satisfied that my conclusion was correct.

Are there age trends regarding the amount of information observers need before they can identify what they have seen? An experimental analogue of the festival example has been carried out in research. The task was to watch a picture that was passing behind a small aperture. The picture was moved at a constant rate, but the size of the opening was varied. When the aperture was wide, the observer could, of course, get more information per unit time than when the aperture was narrow. The whole scene was never visible all at once, but the parts that were seen across time could be integrated to construct the whole scene. Research indicated that the recognition of the whole scene was more difficult for 4-year-olds than for 9-year-olds (Girgus & Hochberg, 1970) and more difficult for older adults than for younger adults (Wallace, 1956). That is, the size of the aperture had to be larger before the young children and older adults could identify the picture.

The difficulty of this kind of task is probably due to the memory load of remembering all the successive parts long enough to piece them together as a whole. An exaggerated version of this task would be to show to someone various pieces of a jigsaw puzzle one after the other one and then to ask the person what the whole picture is. The more proficient problem solver can both remember many more pieces and make inductions based on fewer critical pieces. The search for critical pieces is another means of reconstructing the whole from parts, and there are age trends here also, as the following example indicates.

Suppose Tommy is looking at a comic book. He reads the print and then looks at the picture. Once he sees the spaceship and the blaze of its exhaust, he knows that the picture portrays the launching described in the text. These are critical features used to capture the highlights of the story. His younger brother, Henry, may require more time and more information before he can discern what the picture portrays. Suppose that Henry and Tommy have just turned the page, that neither has seen the next picture, and that Henry accidentally spills grape juice on it. Portions of the picture are obliterated by the stain. All the two children can see is the fin of the ship here, the tip of the blaze there, an orange-purple curve there, and the tip of a crater wall here. Henry cannot make sense out of the stained picture, while Tommy can. Why? Because Tommy needs less information to make an identification—less redundant information—than does his younger brother. The amount of redundant information that is needed to identify a scene is greatest in childhood and middle late adulthood (Verville & Cameron, 1946) and smallest in young adulthood.

The capacity to attend to a few critical features in order to reconstruct the whole, even when pieces are missing, improves our ability to pick up information quickly—also when what we observe is not stained with grape juice. Reading is an example. The proficient reader will skip from key phrase to key phrase quickly and construct the whole message from these pieces. Attention and cognition work together to help us use information efficiently.

The Relationship between Memory, Attention, and Intelligence

Both memory and attention are affected by the qualitative changes described in Piaget's stage theory of intelligence. In their book *Memory and Intelligence,* Piaget and Inhelder (1973) outline the development of memory, and, in his book *The Mechanisms of Perception,* Piaget (1969) outlines the development of attention. Once general intelligence reaches the stage of concrete operations (see Chapter Two), these cognitive structures can influence both the memory trace and the methods of attending.

An interesting example of memory development can be seen in what Piaget calls *long-term memory improvement.* A 4-year-old child is shown ten sticks of different lengths, arranged in stairlike order, increasing in length by equal increments from left to right. The child is asked to copy this seriated row, which he does fairly accurately. One week later, he is asked to remember the set of sticks and draw the set as he recalls it now. Six months later, the child returns to the experimenter, who asks him to draw once again the sticks as he remembers them. (During these six months, the child has never seen the sticks again.)

Piaget, who conducted the experiments, discovered that the test for recall after one week showed many errors of placement and many simplifications of the seriation, while the test after six months showed that the child's memory had greatly improved! The findings were replicated by Altemeyer, Fulton, and Berney (1969). Piaget concluded that the original memory trace had been reorganized by the changes in the structure of general cognition (the onset of the ability to apply the rules of seriation) that had occurred in the period between the two recall tests.

Brainerd (1974a) doubts that these data reflect changes in memory. He gave a similar task to a group of children, but half of his subjects looked at pictures of sticks that were deliberately drawn with distortions and simplifications. These children, too, showed memory "improvement" in the six-month test for recall. That is, these children drew the pictures without distortions or simplifications—as they should have been in the first place, so to speak—although that was not the way the stimulus pictures looked. According to Brainerd (1974a), to say that a memory trace has been reorganized by intelligence is an overstatement of the facts. More probably, the children had learned, in the six-month interval, a particular concept, and this concept interfered with the memory of the actual stimulus presented six months before. For Brainerd, the children were in fact remembering less well.

A clarification of what Piaget means by memory will help us understand both sets of data. Piaget rejects the idea that memory is a simple recall of a mental picture. The child cannot simply call to mind the array of sticks and then, while "looking" at this mental picture, copy the mental picture

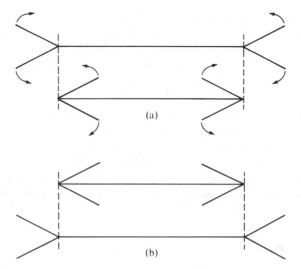

Figure 4-4. If the child has developed an understanding of the schema for reversibility, he or she will attend only to the actual length of the shafts (dashed lines) and ignore the illusion created by the arrowheads.

onto paper. For Piaget, the mental picture itself cannot occur unless the child has a rule that explains how the stimulus array can be reproduced. The rule, or mental schema, in this example might be: first draw the shortest stick, then the next shortest, and so on (the rule for seriation). Without this schema, which organizes the actions needed to reproduce the stimulus array, the child is bound to make distortions.[3] The fact that Brainerd's children, who were given pictures of nonseriated sticks, drew them seriated six months later does not challenge Piaget's viewpoint. In fact, it supports it. These children had evidently learned the seriation rule during the interim and were now applying that rule. Piaget never intended to say that use of these mental schemes invariably leads to more accurate memory; he only insisted that they are invariably used. All memory involves the use of some rule, of some mental schema. Accurate memory involves the use of the correct rule—the rule that reproduces the stimulus array actually presented. Brainerd's subjects were merely overapplying a new rule that they had learned elsewhere.

Piaget (1969) makes similar statements about the interaction between intelligence and perception. What children choose to notice is a function of the schema that they are using at the time. Take, for example, the schema for reversibility (see Chapter Two) illustrated in Figure 4-4. The

[3]Of course, for very simple stimuli, like a single circle, the children could very nearly recall a perfect mental image, without much thought about the rule that explains its reproduction. But the array of seriated sticks taxes this type of photographic imagery.

6-year-old is told to look at the two sticks in Figure 4-4a and asked whether they are of equal length. The child answers that the top stick is longer. Then, when the child watches, the movable arrowheads of the two sticks are changed to the position shown in Figure 4-4b. Now the child first says that the lower stick is longer, then pauses, and finally concludes that the two sticks are the same length.

By using the schema for reversibility, the child understands that the change from 4-4a to 4-4b does not involve a change in the length of the sticks and, therefore, that the apparent change is an illusion. This reasoning causes the child to look at the one-to-one correspondence of the ends of the sticks, ignoring the arrowheads altogether. In other words, reversible thinking directs the child's attention to what is relevant and makes him ignore what is not.

Summary

The development of memory and attention can be explained as the increased ability to organize information. Items to be remembered are chunked, clustered, or otherwise organized to improve retrieval at a later time. Attention is deployed in a systematic manner, so that perceptual biases are eliminated. These developmental changes indicate that the child is taking a more active and deliberately conscious control over his or her mental processes.

A first step in this development is the child's awareness of his or her own thinking, with its patterns and limitations. This child, at this stage, can think about memory as a process (metamemory) and about particular strategies of attention. Improvement in memory and attention comes with the child's ability to treat thinking itself as an object of reflection. Thinking about thinking is a higher-order competence, which is more general than thinking about an object or a class of objects. As we discussed, sometimes poor performance is a result of a failure to think about the process of thinking. "What am I doing to improve recall?" is the question that young children must be taught to ask, that older children think of spontaneously, and that older people often forget to ask.

Does this imply that all age-related differences in memory and attention are washed out when the younger child is taught and the older person is reminded to think about how he or she is thinking? In the last section of this chapter, we concluded that general cognition does set limits on what a person can remember and on what a person is likely to see. The general cognitive ability to make inferences, to understand the implications of the reversibility schema, and to know that dimensions, such as length, are conserved in spite of changes in position makes it possible for the memorizer to remember more and for the viewer to see more. These general strategies actually reduce memory load and eyestrain. Information that previously had to be remembered as a list can now be recalled as a total pattern. Input that had to be viewed as discrete pieces can now be viewed as a series of continuous transformations.

It is not clear whether the decline in memory and attention that occurs in old age is a function of reduced general cognitive competence or of an inadequate problem-solving attitude due to social isolation, fear of failure, and other factors. But it is clear that the error rate of the elderly decreases when tests are not timed and social acceptance is reinforced. We can venture the tentative conclusion that poor performance in the 4-year-old is probably due to lack of general cognitive competence, while poor performance in the 70-year-old is likely the result of an attitude toward solving problems (provided, of course, that the person shows no pathological signs of neurological deterioration).

Chapter Five

The Development
of Logical Operations

Cognitive development is more than a simple improvement in the ways in which we use memory and attention. These information processes are guided by a growing logic. Think of logic as a set of instructions from an "executive" in the brain. Memory and attention are the particular means by which we carry out these executive orders. They are the ways in which we carry out our search through past thoughts and present sights. To paraphrase Flavell's (1977) well-known statement, memory and attention are applied logic. Logic is the plan we use in our attempts to understand the world and ourselves.

The work of Jean Piaget deals almost exclusively with the growth of logical thinking across age. Our discussion of his approach is based on a sampling of his work as well as of the work he has inspired. This chapter is divided into three main sections. The first section deals with *concrete operations*—more specifically, with *classification* and *seriation*. These are logical operations that develop between the ages of 4 and 11 years. The second section discusses *formal operations*. Here, too, we have chosen two operations: *proportionality* and *correlation*. Because formal operations are more complex (see Chapter Two), they are not mastered until after age 11 or 12. The third section takes a life-span view of *conservation*. Conservation concepts begin in infancy and continue to grow in complexity through middle adulthood.

Throughout this chapter we will try to distinguish between two general types of task difficulty. Some tasks are more difficult than others because they make greater demands on attention and memory. For example, a child finds it easier to recognize instances of the concept *animal* than of the concept *mammals* because there are fewer attributes that define the concept *animals*. Therefore, there is less to remember. Some tasks are more difficult than others because they make greater demands on logic. For example, a child finds it easier to think about the difference between robins and blue jays than to think about the difference between robins and birds. In the second case the child must understand more about the logic of part/whole relations. The difficulty is not so much a matter of memory or attention as it is of logic. This distinction between problems of attention/memory and problems of logic will be useful as we try to compare research based on different theoretical perspectives.

Concrete Operations

"I'm G7. I'd like to be promoted to G9," Ms. Kronowski tells her supervisor. "Do you meet the qualifications?" Ms. Coleman asks. "I have learned how to handle the budget and can take dictation by shorthand," says Ms. Kronowski. "But can you program the computer to handle new accounts?" Ms. Kronowski admits that she cannot but is learning. Ms. Coleman recommends that they request a promotion to G8 and make the request for G9 after Ms. Kronowski has learned to program.

There are aspects of this conversation that apply to any everyday attempt to deal with classification systems. One, a class has a set of attributes that define it. In our example G9 is defined by computer-programming skills plus all the skills of lower grades. Two, a classification system includes individual members that possess some or all of these attributes. The particular attributes that an individual possesses determine where that individual is placed in the system. Ms. Kronowski has all of the attributes necessary to make G8 but only some of the attributes needed for G9. Third, a classification system is organized according to order, called a *hierarchy*. The various levels of a classification system are arranged so that higher levels include lower levels, just as all the skills for G8 are included in those needed for G9.

Research into the development of classification logic plays around with these three aspects. Children gradually grow in their ability to discover what attributes define a class, to construct a well-organized classification system, and to deal with the concepts of *some* and *all*. We will discuss these three dimensions of development in reverse order.

Class Inclusion

Adults know that the sum of two or more parts is greater than any of the parts alone. They know that this is true even when the parts are groups of objects. It is obvious to the adult, for example, that the population of Massachusetts must be greater than the population of either Boston or Cape Cod. Children younger than 5 or 6 know that any piece of a cookie is less than the whole cookie. However, this is a different type of part-to-whole relation. The cookie example deals with a spatial relation. It does not require using a rule that defines a class and then including members within that class. The member/class relation is a logical operation; the piece/whole relation is a physical operation. Children younger than 5 or 6 have difficulty with the class-inclusion problem. What is the nature of this difficulty?

Adults know that both swans and ducks are birds. Swans and ducks are subgroups of the larger group *birds*. The adult also knows that there are no swans (or ducks) that are not birds. All swans are birds *by definition*. This is where young children get confused. To young children the labels *swan* and *bird* are names of particular things. They think about these labels much as adults think about the names of people. Suppose that I have two friends—Herbie W. and Bruce J.—both nicknamed Sport. I also have a friend Herbie R., who is not nicknamed Sport. To ask a young child ''Are there more birds than swans?'' is like asking me ''Are there more Sports than Herbies?'' Offhand I would have no way of knowing; I would have to count the Herbies I know and the Sports I know. Young children take the same approach with the question about birds and swans. They treat these labels as names of particular objects—that is, all at the same level of classification.

But we have defined only a symptom of the class-inclusion problem. Let's see if we can't give you a more complete understanding of the problem. If we show a 4-year-old five gumdrops and three peppermints, he will probably have difficulty answering the question ''Are there more gumdrops or more candy?'' (There is also, of course, the possibility that he will say ''None'' after downing the lot!) Let's call the two subsets of gumdrops and peppermints sets A and A', respectively, and the total set of all the candy set B. That is, set B is the combination of set A and set A' (candy equals gumdrops plus peppermints). A and A' are subordinate to and included within set B. When asked whether there are more gumdrops (A) or more candy (B), the child is, formally speaking, being asked to compare A to B. And, since $B = A + A'$, the child is really being asked to compare A (gumdrops) to $A + A'$ (gumdrops plus peppermints).

The child looks at the five gumdrops and then at the three peppermints and answers ''There are more gumdrops.'' What do you think happened? Did the child not listen carefully to the request to compare gumdrops with candy rather than gumdrops with peppermints? Does the child not know the meaning of the words *more* and *less*? Is there something about the way in which the candies are arranged that caused the child to make a mistake? Or, perhaps, does the child not yet have the logical structures that are necessary to coordinate the subset/set relation?

Inattention cannot explain the difficulty. Even children who repeat the question verbatim fail to answer correctly (Inhelder & Piaget, 1964). Nor does the difficulty lie in vocabulary. When you ask a 4-year-old ''If I take out all the gumdrops, will there be any candy left?'' or ''If all the gumdrops were lined up and all the peppermints were lined up, which line would have more?'' she is quite likely to answer correctly. The 4-year-old usually knows the meaning of words like *all* and *more* (Kohnstamm, 1967).

Perhaps the child misinterpreted the question. When asked to compare gumdrops and candy, he simply identified peppermints with candy. He was then comparing gumdrops and candy when he was in fact looking at gumdrops and peppermints (candy). Markman (1973) found that the wording does make a difference. First-graders asked to compare the subgroups *parents* and *children* with the superordinate group *family* found the task-inclusion task easier. The word *family* is not usually used as a substitute for either *parents* or *children* in the same way *candy* can be used as a substitute for *peppermints*. Evidently the label *family* prevents the child from interpreting the original question as a request to compare the two subgroups *parents* and *children* instead of the actual request to compare one subgroup with the superordinate group *family*. ''Who would have more pets—someone who owned the baby dogs or someone who owned the whole family of dogs?'' was a form of questioning that made the class-inclusion relation easier for Markman's subjects. This is not to say that the solution of the class-inclusion problem is solely a matter of listening carefully. Of Markman's subjects 44% still made the typical error and only a few showed any improvement on a second testing of the usual forms of the class-inclusion question—gumdrops versus candy.

Perhaps the perceptual display confuses the child. He sees five gumdrops and three peppermints. The conspicuous abundance of the gumdrops causes him to forget the original question. He *hears* ''gumdrops'' and ''candy'' but sees gumdrops and peppermints. So he answers the question on the basis of what he sees. Wohlwill (1968) tested this hypothesis of perceptual dominance by comparing performance on a class-inclusion problem presented in two different ways—one with pictures and verbal instructions, another with verbal instructions only. Wohlwill surmised that, if the picture display was not there to distract the child from the original question, perhaps performance would improve. It did. Evidently some children do poorly on the class-inclusion problem not because they are unable to relate subset and set but because they are diverted from making the comparison between subset and set.

Winer (1974) points out that the source of the error may be not the pictures but the wording Wohlwill used in the two different conditions. When Wohlwill (1968) presented the pictures, he asked ''Are there more gumdrops or more candy?'' But when he presented the task without the pictures, he said ''If you had five gumdrops and three peppermints, would you have more gumdrops or more candy?'' (Candy, of course, is the sum of gumdrops and peppermints.) Winer tested the idea that the mention of the number of objects and the mention of both subsets in this second condition made the task easier. The absence of pictures, instead, did not seem to contribute to making the task easier. Winer found that, even when the task was presented with the pictures, the question "Here are five gumdrops and three peppermints. Are there more gumdrops or more candy?" made the task easier than when the subjects were simply asked "Are there more gumdrops or more candy?"

These studies (Markman, 1973; Winer, 1974; Wohlwill, 1968) explain why some children don't apply the knowledge they have. The studies, however, don't challenge, nor were they designed to challenge, the notion of general stages of cognitive development. Even under the best of presentation methods, most children under 5 or 6 fail the class-inclusion problem because of an inability to make the correct comparisons between subsets and sets. Children who give evidence of understanding the words *more* and *less*, who listen carefully, who are not distracted by a visual abundance of one subset, and who are not given a mental set with which to compare the two subsets (see Shipley, 1971) still fail to make the correct comparisons. Inhelder and Piaget (1964) conclude that the reason why children rather "stubbornly" compare the two subsets is that they are unable to compare the subset with the superordinate set—an inability due to the complex relations involved in the comparison. One might say that the child does not "hear" the question correctly, because to "hear" the question correctly requires the mental operations necessary to relate a subclass to a superordinate class, which itself includes the subclass!

If the class-inclusion problem is not an instance of poor listening, then what is it? The preoperational child lacks the ability to compare B (candy) with A' (peppermints) because such comparison is impossible when the child is limited by the use of mental imagery. That is, the preoperational child mentally "sees" all the gumdrops (A) being moved away from the group of candy (B), thus leaving only the peppermints (A'). There is no way for the mental imagery of preoperation thought to handle a relation that involves a set of objects (gumdrops) on both sides of a dividing line—the dividing line between gumdrops and gumdrops plus peppermints. When the child is limited by mental imagery, a set of objects cannot be in two "places" at once. The child does not understand that the two "places" are not physical positions but, rather, two different class memberships: gumdrops as gumdrops and gumdrops as candy. The 9-year-old would laugh at instructions to put all the gumdrops over here and all the candy over there. The 4-year-old would probably wear out the gumdrops moving them back and forth.

Free Classification

Preoperational children suffer from the limitations of spatial imagery in a variety of classification tasks—for example, free-classification tasks. In a free-classification task, children are given a bunch of things, like a deck of animal pictures or a pile of plastic shapes of different colors, and asked to "put all those that are alike together." Unlike the class-inclusion task, this task does not give the children any specific classes. The children are asked to classify the objects as they wish (thus "free" classification).

The limits of spatial imagery surface on this task in the following way. A child of about 4 will take five of the circles and make a snowman and then take a triangle and a square and make a pretend house. When asked about the circles she didn't use to make the snowman, the child replies that, since the snowman is complete, she can't add any more circles to it. Putting things together means, to a 4-year-old, piecing physical parts together in a spatial whole.

With 7-year-olds, putting things together is more likely understood as classifying the whole collection of objects by some classification system. Each class in the system is unlimited, because class is not a spatial whole that can be completed. Class is a rule that defines which members are included in that class. Giving a 7-year-old even a thousand new circles would certainly cause fatigue to the child but wouldn't create any conceptual problem. Preoperational children, instead, being limited by spatial imagery, cannot deal with logical extension and would treat the question as a request to make a spatial arrangement—what Inhelder and Piaget (1964) call a *graphic collection.*

Teachers sometimes take the child's ability to name groups of objects as an indication that the child truly understands a classification system. When a child says "All of these are circles," she doesn't necessarily know all there is to know about a classification system. Let's look at an ingenious study by Vygotsky (1962) to make this point clearer.

Vygotsky (1962) made a set of 22 wooden blocks varying in color, shape, height, and width. There were 5 different colors, 6 different shapes, 2 heights (tall and short), and 2 widths (wide and narrow). On the underside of each block, which the children could not see, Vygotsky wrote one of four nonsense words: *lag, bik, mur,* and *cev.* Regardless of color or shape, *lag* was written on all tall wide blocks, *bik* on all short wide blocks, *mur* on all the tall narrow ones, and *cev* on the short narrow ones. These blocks were placed on the table in front of the experimental subject. Vygotsky mixed the blocks up with regard to color, size, and shape. He then turned up one of the blocks (the sample block), showed it to the subject and read the word printed on the underside of the block. Let's say that the sample block was a red, tall, wide block—a *lag.* Then Vygotsky asked the subject to pick out all the blocks that belonged in this same category. The subject could move the blocks on the surface of the table but was not allowed to peek at the names written on the underside.

The subject sorted out all those he believed to be in the same category as the sample block. Let's say that the subject put five red blocks in a group. Vygotsky asked "Why have you put these together?" The subject would answer "Because all of these are red, like that one [the sample block]." Now comes the ingenuity in Vygotsky's study. Vygotsky did not assume that this subject truly understood a classification system. He turned over one of the wrongly placed blocks—say, a red, tall, narrow block—exposing the nonsense word *mur*. "What about this one?" Vygotsky asked.

The older subjects answered. "Oh my! I guess it [the class] is not color!" and immediately began to sort the entire set of blocks on another basis. The younger subjects answered "Well, leave that one out" and were content with just eliminating the one exception from the group of red blocks. The failure of the younger subjects to see the *implication* of the single exception led Vygotsky to label this level of understanding the *pseudoconcept*. In a true classification system all members of one class must have a common property and nonmembers of that class must not have that property. Younger children are hardly ever perturbed by logical contradictions such as "All the red ones are *lags*—except that red one there." For the younger child the exception does not "prove" (disprove) the rule.

Development of Classification Skills beyond Middle Childhood

Consistency of use. How effectively and consistently do older children and adults apply a classification system? Werner and Kaplan (1952) report some interesting examples of how 8- and 9-year-olds fail to sense the inconsistency in their use of new words. They will use a word one way in one sentence and another way in another sentence, without being disconcerted by the fact that the two uses have absolutely nothing in common. That is, 8- and 9-year-olds have no sense of the superordinate meaning of words.

Werner and Kaplan (1952) used tasks similar to those used by Vygotsky. They, too, employed nonsense words for which the children were to discover meaning. Instead of being printed on the bottom of geometric shapes, the words were embedded in sentences. For example, the nonsense word *lidber* was used as a substitute for the word *collect*. The children had to guess the word that *lidber* stood for by listening to the use of *lidber* in several different sentences. For example,

> Jimmy *lidbered* stamps from all countries.
> The police did not allow the people to *lidber* on the street.

After hearing the first sentence, a child would say something like "*Lidber* means 'to collect stamps.'" After the second sentence the same child would say "*Lidber* means 'to throw paper around.'" When asked how the two meanings were related to each other, the child would answer "Well, the police didn't want people like Jimmy to throw stamps around on the streets'' or something similar. The children didn't search for the common denominator of meaning, for the superordinate definition that could apply consistently to both uses of the new word. Although the context of this task is different from that of sorting geometric shapes, the failure to include two things within a common class is the same.

The game of "Twenty Questions" is another way of testing classification skills. If I tell you to ask questions that will help you guess what object I am thinking about, you probably wouldn't start by asking "Is it King Tut's tomb?" Such a question is, to say the least, too focused. You would first try to eliminate large numbers of possibilities. Perhaps you would ask "Is it man-made?" My yes to this question eliminates giant redwoods, Mount Mitchell, George Washington, and everything else that is included in the class of *natural objects*. Children without benefit of a classification system more often ask *focused* questions, while older children (8 or 9) begin to ask *constraint-searching* questions. By 10 or 11, children can play "Twenty Questions" by using a series of constraint-searching questions that truly build on each other to narrow down the number of possibilities (Mosher & Hornsby, 1966). Denney and Denney (1974) found that elderly people (70 to 90 years) showed no evidence of using constraint-searching questions on a pretest but could learn to use them effectively by listening to other people do so. The apparent decline of these skills in the later years was explained as another case of disuse—use it or lose it. If the decline had been due to neurological damage, the modeling wouldn't have been effective.

Research on free classification. Some rather interesting findings have emerged from research on free classification. They relate to how performance varies with the nature of the materials used and with the age of the subjects. Sigel, Anderson, and Shapiro (1966) discovered that some children who have no difficulty classifying real objects cannot do so with life-size color pictures of the same objects! Sigel and his colleagues used pictures of a pipe, a book of matches, a cigarette, a spinning top, a toy car, and a rubber ball. When the children were dealing with the real objects, they had no problem grouping all the "smoking stuff" together and all the "toys" together. But, when they were dealing with the pictures, they would often make what Luria (1976) calls a *functional relation*. That is, they would pair the book of matches with the cigarette, because "you need a match to burn the cigarette." At other times their groupings of pictures were random.

This research has great educational implications, because we take for granted that, if a child can recognize a picture (as these children clearly did), the picture can be a useful substitute for the object. However, Sigel et al.'s work suggests that some children use one system of thinking for objects and another system for the objects' pictures. Sigel and Olmstead (1970) speculate that treating pictures as representations of objects is a skill that must be learned and is more complex than the simple skill of naming pictures.[1]

Functional and categorical classifications. Most researchers assume that a *functional classification,* such as "Hammer goes with nail," is a more concrete and less advanced classification than a *categorical classification,* such as "Hammer goes with saw." A functional classification suggests that the person is thinking about some spatial and temporal whole—for example, the recall of a personal experience when the hammer was hitting a nail. Functional classification is similar to the graphic collection described earlier, which is also the result of the person's thinking about spatial wholes. Categorical classification, instead, results from the person's using a classification system based on common attributes.

The Soviet psychologist Luria (1976) argues that we shouldn't regard one form of classification as more advanced than the other. The two forms are only different expressions of one's economic culture. Luria's research showed, for example, that in some rural regions of Russia functional classifications prevailed. In similar regions nearby, also rural but organized in collectives and using a system of formal education, categorical classifications were found to prevail. Luria's findings represent an interesting challenge to Piaget's assumption that graphic modes of thought are more elementary and invariably precede logical modes of thought.

In a similar vein Denney (1974) discovered that the elderly do not naturally use categorical classifications. They use, instead, functional classifications. Like Luria, Denney inteprets her data in terms of the social demands that are made or not made on the person—in this case, institutionalized elderly people.

One might be tempted to take the Luria and Denney studies to support an environmentalist's position: how you think is determined by what you do. But Denney (1974) is the first to point out that the strength of the environmentalist position rests on subsequent research using either longitudinal sampling or controlled attempts to modify classification styles. Michael Cole, in his foreword to Luria's book, says pretty much the same thing. Nevertheless, the way we earn our living—as farmers with simple field tools or as accountants with pocket calculators—must influence our modes of thought in ways far more profound than we imagine. To cite from Marshall McLuhan (1964), tribes who lived in the rain forest and who had never seen a right angle because their houses were rounded huts and the horizon was obscured by trees, couldn't make a box out of wooden boards. Apparently their environment didn't make the demands on their thinking that cause the

[1]Sigel, now at Educational Testing Service in Princeton, has developed a comprehensive program to teach children various forms of "representational competence," using strategies that encourage children to represent events in actions, pictures, and words.

"construction" of a concept that Euclid thought to be innate—the 90-degree angle. (Anyway, Buckminster Fuller believes that the 60-degree angle is nature's own, and he develops this idea to a Fuller degree in his book *Synergetics*, published in 1975.)

Seriation and Transitivity

Seriation. The basic goal of a classification task is to group similar items together. The relation of these items to one another can be called, in a sort of metaphorical sense, *symmetrical*. There are other relations that are *asymmetrical* in that one element is greater or smaller than another. The asymmetrical relation is the backbone of *seriation*, which is the operation of organizing items in a series of increasing magnitude.

Children vary in their ability to seriate. Inhelder and Piaget (1964) conducted several studies to determine the developmental trends in such ability. They gave their subjects a set of sticks of varying lengths and asked them to seriate them in order of length—that is, from shortest to longest (see also our discussion of memory and intelligence in Chapter Four). In all of these studies Piaget and Inhelder found the same developmental trends. Children younger than 6 would attempt the task but would get several sticks out of order in a series of, say, seven or eight sticks. As children approached age 6, they might eventually get all seven or eight sticks in a staircase arrangement, but the result was achieved by trial and error and without an overall plan. Children older than 6 would systematically search the pile for the shortest stick, place it to the far left, search for the next shortest stick, place it to the right of the first one, and continue this process until all of the sticks had been seriated.

To Piaget "getting the answer" was not the most important goal. The children who systematically created the series obviously were using a system of asymmetrical relations organized as a whole mental structure. Piaget maintains that those children who used a trial-and-error procedure were trying to recreate a "picture," so to speak—a final form that some of them spontaneously called a "staircase." They just arranged and rearranged the sticks, until their "picture" came out right.

To distinguish the *figurative* strategy from the *operative* strategy (see the discussion of the preoperational stage in Chapter Two), Piaget conducted the following experiment. After the children had seriated the first set of sticks, he gave them a second set. The first one was a set of seven sticks increasing in length by 1-inch increments, beginning with a 1-inch stick. The goal was to add the second set to the first one (already seriated in a staircase arrangement) to create one seriated set. The younger children were unable to perform the task and explained their inability with comments such as "My staircase is finished." Giving these children seven additional sticks to add to their "staircase" was just like giving them seven extra pieces to add to an already completed jigsaw puzzle. The older children, however, had no difficulty adding the new series and were able to create a total series of 14 perfectly seriated sticks.

We see here the same difference between preoperational and concrete-operational thinking in free classification. Younger children create spatial arrangements; older children apply rules (a logical operation). Children who make graphic collections, like a snowman, are at the same stage of development as children who make a series that they call a "staircase." Those children who are able to keep adding circles to their "class of circles" are in the same stage as those children who can keep adding items of in-between length to an already seriated row.

When younger children attempt to add the second set of sticks to the first one, they make particular types of errors. They usually place a stick in a way that is correct only in one direction. As Figure 5-1 shows, stick $A\frac{1}{2}$ from the second set should be placed between sticks A and B of the first seriated set. The younger child places it, instead, between sticks B and C simply because $A\frac{1}{2}$ is smaller than C. The child thinks of the relation between $A\frac{1}{2}$ and C but cannot simultaneously think of the relation between $A\frac{1}{2}$ and B—a relation that violates the series. You may recall from our discussion of Piaget in Chapter Two that the more advanced child, who is able to consider both directions of a relation, can use what Piaget terms *reversibility*.

Transitivity. In related research on asymmetrical relations Piaget (1970) maintains that children younger than 6 or 7 cannot deal with *transitivity*. Transitivity is an inference about seriated items—for example, if A is greater than B and B is greater than C, then A is necessarily greater than C. Piaget showed young children sticks A and B, then showed them sticks B and C, and then asked them to make an inference about the relation between sticks A and C, which they had never actually seen paired. The preschoolers insisted that they couldn't possibly know, since the two sticks had never been physically compared. The 6- and 7-year-olds made the correct inference that A was greater than C: "It has to be, since you know that

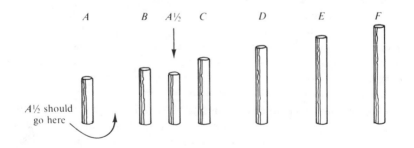

Figure 5-1.

this one [C] is the littlest of all.'' In other words, these children had mentally constructed the seriation and used it in a logical manner.

Several implications emerge from Piaget's research. For one, the child who insists on seeing A and C physically compared is not just stubborn or untrusting. That child is probably the most conscientious and eager to answer. The problem here is conceptual, not attitudinal or motivational. The child doesn't know how to answer the question any other way. The logical necessity of the A-to-C relation depends on mental structures that this child has not yet constructed. For another, Piaget's research shows that getting the answer is not the same as understanding. The preoperational child might be able to seriate seven sticks by trial and error and yet have no understanding of the seriation principle itself. This research supports the approach of those teachers who pay a great deal of attention to how children solve problems, not simply to whether they give the right answers. In so many instances children can give the right answer for the wrong reasons and go unchallenged, unless the teacher has been attentive to the process leading to the answer.

Recent research on seriation and transitivity. Since Piaget's original work on seriation and transitivity, several follow-up studies have taken a closer look at what causes failure and success on these tasks. Siegel (1972) decided that children younger than 6 could seriate items if the verbal instructions were not too complex. Try it yourself. Tell a child to ''put the smallest one here, and then the next smallest here, and then the next smallest here, until you have done them all.'' You're likely to get a wrinkled brow and a ''Huh?''

Siegel (1972) showed Canadian children four sticks in random order and told them simply ''Show me the next-to-smallest.'' If they pointed to the correct stick, they got a Smartie (Smarties are the Canadian equivalent of M & M's). The children continued to point until they finally learned how to get the Smartie every time a new array of four sticks was presented. Even if the children had no idea what the experimenter had asked them to do, they would still learn how to get a lot of Smarties. However, they could do this only if they knew, in their own personal way perhaps, which of the four was the next-to-smallest. The candy reward was always and only under that particular stick. Siegel found that children as young as 3 years of age could make correct choices consistently, but only when they were asked to find the smallest or the largest. The instruction to find the next-to-smallest (or next-to-largest) was too difficult for all but the 6- and 7-year-olds.

Gollin, Moody, and Schadler (1974) reason that Siegel's task ''Show me the next-to-smallest'' was really two tasks in one. Before a child can find the next-to-smallest, he or she first has to find the smallest. The smallest is the *anchor point* from which the child goes one step up in the series to find the next-to-smallest. If children could be helped in establishing this anchor point, perhaps they would find the "next-to-smallest" question easier. These researchers instructed the children to point to the smallest stick first and then find the next-to-smallest. Pointing was supposed to establish the anchor point better. It worked. Children as young as 5 years could then go on to find the next-to-smallest. Children who didn't use the pointing strategy did poorly on the Siegel task. These data suggest that there are sometimes ways to make a task simpler by reducing the load on memory. The children who pointed to the smallest stick probably did not forget which stick was the smallest as they then searched for the next in line. Even children who point to the smallest stick still have to understand the seriation principle, but the clearly established anchor point makes it easier for them to apply what they know.

The whole question of knowing versus remembering has spawned something of a countermovement against Piaget's stage theory. Can we continue to find ways of making a task easier on memory and attention without removing the demands of logical thinking? Bryant (1974) raises the possibility that even very young children can use concrete operations if memory demands are eliminated.

Bryant and Trabasso (1971) looked closely at the way Piaget presented the transitivity problem. Usually the child was given sticks A and B, then sticks B and C, and then he or she was asked about the relation between A and C. If the child couldn't remember that A was longer than B (or that B was longer than C), there was no reason for the child to conclude that A was longer than C. Yet the task was supposed to test the child's ability to make the inference that A was longer than C. Piaget took for granted that the child remembered that A was longer than B and B was longer than C. But it is not fair to conclude that a 4-year-old cannot make an inference when, in fact, the problem is that he or she forgets part of the instructions.

Bryant and Trabasso (1971) circumvented this problem by presenting the $A>B$ and $B>C$ relations so many times that the child would never forget them. Also, each stick was painted a different color. As a further aid, they actually presented sticks A and C when they asked "Which stick is longer?" The children couldn't see the lengths of the sticks, because the sticks were placed upright in a block of wood with drilled holes. The tops of the sticks were the same height, even though the sticks themselves differed in length. With this method children as young as 4 years of age had no trouble making the transitive inference that A was longer than C, even though they had never seen the two sticks paired together. The 4-year-olds could also, with only slightly more difficulty, infer that B was longer than D when they had overlearned the four relations $A>B$, $B>C$, $C>D$, and $D>E$.

These games of seriation and transitivity are much like the games used in a Montessori preschool. These games make use of a "cylinder block," which is a hardwood block with drilled holes that vary in depth.

Each hole contains a knobbed cylinder. The child removes all the cylinders, mixes them up, and then sets out to replace them in the proper holes. A proper fitting is reinforced by a flush match between rim and cylinder. If the cylinder is placed in the wrong hole, it either sticks up above the top of the rim or falls below it.

Do these games also reduce memory load and increase attention to relevant detail? The Montessori game we just described is certainly easier than seriating the same cylinders in open space on the table. Yet the reduction of difficulty here goes so far that it removes the need to use the seriation system as well as the need to make a transitive inference. A child can solve this problem by trial and error, looking only at a single cylinder at a time. And yet even these rote games may eventually develop the seriation concept. As we said before, the teacher needs to observe the procedures the child uses to replace the cylinders and also provide the challenges that truly require seriation and transitivity.

Formal Operations: Proportionality

Often the truth of a statement rests not on absolute figures but on hidden proportions. Take the assertion "It is safer to travel by bus than by plane." This statement is true only if the number of deaths per year are compared to the number of miles traveled per year in each mode of transportation. The statistic that 600 people die annually in planes and only 300 die annually in buses cannot stand alone to confirm the greater safety of buses. The figure for planes could be as little as one death per 10,000 miles in travel compared to three deaths per 10,000 miles for buses.

At what age do children come to realize that absolute figures are sometimes not as important as relative proportions? In Inhelder and Piaget's (1958) original work, children younger than 11 or 12 had difficulty equalizing weights on a balance. They were presented a balance with two unequal weights (W_1 and W_2) at unequal distances (D_1 and D_2) from the fulcrum. First W_1 was placed at distance D_1 from the fulcrum so that it perfectly balanced W_2, which had been placed at distance D_2 from the fulcrum (Figure 5-2a). If W_1 was moved toward the fulcrum (Figure 5-2b), the child under 11 or 12 didn't know how to reestablish balance when limited to changing either D_2 or W_2. The task of balancing weights requires that the child understand that $W_1/W_2 = D_2/D_1$; that is, it requires the coordination of two functions as a proportion. Each element is related to the other three. If W_1, which weighs 10 ounces, is moved to a distance of 5 inches from the fulcrum (D_1), W_2, which weighs 5 ounces, must be placed at a distance of 10 inches from the fulcrum (D_2).

The concept of proportionality involves relating two relations to each other (for example, W_1/W_2 and D_2/D_1). As we stated in Chapter Two, the relation of relations is a formal-operational concept. The two individual

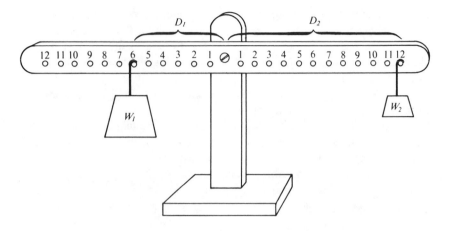

Figure 5-2a. Child is shown how the two unequal weights can balance each other.

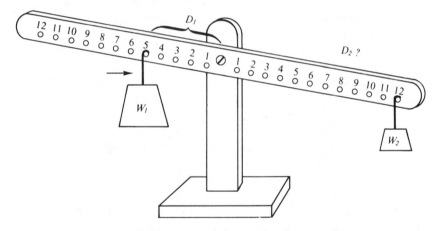

Figure 5-2b. Experimenter moves W_1 to position 5. Child has to figure out where to put W_2 in order to restore the balance.

relations are combined to form a set of implications about every member of the group. That means that the child in formal operations can predict the value of one of the members of the group if she knows the other three. She has related the relations.

Research on Proportionality

Proportionality appears in a variety of problem situations. Lowe, Ranyard, and McDonald (1976) presented children with a problem somewhat similar to the one about planes and buses we discussed earlier. The children were to guess which of two transparent beakers was more likely to yield a red bead on a random draw. Both beakers contained red and green beads, but in different proportions. Could the children understand that a random draw (with eyes closed) from a 20/20 red/green split was less likely to yield a red bead than a random draw from a 10/5 red/green split? Children younger than 11 incorrectly assumed that the chance of getting a red bead was greater for blind draws made from the beaker with the greater absolute number of red beads! They explained their answers by saying "Well, there are more reds in this one." Those children who said "It would be easy to get a red in that one [20/20 split]" probably were not accepting the constraints of the instructions—that is, that the draws were random rather than directed. The inability to accept the hypothetical nature of a verbal proposition is another characteristic of children in stages prior to formal operations.

The concept of proportionality is sometimes so hidden that it is difficult even for most adults to discern. Try this problem on your friends the next time you are having a dull get-together.

> Henrietta was quite proud of herself, because, over the past five weeks, she had lost 15 pounds. This was actually 2 pounds more than her objective. When a friend heard of Henrietta's success, she offered her, as a celebration gift, an 8-ounce slice of lemon meringue pie. "Oh, no, I can't. I would gain at least 2 pounds back. I put on weight so easily" was Henrietta's reply. "You can't gain 2 pounds from eating 8 ounces, Henrietta" said her friend. "Well, I can. It must expand when I eat it" Henrietta replied.

Could Henrietta be right? If everything else was kept constant (like body temperature, no other food, and so on), could our worried weight watcher ever gain more than 8 ounces from eating 8 ounces? Of course not. Yet, adults and children alike don't always see the logic of this answer. The reason is that the answer is based on a hidden proportion. Henrietta was reasoning that the pie once spread out in the body weighs more than the pie in its original form. She was probably thinking about volume and forgetting about density. In actuality, density equals weight per unit volume. If the density decreased (spread out) and the volume remained the same, the weight would actually decrease. If both density and volume increased, the weight could remain the same. Hidden beneath Henrietta's concern and the lemon meringue pie was the proportion $D = W/V$ (rather than the simple relation $W = V$). In many cases, when the problem is personal and emotional, our lack of logic is matched only by our excess of confidence (see Nolen, 1976).

The concept of proportionality has various components. Children younger than 11 years might be able to solve some of the component skills without necessarily being able to deal with the complete concept. (Gagné's model of development would predict as much.) The notion of relative magnitude, as opposed to absolute magnitude, could be one such component.

For example, can children younger than 11 understand that the concept of *larger* depends on what is used as a comparison? A 2-inch square is larger than a 1-inch square but is smaller than a 4-inch square. Brown and Muller (1976) found that 7-year-old children could understand relative magnitude, but children as old as 10 years could not solve proportionality problems.

To test for relative magnitude, these researchers presented the problem as shown in Figure 5-3. Children were shown a 1-inch square and a 2-inch square. They were told to choose the "correct" square—that is, the square that covered a small piece of candy. After the children had made their choices, the experimenter removed the two squares, baited the 2-inch square with a piece of candy (behind a screen), and presented the two squares to the subjects for a second guess. The children made a guess again and, of course, either found or didn't find the candy under the square they had chosen. (It should be noted that the 2-inch square sometimes was on the right of the 1-inch square and sometimes was on the left). Eventually, after a number of guesses, the subjects learned how to get the candy each time they were asked to choose one of the two squares; that is, they always chose the 2-inch square, which was invariably the one that covered the candy. Nothing was said during the experiment about the sizes of the squares. The reasons for determining which square was the "correct" one were left entirely up to the children.

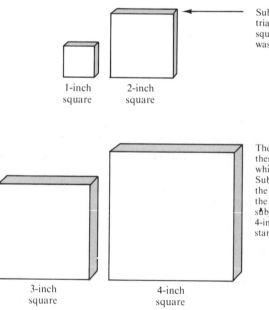

Subjects learned over a number of trials that this was the "correct" square. No mention of size was made.

1-inch square   2-inch square

Then children were presented with these two squares and asked which one was the "correct" one. Subjects younger than 7 chose the 3-inch square (closer to the standard in absolute magnitude); subjects older than 7 chose the 4-inch square (closer to the standard in relative magnitude).

3-inch square   4-inch square

Figure 5-3. Test for relative versus absolute magnitude.

Then, after the subjects had learned how to get the candy every time they were presented with a 1-inch and a 2-inch square, the experimenter gave them a choice between a 3-inch square and a 4-inch square. The children, probably surprised and confused by the change, were reassured that everything was all right, that one of the two squares still covered a piece of candy, and that, as before, they were supposed to guess which one it was.

How would the children go about making their choices? If they chose the 3-inch square, it would probably be because that square had an *absolute* magnitude (3 square inches) that was closer to that of the 2-inch square—the square that in all previous trials had proved to be the correct one. If they chose, instead, the 4-inch square, it would probably be because the 4-inch square was the larger of the two—that is, had the same *relative* magnitude with regard to the 3-inch square that the 2-inch square had with regard to the 1-inch square. Thus, those children who chose the 3-inch square had probably learned on the previous trials to choose the 2-inch square because it had a certain *absolute* magnitude (2 square inches). Similarly, those children who chose the 4-inch square had probably learned on the previous trials to choose the 2-inch square because it was larger in *relative* magnitude. Children younger than 7 typically chose the 3-inch square (indicating that they had learned on the basis of absolute magnitude), and older children typically chose the 4-inch square (indicating that they had learned on the basis of relative magnitude).

Figure 5-4 shows the test that Brown and Muller (1976) used for proportionality. Children between the ages of 9 and 10 were shown a standard pattern—in this case, three red squares and one green square. They then were shown four choice patterns (see Figure 5-4) and asked to match one of the choice patterns with the standard—that is, to choose the one choice

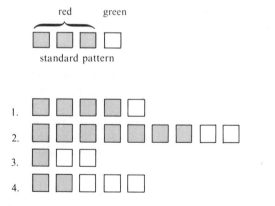

red   green

standard pattern

Subjects were presented with this standard pattern: three red squares and one green square.

1.
2.
3.
4.

Then they were presented with four choice patterns and asked to choose the one that was most similar to the standard above. Most children chose number 1, which preserves the relative magnitude but not the ratio. No children chose number 2, which preserves both relative magnitude and ratio and is, therefore, the correct choice.

Figure 5-4. Test for relative magnitude versus ratio (proportionality).

pattern they thought was most similar to the standard. (Incidentally, no candies were used in this test.) No child younger than 10 chose choice pattern number 2. This pattern preserves both the relative magnitude (more reds than greens) and the ratio of the standard pattern (75% reds and 25% greens) and is, therefore, the best choice. Most of the children chose pattern number 1, which preserves only the relative magnitude of the standard pattern (more reds than greens).

The implication of this research is that children between the ages of 7 and 10 understand relative magnitude without necessarily understanding proportionality. Proportionality involves the coordination of absolute and relative magnitudes. The child who can handle proportionality uses the absolute magnitude of a set to decide (1) which of the two sets is larger and (2) how large the largeness is—that is, what the ratio is. In other words, the child calculates the absolute magnitude of the difference between the two sets—the absolute magnitude of the relative magnitude. This requires an operation on an operation and is therefore a formal-operational task in terms of Piaget's definition of formal operations. It is not enough for the child to know that 3 is more than 1 (relative magnitude only). The child must also know that 3 is 75% of the total 4. Once the child has calculated this ratio, he or she has to reason backward; after seeing a set of eight objects (choice pattern number 2), the child must arrive at the conclusion that 75% of 8 is 6. This last step is an operation on an operation.

You might think that these concepts have little relevance to the child, except as abstract number games. Yet the developmental shift from a single relation to the more complex proportionate relation can explain such things as reading comprehension. In an interesting study by Billow (1975) two groups of children, one in the concrete-operational stage and the other in the formal-operational stage, were read sentences that contained metaphors. The children were asked to explain the metaphors, some of which were easy and others difficult. The easy metaphors involved only a simple relation of similarity—for example, "His hair looks like spaghetti." The children in the concrete-operational stage had no difficulty with this and similarly easy metaphors. They understood that, since both spaghetti and hair are made up of strands and since spaghetti are tangled up, the metaphor evidently meant that the boy's hair was all tangled up.

The difficult metaphors, solved only by children in formal operations, involved a proportionate relation—for example, "Her head is like an apple without a core." To explain this metaphor, the children had to reason "Head is to brain what apple is to core." The analogy of head/brain = apple/core can lead to the conclusion "This means that she is not very smart." Unlike the easier metaphor, which requires only sensing the similarity between two objects (hair and spaghetti), this complex analogy requires the child to relate one relation (head/brain) to another relation (apple/core). As you know, relating relations is a formal-operational skill. Elkind (1976) warns us that authors of readers for young children are sometimes unaware of the complexity of what they write.

Formal Operations: Correlation

Another form of reasoning that becomes possible at the stage of formal operations is *correlation*. Events are correlated—that is, they occur together—in various ways that make it possible to determine whether one causes the other. Call any event, such as a cock crowing, P. Call any other event, like the sun rising, Q. The absence of the event can be designated as $\bar{P}$ (called *P bar*), which in our example is the cock not crowing. $\bar{Q}$ is the absence of the sunrise. Say we see that the cock crows and the sun rises shortly thereafter. Does, in fact, the cock's crow determine the morning light? With the help of these symbols you may think that it is so—that crowing (P) occurs with sunrise (Q). You can write the concurrence of the two events simply as PQ. But does crowing ever occur without the sun rising? That is, do we ever have $P\bar{Q}$—the presence of P in the absence of Q? Alternatively, does the sun ever rise when the cock is still asleep? That is, do we ever have situation $\bar{P}Q$? You already know that the situation $\bar{P}\bar{Q}$ is very common; in other words, you know that the cock is generally silent during the night.

Many everyday questions have the following form: P causes Q only if we have situation PQ but never situations $\bar{P}Q$ and $P\bar{Q}$. (Logicians prefer the less categorical form "P implies Q" to "P causes Q.") Many communication breakdowns result from a failure to see the necessary conditions before one can say with certainty that P implies Q. For example:

> I ask you to do something, and you don't do it. I have to insist and demand before you do what I ask you to do. I wish I didn't have to push you so much. [Assumes that compliance (Q) comes only after pushing (P) but never tests this assumption.]

Perhaps this common assumption reminds you of the wise old man who was sitting on the curb in downtown Tulsa, beating two bamboo sticks together. A curious passerby asked "What are you doing, wise old man?" The wise old man replied "I'm keeping the elephants away." "Elephants? There are no elephants in Tulsa!" And the wise old man, "You see? It works." Before we can safely make statements about P causing Q, we have to test for other possible relations between event P and event Q. If pushing (P) were actually necessary for compliance *(Q)* to occur, the nonoccurrence of pushing would have to result in noncompliance ($\bar{P}Q$). Yet, for reasons deep in the psyche, often the crucial test is not performed. The plaintiff never tries not-pushing, and the wise old man never dares to stop beating his sticks together. After all, each occurrence of P in conjunction with Q is seen as a confirmation of the original hypothesis. After 20 years of successfully keeping elephants out of Tulsa, who's gonna risk the damage?

To solve correlation problems, the individual must transcend the actual and think about the possible. The thinker thinks "Even though I've never seen $P\bar{Q}$, I can consider its possibility and seek out evidence." The ability to accept assumptions (thinking of the possible rather than the actual) gives the thinker the power to consider alternatives that he knows are not actually true or does not believe in. Thus, the individual can step in the role of someone with different values and understand how that person's behavior reflects those values. Or he can look at a set of values that he possesses himself and predict behavior that is consistent with those values (and feel pride or shame when behavior is in or out of phase with such values).

Research on Correlation

There are stages in the development of the ability to deal with the form of an argument independently of its content. For example, Hill (1961) found that fourth-graders could solve the following problems.

1. If this is room 9 *(P)*, then it is fourth grade *(Q)*.
   This is room 9 *(P)*.
   Is this fourth grade? Answer "Yes" or "No."
2. None of the pictures was painted by anyone I know.
   I know Hank's sister.
   Did she paint one of the pictures? Answer "Yes" or "No."
   [This second problem has the general form: All *P*s (painters) are *Q*s (strangers to me). *X* (Hank's sister) is $\bar{Q}$ (not a stranger to me). Is *X* a *P*?]

How could children supposedly still in concrete operations answer these propositional statements correctly? Shapiro and O'Brien (1970) don't think that the questions used by Hill (1961) require formal-operational thinking. These questions, they say, require only that the children recognize a class inclusion. Take the second problem. If the child can reason that Hank's sister is not a subset of class *Q* (strangers), then he or she can easily conclude that Hank's sister is not one of the painters *(P)*, since all *P*s are *Q*s.

Shapiro and O'Brien (1970) made the task more difficult. They reworked Hill's questions so that they were impossible to answer because some essential element was missing. The aim of the experiment was to see whether the children realized that they didn't have sufficient information to answer the questions. Here are Shapiro and O'Brien's questions.

1. If this is room 9, then it is fourth grade.
   This is not room 9.
   Is it fourth grade? Answer "Yes," "No," or "Not enough clues."

2. None of the pictures was painted by anyone I know.
   I don't know this person.
   Did this person paint one of the pictures? Answer "Yes," "No," or "Not enough clues."

Neither of the above questions can be answered with certainty, because they don't provide sufficient information. The first problem states nothing about rooms other than room 9. The second problem states nothing about all the people I don't know. Saying that P (all paintings in this collection) implies Q (people I don't know) doesn't imply the inverse—that is, that all people I don't know (Q) have pictures in this collection (P). But the fourth-grade children who were presented with these questions thought they had sufficient information to reply that the stranger painted one of the pictures. This was like assuming that, since all nickels are coins, then this coin must be a nickel.

Shapiro and O'Brien's (1970) questions were more difficult than Hill's (1961), because here children were asked to compare the information they had with the information they should have had in order to reach a logically necessary conclusion. The added request to state the sufficiency or insufficiency of the information provided made the question more difficult. In Shapiro and O'Brien's view, comparing the information given with the information needed but not given is a formal-operational chore.

Once people acquire the ability to use formal-operational level of thinking about correlations, do they apply it consistently? O'Brien, Shapiro, and Reali (1971) found that they do not. Children in grades four, six, eight, and ten had difficulty solving P-implies-Q problems when such problems were presented as causal statements. The children did much better when the same type of problem was presented as a classification statement. Here is an example.

Causal context: If Judy is neat, she will get a good grade.
                         Judy will get a good grade.
                         Is Judy neat?

Classification context: If it is Jim's car, it is red.
                         It is not Jim's car.
                         Is it red?

As the children approached the usual age for formal-operational thought (around 12 or 13), they did increasingly well on the classification problem. The question above did require comparing $P \longrightarrow Q$ with $Q \longrightarrow P$ and, therefore, were formal-operational problems. However, those same questions presented in a causal context gave the children difficulty, no matter what their ages were. Even young adolescents were apt to reason backward from the cause; that is, the fact that Judy gets a good grade must mean that she is neat.

Even adults with graduate degrees often have difficulty with the logic of implications required by these problems (O'Brien, 1975). Why don't you try the exercise illustrated in Figure 5-5? If you have trouble, feel comforted by the fact that, despite the problem's deceptive simplicity, only about 10% of the college students who were given this problem were able to respond correctly.

Figure 5-5. Look at the four cards above. *Whenever there is a number below the line, there is a letter above the line.* Point to those cards, and only to those cards, that you would need to see fully (by unmasking the black half) in order to find out, once and for all, whether the sentence in italics is untrue.

Cognitive Style

Several times before, we have made a distinction between *having* a skill and *applying* that skill. This distinction becomes more and more important in the years beyond adolescence. There is a great deal of variability in an individual's performance in young adulthood, middle age, and old age. Mood, self-confidence, gaps in education—all contribute to whether an individual solves a particular reasoning problem (Arenberg, 1973).

There is also great variability among individuals of the same age beyond adolescence. Personality characteristics feed into the thinking process and make certain types of problems more or less difficult to solve. Some individuals, because of life experiences, develop a more reflective approach to problems; others are more impulsive. Some individuals develop a tendency to focus on the details of a problem; others back away and study the global picture. These cognitive styles determine whether or not an individual applies a cognitive skill that is well within his or her range of competence. For example, a person who is "field dependent"—that is, who finds it difficult to ignore irrelevant detail—seems to find logical problems difficult, since logical problems also require the individual to ignore the details of the content (Neimark, 1975).

Training in the use of logical notations will not succeed if teachers ignore cognitive style. In order to abstract the form of an argument, students will need to develop the appropriate "mind set." An individualized approach to teaching the art of thinking that includes concern for cognitive style will be more successful in helping students mind their *P*s and *Q*s.

Development of Conservation

Various forms of the conservation concept have been used throughout this book as examples of different theories and research methods. Now we bring these examples together in one place so you won't lose sight of the developmental sequence of the various forms of the conservation concept. The next section is in part a review. The section that follows discusses the use of conservation beyond adolescence. The last two sections deal with four general modification techniques for improving conservation in the adolescent years as well as beyond adolescence.

Development through Adolescence

No matter how much something changes, parts of it remain the same. A demolished office building still contains the same bricks and mortar, only grossly rearranged. My cousin Frank masked for Mardi Gras is still my cousin Frank. Some things change, but others are conserved. Conservation—the ability to identify what remains invariant across change—has received an almost inordinate amount of research attention. Piaget has been studying various forms of conservation for 40 years. Peill (1975) has written an entire book on the subject. And there is hardly a journal dealing with cognitive development that does not contain several articles each month on some variation of conservation. Why the hubbub?

The interest in conservation reflects a major shift in how psychologists see cognitive development. The older theories about how behavior changes and becomes more adaptive are inadequate to explain what it is that the growing child knows. Piaget, and hundreds of researchers since, states that growing children know more and more about the sorts of things that do not change in the world about them. With each new form of conservation that a child understands, the world settles into a more regular and less chopped-up place to live in. Susan is no longer frightened at Halloween, because she now knows that a papier-mâché mask is only an apparent change in her father, not a real one. Günter is no longer fooled by his older brother who tries to take the plate with more cookies by spreading out the fewer cookies on the plate he offers Günter. These are immensely important discoveries, and they occur according to a natural sequence of development. Here is a brief review of the steps that make up such a sequence.

Object permanence. By the age of 10 months the infant realizes that a hidden toy still exists and can be found by removing the cover hiding it. The existence of the object is conserved. Since this form of conservation and the discovery of space are one and the same (the child has discovered that the hidden toy does occupy a place behind the hiding object), it will be discussed more fully in the next chapter.

During the second year of life, children understand that objects usually don't change their shape, size, color, and other such characteristics with a mere change of position. Children at this age, in fact, will show surprise if, say, a striped ball rolls behind a chest and hits a polka-dot ball that was lying behind it, so that the latter rolls out into view on the other side of the chest. They will show surprise because they know that something is wrong —that the qualitative identity of the ball has not been conserved. But sometimes the change in the qualitative features of something is too much. Even children who understand the above situation might be frightened if their pet cat appeared one morning wearing a dog's mask (see DeVries, 1969). Once children are 3 or 4, however, if they can witness the transformation of a familiar object, they are seldom confused by a change in its appearance.

More complex forms of qualitative identity concern the metamorphic changes of certain animals. A caterpillar changes into a butterfly and, yet, is still the same animal. Can children conserve the identity of the animal across changes that are this great? Langford (1976) found that 4-year-old children knew that a tadpole was still a tadpole when it changed in size (got bigger) and also when it changed in form (added legs and lost tail). But it was not until they were 7 years old that children could coordinate quantitative changes (size) with qualitative changes (form). Evidently the coordination of size and form changes requires the class-inclusion skills of concrete-operational intelligence.

The following example, cited in Forman and Kuschner (1977, p. 62), illustrates this point. A 4-year-old boy was totally confused by a teacher who, holding a caterpillar in one hand and a butterfly in the other, said "This butterfly used to be a caterpillar." The little boy thought that he had seen the very same animal at two points in its life cycle; that is, he thought that a single organism can be preserved as a specimen at two different stages of development.

Discontinuous quantity. Once the child enters the stage of concrete operations, changes in the distribution of objects are not confused with changes in the total number of objects. The child knows that the quantity remains the same. We are speaking here of *discontinuous quantity*, so called because the objects constituting the collection are separate and countable.

Continuous quantity. Shortly after mastering the conservation of discontinuous quantity (around 7 to 8 years), the child becomes capable of generalizing quantity conservation to continuous media, such as sand and clay. That is, the child understands that change in the shape of the clay does not imply a change in its amount. Continuous quantity is more difficult, as Klahr and Wallace (1976) explain, because continuous media need to be mentally converted into a collection of unit particles (see Chapter Three). In the section on modification techniques we will discuss how Inhelder, Sinclair, and Bovet (1974) create conflict between continuous- and discontinuous-quantity conservation in order to get children to better understand both types of conservation.

Weight conservation. For some reason conservation of weight is more difficult than conservation of discontinuous quantity.[2] Children who know that the total number of a group of objects does not change when the objects are spread out may still believe that their total weight does change when the objects are spread out. Perhaps the difficulty lies in the fact that *hefting* a group of spread-out objects (for example, on a tray) feels very different from hefting a group of objects close together. The two arrangements produce different feelings of balance. These different feelings are very noticeable and more difficult to overcome, when making judgments about total weight, than those related to just *seeing* the group spread out, as is the case in conservation of discontinuous quantity. These apparent differences in weight have to be put aside in order to develop an objective concept of weight.

Volume conservation. The volume of an object remains the same no matter what change in shape the object undergoes. A ball of clay rolled in the shape of a sausage will still displace the same amount of water it displaced as a ball. This seems obvious enough. Then why is volume conservation usually not achieved until age 11 or 12? Because volume, like proportionality, involves an operation on an operation—something that is not possible until the period of formal-operational thinking. Consider the steps a child must take to solve the following problem.

The experimenter shows a child a square piece of wax $4 \times 4 \times 2$. The wax is tied to a wire and immersed in a glass, brimful with water, set in a receptacle that catches all the displaced water (Figure 5-6a). The displaced water is then poured into a graduated cylinder. Then the experimenter reshapes the square piece of wax into a rectangle $1 \times 4 \times 8$ (Figure 5-6b). Just before the experimenter lowers the reshaped wax into the same glass, which has been refilled to the brim, she asks the child to predict how much water will be displaced this time. The child thinks for a moment. Since the wax is now thinner (1 inch instead of 4 inches), it will push less water to the sides (call this W for width). But, since the wax is taller now (8 inches instead of 4), it will push more water to the top and bottom (call this H for height). The increase in H does not appear to offset the decrease in W. But, wait a minute! The wax has also changed in its front-to-back dimension (call this D for depth). Can the child integrate all three of these dimensions—W, H, and D? If the child considers only two dimensions, he will make a mis-

---

[2]It should be noted that, depending on the particular features of the task, conservation of weight may appear at the same period of development as conservation of continuous quantity.

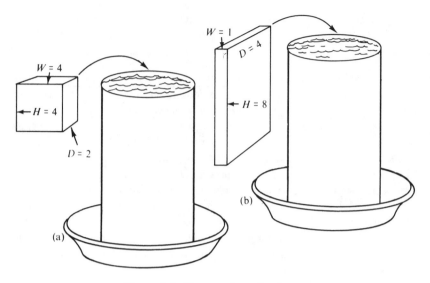

Figure 5-6. Conservation of volume.

take. The area of the individual sides has not been conserved—that is, 4 × 4 does not equal 8 × 1 (see Figure 5-6). Does the child automatically conclude, therefore, that the volume is not conserved? Actually, the volume is conserved (4 × 4 × 2 = 4 × 1 × 8). In order to give a conserving answer—that is, to predict the possibility that the area of one side can change without changing the total volume—the child must make an operation on an operation. The first operation is considering the relation between two areas (*H* × *W* of the square and *H* × *W* of the rectangle); the second operation is considering how the third dimension (*D*) relates to the change in these two areas. This last step is indeed an operation on an operation, or the coordination of one relation with another.

This particular task presents the added difficulty of having to compare the amount of displaced water with the amount of space occupied by the piece of wax. That is, the child must consider the amount of space that the piece of wax "takes up." In fact, the child has not been asked about the volume of the wax; he has been asked about the volume of the "hole" that the wax creates in the water. The child could have been asked to compare the amount of liquid produced by melting the wax in both shapes, the square and the rectangle. This form of questioning deals with "interior volume" and is a little easier than the more indirect question regarding volume measured by the displacement of a second substance (see Lovell & Ogilvie, 1960, 1961).

Density conservation. Density is the relation between weight and volume. The denser an object, the less likely it will float on water. If the particles of the object are packed together tightly, the object will weigh more than an equal volume of water. Therefore, it will sink. If the particles are not tightly packed—that is, if the substance of which the object is made has tiny air chambers—the object will weigh less than an equal volume of water. Therefore, it will float.

Does changing the shape of a substance change its density or its relation to an equal volume of water? Children in the concrete-operational stage think that a clay ball that sinks will float when changed into the shape of a pancake. These children also think that, if the whole ball will not float, then a cut-off half or maybe a fourth of it will. The fact is that conservation of density is based on a complex relation between two relations involving volume and weight of the object and volume and weight of water. These two relations must be related to each other—a problem at the level of formal operations.

The development of the various forms of conservation is a gradual process that goes on until the child reaches adolescence. Each developmental theorist, as we discussed in Chapters Two and Three, takes a slightly different perspective in accounting for the sequence in which the various forms of conservation emerge. Whichever perspective is chosen, it cannot be denied that conservation has become a "master task" that has put into relief our changing view of cognitive development. The growing child learns how to deal with *change* at successively increasing levels of sophistication. The emphasis on conservation in developmental psychology is a concomitant of the new approach in physics, which treats the laws of conservation (matter, energy, and existence) as one of the foundations of science.

Development of Conservation beyond Adolescence

As in so many other areas of cognitive development, changes in the use of conservation beyond adolescence present some interesting contrasts. Adults who can conserve volume and density in one content area have difficulty in others. Even those who seem to be able to firmly conserve in one area can be led to make nonconservation errors. Educational level, social demands, and living arrangements are only a few of the many factors that influence the individual's successful application of the conservation concept. Besides, it should be remembered that not every adult seems to reach formal operations, a prerequisite for the higher forms of conservation. In a nutshell, it may be inappropriate to talk about development of conservation beyond age 16 or 17. Here is a sample of the research that supports this summary statement.

Chiapetta (1976), in a review of several studies, maintains that many American youths do not reach formal-operational forms of conservation even by the age of 20 years. Furthermore a large percentage of secondary- and college-level teachers fail formal-operational tasks of conservation. McKinnon (1971) found that 50% of the college freshmen he studied

could not conserve density or volume. The same kinds of findings are repeated in other works as well (see, for example, Renner, Stafford, Lawson,
McKinnon, Friot, & Kellogg, 1976). The development of formal-operational
proficiency on conservation tasks doesn't appear to be a natural "unfolding"
of a biological urge resulting from living in any environment. Obviously the
environment must include language, reasons to conserve, social interaction,
and perhaps a preference for the Western mode of thought, which values
objective measurement.[3] The use of formal operations depends on many
essential environmental factors, but, as Piaget has explained, the concept
that volume or density is conserved by virtue of *logical necessity* cannot
itself be taught.

    With regard to this last point, to what degree is an adult's conserva-
tion answer based on a logical deduction demanding that answer by logical
necessity? In a conservation-of-weight task Chiseri (1975) found that college
students had no trouble making the conservation response. But when they
were confronted with the fact, actually a bogus, that a reshaped ball of clay
didn't weigh the same as it did before, they changed their answers altogether. Chiseri reasoned, as Smedslund (1961) had done before him, that,
had conservation resulted from a logical principle, the sleight-of-hand bogus
wouldn't have caused the students to change their answers. On the contrary,
they would have accused the experimenter of tampering with the evidence,
so to speak. These studies help to distinguish answers that come from rote
learning from answers that derive from a well-integrated understanding of
physical laws.

    Research on conservation in the later years. To what extent do
those adults who have achieved a well-integrated understanding of conservation maintain their ability to use this concept as they grow older? We preface
our review of the following studies with the usual disclaimer that the use of
cross-sectional sampling often confounds age changes with generation differences.

    Papalia (1972) tested conservation in subjects ranging in age from 6
to 65 years and beyond. He found that the ability to conserve volume
showed a decrease beyond age 64. His subjects would answer that a certain
object—such as a 100-cc piece of clay—would displace more water when
immersed shaped as a ball than immersed reshaped into, say, a sausage.
However, they could answer questions of weight and substance correctly—
for example, "Does the clay weigh the same now that its shape has
changed?" and "Has the quantity of the clay changed together with its
shape?" The volume problem, defined by researchers as a formal-

---

[3]See Buck-Morss (1975) for an interesting discussion of why she thinks Piaget's
theory of cognitive development is an expression of Western culture's tendency to separate form
from content.

operational problem, taxed the elderly person's thinking more than the concrete-operational tasks of weight and substance conservation.

This study does suggest that conservation skills decrease with age, at least with regard to the more complex forms of conservation. Why the decrease occurs is not clearly understood. In an attempt to test the relative effects of neurological deterioration versus social isolation, Rubin (1973) conducted a study with institutionalized as well as noninstitutionalized elderly people. He reasoned that, if the noninstitutionalized elderly subjects did better than those confined in nursing homes, he would have a clear indication that social isolation reduces conservation skills. Rubin did find poorer performance in tasks relating to conservation of number, substance, and weight on the part of the institutionalized subjects. His conclusions, however, don't take into account the possibility that those elderly people who are institutionalized may suffer from more serious neurological deterioration than those elderly people who continue to live in the community. Nor does the study report the quality of the institution versus the quality of the community life. In other words, the decline in the elderly could be due to neurological or to sociological causes.

Imagine a young graduate student testing elderly patients in a nursing home. He whips out his kit of conservation tasks, sits down with an 80-year-old woman dressed in her day robe, and spreads out two green pieces of felt, each a square foot. He places a toy cow on each piece of felt and asks "Do these two cows have the same amount of grass to eat?" The elderly woman looks quizzically at the young man, grins at his rather childish game, and nods her head. Now the doctoral candidate, strong in his conviction that he is gathering priceless experimental data, places two toy barns close together on one piece of felt and two toy barns far apart on the other piece of felt. This arrangement creates the illusion that less grass is available on one "pasture" than in the other. The question is repeated: "Do these two cows have the same amount of grass to eat?" The woman gives the bearded young man a look that clearly indicates her view that he is a bit too old to be playing with toy animals and capriciously says no without further explanations. We may be justified in wondering how much serious effort this woman puts in trying to answer a conservation problem disguised as a childish game.

Garber, Simmons, and Robinson (1974) not only changed the materials from toy animals to geometric blocks (more "adult" objects) but also convinced their elderly subjects that they were capable of solving logical problems. With these changes, the elderly subjects performed better. Thus, poor performance by the elderly may have more to do with their attitudes toward taking the tests than with any general inability to think logically.

Perhaps this is a good place to make a short digression and talk about the research methods of developmental psychology in general. The leading article in the July 1977 issue of *The American Psychologist* is a plea by Urie Bronfenbrenner for a new methodology in developmental research. He decries the fact that the American emphasis on scientific rigor has caused us to study tasks that are limited in scope and general relevance. He states:

> This limitation derives from the fact that many of these experiments involve situations that are unfamiliar, artificial, and short-lived and that call for unusual behaviors that are difficult to generalize to other settings. From this perspective, it can be said that much of the contemporary developmental psychology is *the science of the strange behavior of children in strange situations with strange adults for the briefest possible periods of time* [Bronfenbrenner, 1977, p. 513].

Bronfenbrenner goes on to advocate a new method, which he calls an "experimental ecology of human development." This new approach would focus on the "progressive accommodation, throughout the life span, between the growing human organism and the changing environments in which it actually lives and grows" (p. 514). The phrase "experimental ecology" is meant to communicate that this new approach would neither reject the rigor of the scientific method nor ignore the social and ecological relevance of what is researched. Certainly Bronfenbrenner's proposal and commentary apply also to research in the development of conservation.

Modification of Conservation Ability

We have discussed a large number of studies that plot the stages through which most people pass as they move toward greater cognitive ability. Can we, as educators, facilitate this development? Since cognition is a general ability, can we improve the child's understanding of conservation? Many research projects in the 1960s tried and failed. But we are now finding techniques that do seem to improve this cognitive operation. What are these new techniques, and how do they work? In order to discuss and compare their varying degrees of effectiveness, let's outline some of their distinguishing features.

The first distinction is between techniques that take a *direct* approach and techniques that take a *component-skill* approach. A teacher who follows the direct approach will take a conservation problem and let the children work directly at it. If, instead, a teacher follows the component-skill approach, he or she will first train the children in the simpler skills that are combined to form the more complex, ultimate skill—in this case, the conservation problem at hand. Gagné, for example, would follow this approach (see Chapter Three).

The second distinction is between *expository* and *corrective* techniques. A teacher who follows the expository method will offer explanations and instructions before the children attempt to solve the problem. This teacher assumes that the children can learn by simply listening and watching—a common classroom assumption. A teacher who follows a corrective procedure will, instead, let the children try to solve the problem by themselves. He or she says little before the child makes a guess. If the child is incorrect, then the teacher corrects the mistake and offers explanations.

The third distinction concerns what the teacher does to transmit information to the child. The teacher may say "Yes, that's correct" or "No, that's wrong." We call this the *yes/no* method. This method may be used as a form of the corrective procedure if the teacher says yes or no after the child guesses. It may also be used with the expository procedure if the child is listening to the teacher answer yes or no to someone else's questions. The teacher, of course, can do more than just say yes or no. He or she may give a *verbal rule* or a *physical demonstration*. Both of these forms can be used either in the expository procedure (for example, by explaining or modeling before the child attempts the task) or in the corrective procedure (for example, by telling or showing to the child the nature of his or her incorrect guess).

Finally, the teacher may do none of these things. After the child makes a guess, the teacher can give the child a second problem that is specifically designed to cause the child to contradict his or her first guess. The goal of this approach is to have the child eventually realize that his or her contradictory answers cannot be both correct. This is called the *conflict-inducement* procedure. Conflict inducement can, in a sense, be considered a corrective procedure, albeit the child corrects himself or herself. It doesn't fall neatly into the expository procedure, nor have there been attempts to use it in combination with the component-skills method.

Direct Designs—Corrective

In the studies conducted to test these techniques, the experimenter works directly on the conservation task that the child is supposed to learn. This is done by first allowing the child to guess and then correcting the child's guesses. When the child hears or sees that she has made an error, she

	Expository	Corrective
Direct design	yes/no	yes/no
	rule	rule
	demonstration	demonstration
		conflict
Component-skills design	yes/no	yes/no
	rule	rule
	demonstration	demonstration

Figure 5-7. Four general categories of techniques used to improve conservation ability.

experiences surprise, tension, and perhaps a conflict between her guess and the feedback she receives. It should be noted that the feedback here is not corrective in a strict sense; rather, it has the potential of being used by the child to correct her own guess. Recall Bruner's procedure discussed in Chapter Three. Children were asked to guess whether the level of the water poured from a tall skinny glass into a short wide glass (covered by a shield) would remain constant. After the children guessed that the two levels would be the same, the shield was removed and the children could see that the water level in the wide glass was lower. This study deliberately attempted to place the children's verbal guesses in conflict with their perceptual experience. Such a conflict enabled the children to reevaluate their original guesses and understand that they were dealing with "the same water." This, in turn, allowed them to ignore the apparent difference in amount due to the real difference in level.

Inhelder, Sinclair, and Bovet (1974) also used a conflict procedure, but with a slightly different focus. Their goal was to help the children understand why the water level was lower in one glass, when the amount of water was the same. They wanted the children not to ignore the water level but to understand that the lower level was due to the greater width of the second container. To achieve their goal, these researchers had their subjects watch very carefully while the water was being poured from one vessel into the other. As soon as the children guessed that the water in skinny jar A would be "less" when poured in fat jar B, the experimenter simply poured the water back from jar B into jar A, without making any comment. By alternating between problems that caused the children to contradict themselves, the experimenter actually led them to conclude that the amount of liquid in the two containers was the same. What the water lost in height it gained in width.

Inhelder, Sinclair, and Bovet (1974) used other ingenious procedures to generate conflict. In one activity the subjects were asked to place ten small balls of clay into a narrow glass and ten small balls of clay into a wide glass by dropping a ball from each hand into each glass simultaneously. If the children focused on the one-to-one correspondence of the activity, they would say that the two glasses contained the same amount of clay balls. If, instead, they focused on the faster rise of the level in the narrow glass, they would conclude that the two glasses contained different amounts of clay balls. The ensuing conflict eventually led the children to understand that the higher level in one glass was compensated for by the greater width of the other glass. Other studies that have found cognitive conflict successful in inducing conservation concepts are Berndt and Wood (1974), Murray (1968), Smedslund (1961), and Strauss and Rimalt (1974).

In a review of the literature Brainerd and Allen (1971) cite several unsuccessful training procedures that didn't alternate the child between conflicting judgments. Instead of asking a follow-up question that was the direct opposite of the original question, these procedures used a follow-up question that was a direct extension of the original one. For example, if the child said that a slightly bent piece of string was the same length as a straight piece of string (a correct answer under the circumstances), the follow-up consisted of successively bending the string more and more until the child changed his answer to a nonconserving one. Under these procedures children were less likely to sense the contradiction, probably because the discrepant answers did not alternate back and forth in rapid succession. Having to change one's mind after a while is not as disconcerting as having to change one's mind on every other question.

The experimenter can give corrective feedback without waiting for the child to attempt to deal with the problem. Brainerd (1974b) showed 5-year-olds two identical sticks placed side by side with their ends exactly aligned. He then pushed one of the sticks slightly forward so it appeared to be longer (on one side only, of course). Brainerd asked his subjects whether the two sticks were still the same length. Whenever a child said that one of the sticks was longer (or shorter, as the case might be), Brainerd would simply say "No, you're wrong. The top stick is still as long as the bottom one." These procedures resulted in a conservation-performance improvement that endured at least until a second testing a week later. Brainerd (1974b) states that the experimenter-provided correction can be an effective way of causing enough tension for the children to rethink their answers. The conflict here is between the child's answer and the experimenter's answer rather than between the child's two answers. This conflict between child and adult can make the child search for an alternative on which to base his or her answer. In Brainerd's study, for example, the child would find such an alternative in looking at both ends of the sticks, not just at the ends on one side. The danger, of course, is that the child might learn some method of answering the questions correctly without explicitly knowing the reasons why—for example, without knowing the rule of compensation. What the stick gains in apparent length on one end is compensated by what it loses at the other end.

Correction need not come from an adult. Silverman and Geiringer (1973) and Silverman and Stone (1972) placed the nonconserving child in a problem-solving situation with more advanced, conserving children. They found that, when nonconservers and conservers disagreed, the nonconservers were more likely to change in the direction of the conservers than the other way around. Relevant measures indicated that this shift to a higher level of thinking was not due to a rote acceptance of peers' opinions. Rather, the disagreement generated a type of conflict that could be resolved only by the better logic of the conservation concept. Murray (1972) discovered that, when two conservers and one nonconserver try to reach consensus, all three children show improvements! These studies provide support for Piaget's hypothesis that social interaction, through the dialectics of disagreements, is an important source of cognitive development (Piaget, 1967).

Some studies have corrected the child's erroneous guess with a verbal rule and/or a physical demonstration. Each time the child said that the number of some spread-out objects was greater than an equal number of compactly spaced objects, Beilin (1965) gave the child the conservation rule and also demonstrated that the spread-out row of objects could be compressed into a shorter row. This procedure proved to be more effective than the expository procedure of telling the child beforehand what dimensions of the task to attend to and what to ignore. The combination of verbal rule and physical demonstrations also proved to be a better corrective procedure than simply indicating that a response was wrong or correct. Evidently the yes/no corrective procedure used by Beilin was not as effective as Brainerd's yes/no procedure mentioned earlier.

Direct Designs—Expository

When we think of teaching a child something new we often wonder whether giving the child the right introduction to the task will help his or her learning process. When does the expository procedure work? And does it short-circuit meaningful learning and cause rote learning? Several studies have focused on these questions. The results of one of them suggest that the expository procedure does not lead to rote learning. Zimmerman and Rosenthal (1974) had an adult work on conservation problems and explain the various steps while the children watched and listened. These children, about 6 years old, understood what they saw and heard well enough to apply what they had learned to a different task. To the question "How would you show a friend that these two sticks [arranged in a T] are still the same length?" the children gave the answer "Turn them back around like they were before [parallel and aligned]." These children had never seen the adult do just this, so it cannot be said that what they had learned by watching the experimenter was mere rote learning. They had seen and heard the adult deal with a conservation-of-length problem created by pushing one of the sticks forward, not by rotating one of the sticks to make a T. It is true that the two problems were similar, but they were not identical. The study also showed that the expository procedure worked equally well as a corrective procedure when the rule was given after each wrong guess by the children.

Component-Skills Designs—Corrective

Instead of teaching conservation directly as a whole, the teacher may decide to look closely at the conservation problem, decide what component skills are needed to solve it, and begin by teaching the component skills one at a time. This means that students first will be trained on a particular component skill and then will be tested on the whole task to see if learning the component helped their overall performance.

Halford and Fullerton (1970) taught young children to say "Same!" if two cards had an equal number of dots and "Different!" if two cards had an unequal number of dots. The experimenter simply said no if the child counted and compared incorrectly and yes if the child counted and compared correctly. This was not a conservation task, since neither set of dots was spread out to see whether the child realized that, no matter how spatially arranged the dots were, the number of dots was still the same in the two sets. Counting two sets of something is necessary but not sufficient for true conservation. In fact, children can sometimes count the elements in both sets correctly after one set has been spread out and still give nonconserving answers. They will say something like "This row has eight and this row has eight, but this one [the spread-out one] has more." In other words, they both have eight elements, but these eight are more than those eight! The recognition that two sets have the same number of components—what Inhelder, Sinclair, and Bovet (1974) term *quotity*—is therefore a necessary component of number conservation, but it is not sufficient. Halford and Fullerton (1970) found that quotity training (counting both sets to determine equality/inequality) improved performance on a subsequent number-conservation test in which one of the two sets was spread out.

Pufall (1973), on a task requiring children to conserve the order of three colored balls, didn't find certain component skills effective. Some children were given component-skill training on discrimination of order—a fairly easy task. All the children had to do was to decide whether two rows of colored balls were in the same order left to right. Other children were shown a standard row and asked to construct a row that had either the same or the reverse order of the standard. The two groups were then given the test of order conservation. The experimenter put three balls, each of a different color, into a tube. The children, who were watching the experimenter, had to remember the order of the colors. Then the experimenter rotated the tube either 180 degrees (thus reversing the order) or 180 degrees and then another 180 degrees (thus first reversing and then restoring the original order). The subjects were to say whether the rotations did or didn't change the order of the colored balls. After the children had given their answers, the experimenter removed the balls from the tube. The children who had had discrimination training did less well than those who had been trained to construct rows in the same or in the reverse order of the standard row. Neither group did as well as a third group, who had been trained from the beginning with the rotating tube—that is, who had had preliminary trials with the conservation-of-order task. In other words, this third group had followed a direct-design procedure, while the other two groups had been trained according to a component-skill design.

Evidently the type of component skills chosen makes a big difference. So does the type of correction, as shown by Gelman (1969). She used a simple yes/no correction to help children discriminate changes in length and height. Orienting the children's attention to changes in these dimensions (a component skill of conservation) improved the children's ability to conserve quantity. However, Field (1974) showed that the gains resulting from Gelman's yes/no procedure didn't last as long as gains resulting from giving the children a verbal rule after an incorrect response.

It is not clear why these studies have conflicting evidence for the value of component-skills training. Several possibilities exist. In some cases the component skills are so similar to the ultimate whole task that training the children in component skills is almost like giving them the answer (Halford & Fullerton, 1970). In other studies the difference between training and testing is greater (as in the first two conditions in Pufall, 1973). The form of correction, too, may make a difference. A simple yes/no correction, although it results in immediate gains, may not be as effective in the long run as correcting the component skills with verbal rules. But some component skills are so simple—the discrimination of order, for example—that a verbal rule would be a case of overkill. With such simple tasks, a yes/no correction works better.

Component-Skills Designs—Expository

One way to teach a new concept is to take a component skill of the concept and tell the child as much as possible about that component. Placing objects in one-to-one correspondence—one for you, one for me; one for you, one for me; and so on—is a component skill of number conservation. Why not just demonstrate this component skill for the child? Wallach, Wall, and Anderson (1967) did so with success. They showed the children how two sets of objects could be placed in one-to-one correspondence even when one set was spread out or arranged in different ways. They demonstrated the component skill of one-to-one correspondence but said nothing about conservation of number. Note that it would still be possible for a child to learn to match each element in one set with just one element in another set and still believe that one set had more elements. Wallach, Wall, and Anderson (1967) did find that the training on one-to-one correspondence did improve performance on number conservation. The children knew that spreading out a row of objects or pushing them close together didn't change the equality relation between the two sets. However, the children seemed to have only a limited understanding of number conservation. They had learned to ignore the apparent differences in number (the illusion created by the spread-out row) but hadn't learned to explain the reason for the apparent difference. Few of the children said something like "The two rows only look different. If you push together the top row as it was before, the two rows look the same again." In sum, these children may have learned how to give a correct answer, but it is not clear that they understood the reasons for their answers.

One way of defining conservation is to say that the child understands that an object, or set of objects, can change in two ways at once. A piece of clay can be reshaped so both its height and width change, thus remaining the same in quantity. The row of objects can change in length and in density at the same time, thereby retaining the same number of components. The component skill of classifying objects in more than one way was used by Sigel, Roeper, and Hooper (1966) as a training procedure. Encouraged and stimulated by their teachers, a group of 5-year-olds learned to call an orange "orange," "fruit," "something you get juice from," and so forth. This training on multiple classification improved the children's performance on subsequent tests of conservation. Although this study represents one of the clearest proofs that conservation performance can be enhanced by component-skills training, it must be noted that its subjects were children with IQs of over 130.

Implications of Modification Research

What generalizations can we make on the basis of this brief review of selected research? First of all, it should be said that the variety of methods and materials used in these studies makes it difficult to rank one technique as better than another. Also, we should keep in mind the qualifying comments we made when we described the various studies. Having said that, we can venture some broad generalizations.

Attempts to teach the whole task (direct designs) seemed to fare better than those that broke the conservation task down into subparts (component-skills designs). This conclusion is based on the fact that the studies using the component-skills design showed success only inconsistently. The reason (if our conclusion is correct) may be that learning a subpart of a problem is difficult because the student still has to relate the parts to the whole task. For example, after children are taught to count, they still have to relate the number of a set to the conservation of a changed set.

Another possible reason for these inconsistent findings rests in the nature of the component skill. Teaching the wrong component doesn't help the child perform successfully the whole task later. Here is a great challenge for educators: what skill helps the child to learn what higher skill? Does *identifying* the reversed order of a row or *constructing* the reversed order facilitate attempts to predict the order of a rotated row of balls in a tube (see Pufall, 1973)? Perhaps, if we give children all of the component skills—which is in essence the whole task, or the "direct design"—children can select for themselves those components on which they need practice.

We tentatively conclude that the whole-task method is better than the component-skills method because (1) the whole-task method lets the child select troublesome components that need rehearsing and (2) the whole-task method not only presents all of the components but presents them organized together. Learning a component skill in isolation still leaves the child with the chore of integrating that skill into the organized whole task at a later time.

What are the relative merits of having children relate a rule to a response that they have already made (corrective design) and having children relate their responses to a rule that they have already heard (expository design)? In one case, the children consider how they should "reshape" a response they have already made; in the other, how they should "shape" a response they have not yet made. The research supports both approaches but with the qualification that correction or exposition must be explanatory. Correcting children with a simple yes or no is not as helpful as explaining to them why they are right or wrong.

Perhaps the value of providing an explanation is not as great in those cases in which the component-skills design was successfully used (Gelman, 1969). One might speculate that, if a teacher has decided to break a task down in many small subtasks, a quick yes/no correction moves the child rapidly through many small steps toward the ultimate whole task. Providing the child with an explanation for each small step may slow down learning, create interference, and prevent the child from making the integration of parts that is necessary for performing the organized whole.

Explanations differ in form, timing, and source. Their form can be a simple yes/no, a rule, or a staged demonstration. With regard to timing, explanations can be offered before or after the child has attempted to answer. The source can be found in the materials themselves, in an adult, or in other children. All three sources work well. Bruner, Olver, and Greenfield (1966) and Inhelder, Sinclair, and Bovet (1974) presented the materials in such a way that the children were forced to find their own explanations in order to reduce the conflict generated by the materials. When the outcome of their manipulation of the materials caused the children to contradict themselves, they often began to seek a higher-level explanation. This didn't happen when the children were led gradually into contradiction. These studies suggest that we should distinguish between a change in a child's answer without perplexity and a change in a child's answer with perplexity. Being led gradually to give a different answer to what seems to be the same question causes the child no perplexity, thus no conflict, and thus no need to seek a higher form of explanation.

The other sources of explanation—adults and other children—work well only under certain circumstances. Watching other children solve conservation problems is helpful when the viewer can actively participate in a discussion of what is going on (Murray, 1972). Watching adults solve conservation tasks helps even when the viewer is somewhat passive (Zimmerman & Rosenthal, 1974). The reason for this difference could be that the source of explanation is not as important as its clarity. Adults can demonstrate with precision and give rules that are well timed with a child's guesses. This distinction, however, should not be carried too far. Anything that helps the child systematize the relations that make up the conservation task is useful. Such help can come from an adult, from a more advanced peer, or even from the materials themselves when conflict occurs.

Modification Studies with the Elderly

The difference between poor performance due to neurological deterioration and poor performance due to social isolation can be decided by modification studies. If the elderly can be taught to think logically and if they can generalize that learning across a variety of tasks, we assume that their initial difficulty was not due to the irreversible effects of neurological regression and deterioration. Hooper and Sheehan (1976) review several studies that have been conducted to test modification of logical abilities in the elderly. Noteworthy is the fact that most of these studies were more successful when transfer tasks were not too dissimilar from the original training task.

Using a direct-design corrective procedure, Hornblum and Overton (1975) tested elderly females living in the community. Those who could not conserve volume were given a training procedure with feedback or a control procedure with no feedback. Feedback was simply a matter of correcting the subject's guess after each transformation of the object's shape. Training was not on volume conservation but on surface area. The subjects in the feedback group did better both on tasks similar to the training tasks and on tasks different from the training task, thus indicating general transfer of training. These improvements held on a posttest six weeks later. The Hornblum and Overton (1975) study suggests that the initial poor performance was not due to structural changes in the brain.

Other training studies using elderly subjects have been successful with different types of logical abilities. Denney (1974) trained elderly people in a nursing home to sort objects according to the class membership of many objects rather than to the similarity of two adjacent objects. Vief and Gonda (1975) improved the elderly's ability to think in terms of variables and classes. Denney and Denney (1974) trained their subjects to ask questions yielding more information. While neurological deterioration may be a fact of old age in a few cases, we cannot write off a low score on a test as *prima facie* evidence for an irreversible difficulty. Engaging the elderly in logical thinking in a form that is appropriate to their advanced years seems to work when neurological pathology is not an obviously limiting factor.

Summary

In this chapter we have discussed the structure of several logical operations. Two of these, classification and seriation, are concrete operations in the Piagetian sense. The difficulty of the classification problem, in both class inclusion and free classification, rests in the 4- or 5-year-olds' tendency to use spatial part/whole relations when they should be using member/class relations. The latter is a logical, not a physical, relation and requires that the child think about an object being in two categories at the same time—for example, an object being both red and wooden. Research on classification skills of older adults indicates that, while older adults classify objects in ways similar to young children's, these ways represent preferences, not an upper limit of the subjects' competence.

Research on seriation and transitivity—two additional concrete operations—show much the same trends. While young children can construct a seriated set of sticks by using the spatial image of a staircase, they have difficulty inserting an additional set of sticks. To do the latter, the child needs a general rule that is logical, not spatial. As in classification, the child needs to think about an object (in this case a stick) being in two relations at once. Each stick is both *smaller* than one stick and *larger* than another stick. While practice on this task can improve young children's memory with regard to the absolute length of each stick, it cannot completely compensate for young children's inability to understand the relations involved.

Proportionality and correlation are formal-operational problems. Children still in concrete operations confuse a comparison between two ratios (proportionality) with a comparison between two whole numbers. For example, they think that the probabilities of drawing a red bead are greater with a jar containing 20 red beads and 20 green beads than with a jar containing 10 red beads and 5 green beads. The concrete-operational child compares only the numbers of red beads (20 versus 10) when, in fact, the task calls for a comparison of two ratios. Proportionality—that is, ratio comparison—is a formal-operational task because it involves a comparison of two comparisons, which is a variation on the theme of formal operations (an operation on an operation).

Correlations, too, involve formal-operational thinking. A relation between two events, P and Q, must be compared to other forms of the P/Q relation in order for the child to decide if P causes Q. Concrete-operational children often make the mistake of thinking that, if P occurs with Q (say, a hot day and a flat bicycle tire), then P causes Q: heat causes flat tires. They fail to test for cold days with flat tires or hot days with full tires. Formal-operational children, instead, compare the observed relation with other possible relations; they can mentally operate on an operation.

Conservation is a fundamental concept that spans all four developmental stages of cognition, beginning with the sensorimotor stage. In essence, conservation involves knowledge of the invariance within things that change. In the sensorimotor stage children learn that an object continues to exist even when it changes position or is hidden. As children become more and more aware of the invariants in a changing world, they come to understand that number, weight, volume, and density stay the same regardless of certain types of transformations. Ideally adolescents will begin to see these constancies as logically necessary and not just as highly probable. Yet, not all adolescents—or, for that matter, not even all adults—reach this level of understanding. Older adults might reach this level in some areas but not in others. We emphasized that it might be a mistake to think that, once a person "has" conservation, he or she will always and appropriately apply it, regardless of the situation. Whether the conservation concept is applied depends on the attitude of the person toward the situation as well as on the general competence of that person.

Modification studies using conservation represent a direct test of this difference between performance and competence. If a person can be taught conservation during the course of the training study, the techniques of training tell us what performance obstacles the person has overcome. For example, training to look more closely, if successful, indicates that conservation requires close attention to changing dimensions such as height and width. Not only do training studies define the concept of conservation; they also give suggestions for educational practices in general. We reached the tentative conclusion that breaking a task down into its component parts leaves the child with the burden of trying to synthesize those parts later. A more direct approach—one in which the task as a coherent whole is not lost—seems preferable. The direct approach appears to work well when one either tells the student beforehand how to solve the problem or corrects the student's answers afterward. But in both procedures the students should receive enough information so that they can experience some conflict, conflict either between themselves and the teacher or between their own contradictory answers. Modification studies with older adults once again confirm that the initially poor performance of the elderly is more likely to be due to disuse of cognitive skills than to a complete loss of ability.

Chapter Six

The Development
of Basic Knowledge:
Space, Time, and Causality

The information processes of attention and memory (Chapter Four) and the logical operations (Chapter Five) are the means by which the child constructs basic knowledge about space, time, and causality. For example, in order to anticipate that pulling a string will cause a toy to make a noise, the infant must remember past occurrences of these two events in a "first-pull, then-noise" sequence. If the infant can neither remember the independent events nor reconstruct the sequence, he or she will not pull-in-order-to-hear.

Concepts of space, time, and causality are fundamental to all other types of knowledge. They are basic. No matter what it is that you choose to learn, you are going to use some or all of these three basic concepts. For example, carpentry involves the basic relations of space, such as fitting parts to make a whole. Law involves the basic concepts of causality, such as the determination of a crime's motive. Film making involves the basic concepts of time, such as editing segments to show flashbacks or using a dissolve to portray a break in the continuity of time. The development of these basic concepts merits our attention.

There may be some debate regarding the development of these concepts, since some thinkers maintain that they are innate. For example, Immanuel Kant (see Edwards, 1967) held the position that nothing could be learned without already knowing that things exist in space, pass through time, and cause other things. The concepts of time, space, and causality are givens—givens that must be there before one can learn facts about the environment. For example, the fact that "Mother will bring me food" can be understood by the infant only if he *first* knows that the face of Mother is an external object and not a film of dirt on his eyeballs, that the face endures across time, and that an event that invariably follows another is caused by the first one. These three categories of knowledge (the givens) cannot themselves be learned, Kant maintained, since they themselves are necessary for all learning.

Piaget (1970) agrees that the concepts of time, space, and causality are indeed fundamental categories of knowledge but disagrees with Kant on their innate existence. According to Piaget, even those most basic forms of knowledge are constructed by the infant through his or her interactions with the environment. In this chapter we will discuss the research performed or inspired by Piaget on the development of the concepts of space, time, and causality. The two main sections, one on space and time and the other on causality, are each organized developmentally. In the section on space and time the discussion of the infant's understanding of space precedes that of the understanding of space and time by young children, adolescents, and adults, respectively. Since it is meaningless to talk about space independently of time, we have chosen not to write a separate section on the development of temporal concepts. The section on causality follows the same developmental order as that on space and time; that is, it discusses how the concept of causality evolves from infancy through adulthood.

Space and Time: Spatial Development

Space is frozen time, and time is movement through space. The statement "The ink bottle is on the desk" really means that, if I were to move in space from above to below, I would get to the ink bottle *first* and then to the desk. I could have described that same spatial relation as "The desk is under the ink bottle," which means that, if I were to move from above to below, I would get to the desk *second*. So, even in what appears to be a purely spatial relation, the temporal concepts of *first* and *second* are implicit. The same can be said about what seems to be purely temporal relations. "Newman runs faster than Kirk" implies that for a given interval of time Newman covers more *space*. Most of this section is devoted to what has conventionally been called *spatial development*. However, since in the final analysis time and space are inseparable, our discussion is essentially a discussion of both space and time.

The development of spatial concepts across age can be approached in a variety of ways. For example, we could look at spatial development as a series of ever-widening circles of awareness, beginning with infants' awareness of their own bodies, through young children's awareness of their neighborhood, to adults' awareness of their town, state, nation, and planet. While this course of development does occur, such an approach doesn't tell us much about general cognitive development. This circles-of-awareness model portrays spatial development as a rather mundane process of learning more and more. Piaget presents an alternative way of viewing spatial development. According to this view, children develop awareness of space because they (1) learn ways to represent spatial relations and consequently (2) inter-relate more aspects of space. In the following subsections spatial development is outlined according to the different ways in which children represent space. The similarities between Bruner and Piaget will become apparent in the course of our discussion.

Perceptual Space

Looking at a person's face and recognizing that person as familiar doesn't require much in the way of representation. An infant who smiles at the sight of his mother's face and cries at the sight of strangers is telling us that he knows the shape of those faces. This "knowledge" doesn't imply that the child could draw the faces from memory or describe them to the police. The child can simply distinguish some shapes from others.

Within the first several months of life infants acquire a host of non-representational spatial skills. They can distinguish a large faraway object from a small nearby object (Bower, 1964). That is, infants don't think that an object moving farther and farther away shrinks in size, even though the size of the image the object casts on the retina gets smaller and smaller. Depth perception helps infants learn not to grasp at objects that are out of their reach.

Infants can also perceive direction of movement. Ball and Tronick (1971) placed infants in front of a screen onto which a circle of light was cast from the rear. The circle was made to expand in such a way that it created the illusion of an object either heading directly toward the child on a collision course or heading toward one side. When the "object" appeared to be on a collision course, the infants would begin to fret. But when it appeared to be a "miss course," the infants were less upset. The evolutionary advantage of this type of reflexive arousal should be apparent.

Even at the age of 1 minute neonates will reflexively glance toward the source of a sound to the right or to the left. Seldom do infants turn their heads to the left if the sound comes from the right (Wertheimer, 1961). But this is a reflex and does not mean that infants will search for a hidden object or move their fingers when hearing the sound, in anticipation of seeing an object they know they can grasp. These latter skills denote a higher level of spatial understanding.

During the first year of life the infant who has no difficulty distinguishing two different objects at rest has some difficulty coping with the movement of one object. If her teething ring was originally near her knee but then is slowly moved elsewhere within reach, the baby will visually track the ring but will still "search" for it near her knee, where it was before (Bower, 1974). Perhaps moving the teething ring changes its perspective so much that the infant doesn't recognize it as the same ring.

Once static objects become moving objects, the child has to deal with time. Is this a new teething ring or the same one in a *new* place? The new place is the second place the object occupies in time. To the young infant the moving object may just as well be a different object altogether. She has no trouble distinguishing that the object(s) differ(s) in distance (space). But, in order to make the distinction regarding the object's identity, the child must take time into consideration (then versus now).

The recognition of depth develops early, but the understanding of depth takes longer. The fact that infants can distinguish the nearness of the bedsheets from the farness of the floor doesn't necessarily carry practical implications. Long before infants can walk, crawl, or even pull their heads up, they show a slowing down (deceleration) of the heart rate when exposed to a far surface, such as a view of the floor from above, after a series of near surfaces. The heart-rate deceleration simply means that the "cliff" is distinguished as a novel stimulus in comparison to the series of near surfaces. However, when children reach 8 months or so, the heart-rate deceleration changes to an acceleration when they approach a cliff's edge (Yonas & Pick, 1975). While deceleration is only a diffuse reaction to anything that is novel, an increase in the heart rate is indicative of fear. Depth takes on meaning.

Practical Space

Practical space involves more than the visual recognition of shape and depth. A practical knowledge of space guides action. The infant who can rotate her inverted bottle to find the nipple has a practical knowledge of the spatial relation between the nipple and the bottle's bottom, which was temporarily hiding the nipple. Practical knowledge of space involves doing. Practical space, like perceptual space, doesn't necessitate either graphic or linguistic representation. But there does exist at this level of spatial knowledge a very elementary type of representation—*position.*

Position is not a shape. We don't say, except in a most academic way, "This is a familiar position." Position is a relation—a relation between an object and other objects or between an object and a frame of reference. You can remove an object and leave its position there, so to speak. "Your pipe was next to the telephone"; the position once occupied by the pipe is indicated by some imaginary spot adjacent to the tangible telephone. In this elementary sense the telephone *indicates* the position of the object; that is, the telephone represents the position. In the sense that a representation is a stand-in for something else, representation occurs when the child discovers that objects occupy positions. The empty chair or the vacant space between two front teeth is a reference for the position of a missing object. During the first two years of life the child makes great strides in dealing with position and changes of position across time.

Hidden objects. As we said earlier, the search for hidden objects is the first indication that the child has knowledge of spatial position, position that exists independently of visual contact with the object itself. The box that hides the toy covers the place where the permanent object rests. The child knows that the toy is still there in space, which is more than knowing that the object is there in sight. The child understands that the object has a position and this position is "under the box." The box is an index (a representation) of the toy's position but is not the toy itself. The 8-month-old knocks over the box, uninterested in the box itself, and grabs the toy.

But objects move about. Can the infant cope with changes in positions? Hide a favorite toy under cover *A*, let the child find it, hide it again under *A*, let the child find it again, and then hide the toy under cover *B* nearby. Piaget (1954), who conducted this experiment with his own daughter, Jacqueline, reported that she searched for the toy under cover *A*. Why? There are two possible, and quite different, explanations. One is that Jacqueline was unable to register the new hiding place; the other, that she did register it but forgot before she was given the chance to search for it.

Gerald Gratch (1975) has reviewed research that bears on both of these interpretations. Piaget prefers the first explanation. He reasons that, since the 9-month-old doesn't know position as something independent of her personal actions, she searches for the toy where she had searched before. If Piaget is correct, a delay between the time Jacqueline saw the object being hidden under *B* and the time she was allowed to remove the cover of her choice should make no difference. She should do just as poorly with zero delay as she would with a delay of several seconds. Piaget reasons that her problem results from her inability to understand what she sees (a problem of registering the correct information in the first place). On the other hand, if Jacqueline did register the toy's new position by watching it disappear under *B*, she should do better with a zero delay than she did with a delay of a few seconds. She would do poorly when forced to wait, simply because she would forget what she had initially registered. She would then choose cover *A* because she remembers that better, having found the toy there on two previous occasions.

Gratch's (1975) review leads to the conclusion that both interpretations are correct, depending on the age of the infant. A 10-month-old will keep searching under *A* only when the delay is longer, thus indicating an initial registration of position and a subsequent forgetting. A younger child will make the error regardless of delay, thus indicating that, for some reason, viewing the object disappear under *B* was not registered as *B* being the new place where the toy now exists. Piaget would say that the child younger than 10 months codes the position of the toy as "movement of self toward *A*." Older infants understand that position can also be referenced by proximity to other objects and not necessarily by personal action. In other words, position loses its egocentric reference as the child matures. This reduction in egocentricity is a theme that we will trace throughout the remainder of this chapter as well as in Chapter Seven, in which we discuss the development of nonegocentric awareness of another person's viewpoint.

Invisible displacement. Not only does the child's understanding of position become less egocentric; it also becomes very inferential. We briefly mentioned the significance of invisible displacements in Chapter Two. We speak of invisible displacement when the child doesn't observe the change of position of an object. For example, place a toy under a cup and then, as the child watches, move the cup behind a screen. Out of the infant's view remove the toy from under the cup and leave it behind the screen. Then move the cup near the child again. When the child searches under the cup and discovers that the toy is missing, will he infer that the toy is behind the screen? This is a difficult task indeed. It requires an elementary form of a "transitive" relation—that is, if A (toy) is in B (cup) and if B disappears behind C (screen), then A was at one time behind C. And this is not all. Having constructed these relevant spatial relations, the child still has to conclude that A could have been released behind C. The release behind the screen was the invisible displacement.

If infants can manage invisible displacements by the age of 18 months (Gratch, 1975), the question is "How do they do it?" Do they search behind the screen because that is the only unturned stone around or because they have decided that the screen is the only possible place? The first interpretation suggests the learning of a simple habit: when the object disappears, knock over all barriers. The second interpretation suggests a deduction: if A is in B and B is in C, then A is in C. How can we know which of these two interpretations is correct?

An ingenious study designed by John Watson of the University of California at Berkeley suggests a possible answer.[1] Put three cups upside down on a flat surface near the infant, hide a pea under one of them, and shuffle the cups. Now the child starts lifting the cups, one after the other one, looking for the pea. (The game can be rigged so that the pea is hidden under the last cup the child is likely to lift.) How quickly does the child lift each cup? If the child is picking up the cups on the basis of habit (rather than deduction), the speed at which he picks up the last cup should be slightly slower than the speed at which he lifted the other two cups. After all, he has tried twice and failed. The habit has gone unreinforced and should be weakening slightly. If, however, the child is using deduction, he should pick up the last cup more quickly than the previous ones. Having eliminated the first two cups as the pea's hiding place, he *knows,* even before lifting the third

---

[1]At the time this book was written, the study was still under development.

cup, where the pea is. He literally pounces on the last cup with certainty. The child didn't see the pea being placed under that cup (that is, it is an invisible-displacement situation), but he is certain that it is there.

Gratch (1975) reports research that confirms Watson's prediction concerning increase in certainty (reduced reaction time) in simple-hiding situations (without invisible displacement). Perhaps Watson's more complicated task would also show the predicted reduction in reaction time. Such reduction would substantiate Piaget's theory that the 18-month-old can handle the discontinuity of space (invisible displacements) by using an early form of inference. The use of inference at this early age foretells an increasing use of inference and logical operations in the higher, more representational forms of spatial knowledge.

Active reconstruction of spatial relations. The various forms of practical knowledge of space mentioned so far—finding hidden objects and inferring an invisible displacement—involve very simple responses. The child watches and then lifts a cover to find the object. But children can also demonstrate their practical knowledge of space by more complex responses, such as actively reconstructing a spatial pattern they see or by actively building a pattern they spontaneously choose. Research using tasks that require active manipulation of sticks and blocks portrays an interesting developmental picture.

Greenfield and Schneider (1977) asked children ranging in age from 3 to 11 to reconstruct a design made of straws, which looked somewhat like a family tree. Their most interesting finding concerned the order the children followed to join the straws. The 6-year-olds reconstructed the "family tree" starting at the lower right, moving upward, and then going down the other side (Figure 6-1a). The 11-year-olds began at the top left, shifted to the right side, went back to the left, and so forth (Figure 6-1b). The 11-year-olds started with one segment of the tree, stopped working at that segment, shifted to another, and then came back to the original one. The 9-year-olds followed the same sequence as the 6-year-olds but could be encouraged to build the tree structure in the same way the 11-year-olds built it. The 6-year-olds, instead, were not influenced by such suggestions.

The conclusion drawn by the researchers from this developmental picture relates to the structure of thought itself. Evidently the 11-year-olds could use an "interrupted" pattern of thinking. They would begin to construct a subunit of the family tree on the left side of the mobile, interrupt the completion of that side, and shift to the right side. They would make a few additions on the right side, interrupt completion again, and shift to the left side. The 6-year-olds would begin, instead, in an uninterrupted fashion—a more linear fashion—starting at one end and following through down the line to the other end. They didn't think about the whole pattern in terms of subunits embedded within larger units. For example, in Figure 6-1b, it

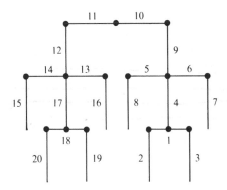

Figure 6-1a. Typical strategy used by 6-year-olds to reconstruct a "family tree" design. Numbers represent order of placement.

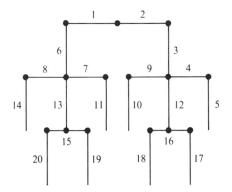

Figure 6-1b. Typical strategy used by 11-year-olds to reconstruct a "family tree" design.

seems that the 11-year-olds considered the bottom four sticks to be two pairs—17 and 18 on the right and 19 and 20 on the left. These two pairs are each embedded as subparts of the two main branches of the whole design. No such thinking was evidenced by the 6-year-olds.

Greenfield and Schneider (1977) state that this same developmental picture, from uninterrupted to interrupted thinking, occurs in language development. Take the sentence "Herbie, who cried, came to my party." Compare it to the sentence "Herbie cried and came to my party." The first sentence contains an "interrupting" clause. "Herbie came to my party" is interrupted by the dependent clause "who cried." That is, the sentence begins with one thought, shifts to another, and then comes back to the first. The clause "who cried" is embedded within the larger whole. The second sentence has a linear construction—first one thought and then the other—

with no interruption of either. The ability to understand sentences with embedded clauses comes later in development than the ability to understand the
more linear construction (Slobin & Welsh, 1973). Since the structures in
action and in language have similar forms and similar orders of development, Greenfield and Schneider (1977) conclude that there may be common
principles of organization that underlie both the reconstruction of spatial relations and the comprehension of language.

That the construction of spatial relations and the construction of
language share underlying principles is an intriguing hypothesis. We can
relate this hypothesis to Piaget's view of the relationship between the structure of sensorimotor action and the structure of logical thought, which we
discussed in Chapter Two. Piaget's more general hypothesis implies that the
spatial organization of action on objects is essential for the construction of
logic, which transcends spatial organization.

Spontaneous construction of symmetry. Forman, Kuschner, and
Dempsey (1975b) present data on a developmental sequence that confirm this
gradual shift from action to logic. The subjects of this study, 65 children aged
from 7 to 24 months, were invited to play with a set of five small geometric
blocks. The children returned for a second and third visit at four-month
intervals. Everything they did with the blocks was filmed, and each action
and production was coded, computerized, and counted. With regard to the
specific topic of action and thought, Forman and his colleagues looked,
among many other things, at the changing methods children used to create
symmetry. Figure 6-2 illustrates these changing methods.

Grasping a single block with one hand on each side (Stage 1) is
symmetry in action. Banging together two blocks, holding a block in each
hand (Stage 2), is also symmetry in action. Here, however, it is the objects
rather than the hands themselves that are the content of the action. Bilateral
banging is less "egocentric" than bilateral grasping. Placing two objects
side by side and then releasing them (Stage 3) is the first case of a bilateral
production. (Production, in this context, means a tangible spatial pattern of
objects, not actions.) The bilateral-placement symmetry is a symmetry of
frozen movement (that is, space). It exists even after the initial action ceases
(hands release grasp, but symmetry remains). It should be noted, however,
that in the bilateral placement the axis of symmetry is the very tangible
vertical face of each block. Thus, symmetry is produced because one block
physically resists the other when the two vertical surfaces are placed against
each other.

In the next form of symmetry, bisection symmetry (Stage 4), the
axis of symmetry is not so tangible. One block is centered on top of
another. The center of the foundation object is not visible; rather, it is esti-
mated. Even though bisection symmetry is an advance over bilateral placement, it requires only a position adjustment. In the highest form of sym-

Stage 1:   Bilateral grasping. Each hand grasps one side of the same object. The hands themselves are symmetrically placed. The entire object serves as the axis of symmetry.

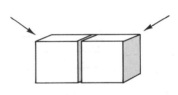

Stage 2:   Bilateral banging. Each hand holds an object. The two objects are banged together in midair, without being released.

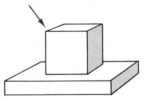

Stage 3:   Bilateral placement. Two objects are aligned side by side and released. This is the first symmetrical production.

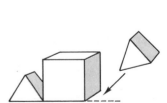

Stage 4:   Bisection symmetry. One object is placed on the imaginary midline axis of another object. The empty spaces on both sides of the small cube are equal; thus the production is symmetrical. The shape of the objects is irrelevant.

Stage 5:   Reiterative symmetry. An object of a particular shape is placed so it "balances" the "equation" represented by the relation between the two blocks already placed. This is achieved by placing the triangle on the right side of the square.

Figure 6-2. Stages in symmetrical actions and productions of children from 7 to 32 months. (From *Transformations in the Manipulations and Productions Performed with Geometric Objects: An Early System of Logic in Young Children,* by G. E. Forman, D. S. Kuschner, and J. Dempsey. Final report to the National Institute of Education, 1975.)

metry, reiterative symmetry (Stage 5), the child has to do more than choose the correct position. The child also deliberately chooses a particular shape. If a small triangle rests to the left of a large square, the child will sense that the space to the right of the large square is "empty." The nature of this "emptiness" is peculiar indeed, because it is not an emptiness meant to be filled, like the inside of a cup or dish. The "emptiness" on the right side of the large square results from a relationship between the square and the triangle on the left. The construction of reiterative symmetry is in fact the completion of a sequence, not just the filling of a space.

In the Forman et al. study (1975b), these various forms of symmetry appeared in the spontaneous play of the children in the order of development presented above. Bilateral grasping was at its peak around age 7 months; the other forms peaked at 11, 27, and 32 months, respectively, with reiterative symmetry just beginning to occur at 32 months. How can the implications of this developmental sequence be summarized? Forman and his co-workers reasoned that expression of symmetry—and spatial relations in general—progresses from body actions to object actions to object products. The bilateral anatomy of the human body—especially the hands, one on each side of a middle axis—prestructures the form of action itself. The opposing hands eventually clap together; clapping hands eventually trap an object between them; and two hands, each holding one block, eventually bang the two blocks together. The anatomy of the body determines the form of the body actions, which, in turn, determine the form of the object actions. Then the form of the object actions determines the form of the placement and release of the blocks—a symmetrical production.

Object products themselves progress to more advanced levels. The first form, bilateral placement, is frozen time; that is, the action of bilateral banging is frozen in the form of the bilateral placement. The bisection is more advanced, since the child, now some 2½ years old, constructs an imaginary axis of symmetry. He has transcended physical boundaries of tangible edges. The reiterative symmetry, as we explained, is still more advanced, since it implicitly involves the use of a relation between two objects to establish the position and shape of a third object. Object products, then, progress from use of physical edges, to imaginary axes, to a "logical" sequence (logical in the sense that a relation must be used to complete the sequence). In other words, the factors that determine symmetrical products become less spatial and more logical. To make the bold leap, one could say, as Forman et al. did say, that the anatomy of the body (the spatial arrangement of its parts) determines the structure of thought and perhaps even the structure of that elegant algebraic formula $A = A$. The mathematical concept of equivalence doesn't feel too far removed from the sensation of holding two identical blocks, one in each hand. Could it be that the elegance of mathematics is so appealing, and so workable, because after all it is no less than a mirror of our body? This, to be sure, is a highly speculative possibility, but one advanced by authors like Buckminster Fuller (1975), Martin Gardner (1969), and, of course, Jean Piaget (1971).

Representational Space

The understanding of representations of spatial relations is necessary to all kinds of everyday activities. Identifying depth, size, and position in photographs, interpreting a series of cartoon pictures as one person changing position across time, and using language to describe space and change are just a few examples. In this section we discuss two of these examples, both included in Figure 6-1: recognition of a change of position in pictures and the receptive and expressive understanding of words that describe position and change of position. The fact that real objects may be used in a task dealing with representation should not confuse you. If the goal of the task is to understand how the pictures or the words "stand for" those objects, the task is one of representational space. Reconstructing a toy Ferris wheel by looking at its blueprint is indeed a representational task, since it involves translating the picture (blueprint) into the real object.

Notational and nonnotational systems of representation. How do children judge whether a picture represents a rotated perspective of an object or a different object altogether? If you take a full front-line drawing of a telephone, showing dial and receiver, such full front view appears symmetrical. How does the child recognize a 45-degree or 90-degree rotation of the same object in a second drawing? There are at least two possibilities, with profoundly different implications. For one, the child may look for common features between the two pictures—the dial, the little lip that holds the receiver, and so forth. She labels these features, makes a list of features that describe the familiar perspective, and then checks the second picture to match the list of features. If she finds that most of the features in the list exist in the second picture, the child concludes that the second picture is a picture of the same phone in a new perspective rather than a picture of a different phone in a different perspective. The other possibility is that the child may engage in a type of mental rotation (kinetic imagery). She looks closely at the second picture and begins to mentally rotate it back toward a full front perspective. At the end of this mental rotation, the child checks to see whether the imagined full front view in the second picture matches the existing full front view in the first picture. She doesn't use a list of discrete (separate) features but, rather, responds to the form in action of the telephone as a whole.

These are two very different mental processes. The first is usually called a *notational system of representation.* The units are discrete, discontinuous pieces that have no particular spatial relation to one another. The printed word, the spoken word, and numerals are other types of notational representations. The second process is *nonnotational* and continuous, and the change of form is a matter of preserving the spatial relations of all the parts throughout the mental rotation. It is the movement itself that is represented, not just the static features in two different perspectives. How do we know which process a child uses?

If a child uses the nonnotational process of kinetic imagery, it should take her longer to recognize a 90-degree rotation than a 45-degree rotation. To make the match between the frontal-view picture and the picture that has been rotated 90 degrees, the child has to mentally rotate the second picture through 90 degrees of arc, as opposed to 45 degrees. If a child uses the notational process (matching features), it shouldn't make any difference, as far as the amount of time needed to identify the two pictures as the same or different objects, whether the picture has been rotated 45 or 90 degrees.

We are assuming, of course, that the number of identifiable features is the same in both degrees of rotation. In research that controlled for this last factor, Shepard and Metzler (1971) found that adults take longer to match two pictures when the angle of rotation is greater. Marmor (1977) obtained the same results with 4- and 5-year-olds. Both children and adults seem to be using a nonnotational, kinetic imagery on these tasks. The significance of these findings can be better understood if we shift now to David Olson's (1975) work on the relation between language media and spatial media.

Language and kinetic imagery. Could it be that a premature emphasis on reading and the verbal description of space inhibits the use of kinetic imagery? Olson (1975) proposes that the structure of the medium itself influences thought. Language is by necessity composed of discrete units; that is, language is a notational mode of expression. Kinetic imagery operates in a continuous, nonnotational fashion. There is some evidence that the notational system of language and the nonnotational system of kinetic imagery are two separate systems. Ostensibly, the left hemisphere of the brain directs notational (language) representations, and the right hemisphere of the brain directs nonnotational (spatial) representations (Cohen, 1973). Furthermore, Levy (1972) provides evidence that, if the functions of the right and left hemispheres are not well separated (both exist in the same hemisphere), then spatial representation suffers. Can the same thing be said of early emphasis on the use of notational representation (reading) in early education? It might be that the notational nature of speech and reading inhibits the use of kinetic imagery before the latter becomes fully developed.

Forman and Kuschner (1977) have taken this possibility seriously and have designed a preschool curriculum that emphasizes kinetic phenomena. Children 2 or 3 years old are encouraged to draw the motion of objects rather than their static features. The children also observe the trail left by a spool that has been dipped in finger paint, reconstruct a wire circle back into its original square shape rather than simply copying a static square, and engage in other activities that emphasize the transformations and kinetic aspects of space. Forman and Kuschner (1977) explain why the emphasis on the transformations of objects is so important to cognitive development. The explanation is based on Piaget's work on early forms of conservation and kinetic imagery (see in particular Piaget & Inhelder, 1971).

Language and space don't have to be at odds. Olson (1975) simply advises us to value both modes of thought, notational and nonnotational. He then poses some questions about the development of language and thought. To what degree is language structured by our practical interactions with space, and to what degree is our understanding of space determined by learning a spatial vocabulary? Benjamin Whorf (1956) argued that the particular language we learn as young children determines how we organize the undivided flow of time and space. According to Whorf, if someone's language doesn't contain tense markers (such as -ed), his or her view of time is completely different from that of English-speaking people. If someone's language doesn't emphasize directions (such as *up* and *down*) but emphasizes, instead, personal effort in movement (such as *strained* and *relaxed*), that individual's conception of space will be completely different from our own.

Olson sees the influence between language and space/time in the opposite way. What we do as young children (or as a young species) influences the true meaning of our language that refers to space. For example, the two words *high* and *low* are not actually perfect opposites. One of the two words is more general than the other. The word *high* refers not only to the position *above* but also to the entire range of height, as in the question "How high is the kite?" Only in special circumstances do we ask "How low are you?" "How short are you?" or "How low is the kite?" Citing work by Clark (1973) and Fillmore (1971), Olson relates these linguistic conventions to early practical experiences with spatial relations.

Why is *high* more general than *low*? Perhaps because one can move indefinitely in an upward direction but one can move downward only to the point of contact with the ground. The spatial term *low* is marked (Clark's term); the spatial term *high* is indefinite and better suited to refer to an entire range across the vertical dimension. The same can be said of the two spatial terms *near* and *far*. We generally say "How *far* are you from me?" not "How near are you to me?" The term *near* is marked by the position of the self; the term *far* refers to a horizontal direction that can refer to an indefinite extension.

If Olson (1975) and Clark (1973) are correct in assuming that spatial words derive their meaning from earlier experiences of moving oneself, as well as objects, in space, then the order in which spatial terms are learned should reflect such earlier practical experience. For example, in the physical placement of two objects it is easier to intentionally place one object *next* to another than to intentionally place one object *between* two others. A child trying to place an object *between* two others has more opportunities for mistakes, since he has more alternatives to eliminate. But all he has to do to place an object next to another is to release one object so that it touches the other. He doesn't have to place the object in a particular position that is defined by two other objects spread apart. Words that refer to complex actions are learned later than words that refer to simpler actions. The word *at* should be learned before the word *on,* since *on* refers to two dimensions (one plane on another plane) while *at* refers to a single dimension (for example, the act of pointing *at* something). Similarly, the word *in* should be learned after the word *on,* since *in* refers to the action of placing one thing within a three-dimensional space, such as a cup or a room. We say "The deer is on the grass" but not "The deer is on the forest."

The order in which spatial terms are learned may also be influenced by whether the denoted direction of movement is egocentric or not. Movement toward the self has more practical value in the early years than movement away from the self. This suggests that *to* is understood earlier than *from, on* earlier than *off,* and *into* earlier than *out.* In these last two examples the more difficult direction is the direction away from the target object, which assumes the status of a substitute self (see Werner & Kaplan, 1963). Both David Olson and Herbert Clark are continuing their research to substantiate their suggestion that the difficulty of spatial language is a reflection of the difficulty in carrying out the actions to which the words refer. The research of Greenfield and Schneider (1977) and of Forman, Kuschner, and Dempsey (1975b) also bears on the more general issue of the relation between actions in space and the logic of thought.

Degrees of difficulty in spatial representation. The difficulty of representing spatial relations depends on (1) the number of spatial properties that must be preserved to reconstruct the object being represented and (2) the demand for an interrelation of these spatial properties. Give a 5-year-old child a map of the classroom that also includes the furniture. Then ask the child to place an *x* on the map where her friend Lucy is now standing. Since Lucy is standing next to the painting easel, the 5-year-old is likely to place an *x* next to the painting easel. Now give the same child a map of the classroom that doesn't include the furniture. Ask the child to put an *x* on the map where the painting easel is standing. Since the map is little more than a rectangular outline of the room, the child has to estimate how far the easel is from *both* the front wall and the side wall. Most children this age can consider one relation or the other but not both; that is, they cannot coordinate the distances from both walls simultaneously (Laurendeau & Pinard, 1970). This inability to coordinate two dimensions simultaneously is an example of the second element in the degree of difficulty of spatial representation—the demand for an interrelation of spatial properties.

With regard to the first element, some spatial tasks may essentially differ only in the absolute number of spatial dimensions to be represented.

Take the task of drawing a rectangle that the child has seen recently but that is no longer present. To perform this task accurately, the child needs to preserve the spatial properties listed in Figure 6-3c. However, before achieving the stage at which all the necessary properties are preserved (Figure 6-3c), the child goes through two stages at which only some of the properties are preserved (Figure 6-3a and 6-3b). As Figure 6-3 illustrates, these three stages follow one another in a sequence of increasing mastery of the task.

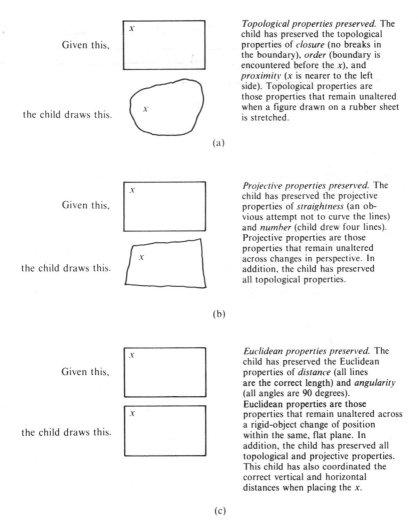

Given this,

the child draws this.

Topological properties preserved. The child has preserved the topological properties of *closure* (no breaks in the boundary), *order* (boundary is encountered before the *x*), and *proximity* (*x* is nearer to the left side). Topological properties are those properties that remain unaltered when a figure drawn on a rubber sheet is stretched.

(a)

Given this,

the child draws this.

Projective properties preserved. The child has preserved the projective properties of *straightness* (an obvious attempt not to curve the lines) and *number* (child drew four lines). Projective properties are those properties that remain unaltered across changes in perspective. In addition, the child has preserved all topological properties.

(b)

Given this,

the child draws this.

Euclidean properties preserved. The child has preserved the Euclidean properties of *distance* (all lines are the correct length) and *angularity* (all angles are 90 degrees). Euclidean properties are those properties that remain unaltered across a rigid-object change of position within the same, flat plane. In addition, the child has preserved all topological and projective properties. This child has also coordinated the correct vertical and horizontal distances when placing the *x*.

(c)

Figure 6-3. Three stages in the copying of geometric figures. Topological features are preserved during the preschool years; projective and Euclidean features, during the elementary-school years.

To accurately draw a single object, the child requires the use of all of these properties—topological, projective, and Euclidean. To place an object in a frame of reference, as in the map example above, the child requires either a point-to-point reference (place *x* near easel) or the use of a coordinate system (the intersection of the distance from both walls). The latter requires concrete operations.

Spatial Relations in Adolescence

Although children younger than 14 or 15 are usually able to use a coordinate system to locate objects in space, most concrete-operational children cannot think about the assumptions of the coordinate system itself. Thinking about the propositions that underlie a set of relations is more the province of formal-operational thinking. At what age should geometry teachers ask students to reflect on the basic axioms of Euclidean geometry? At what age does the student begin to understand that any system of spatial representation is based on arbitrary givens, such as the given that two parallel lines infinitely extended will never intersect? Comprehending the concept of infinite extension goes beyond purely concrete-operational thinking. Looking at axioms as arbitrary givens also goes beyond purely concrete-operational thinking.

Although the student doesn't need to know the basic assumptions of Euclidean geometry in order to *use* it, he or she cannot *understand* Euclidean geometry without knowing these basic assumptions. If the student is not aware that Euclidean geometry presupposes that straight lines are "drawn" on flat surfaces, the idea of parallel lines eventually intersecting will appear absurd and impossible to understand. However, if one changes the basic assumption that straight lines are drawn on flat surfaces to the proposition that extended space is curved, then a whole new set of corollaries result through deduction. Parallel lines drawn on curved space eventually intersect. If parallel lines intersect, then an object traveling away from earth will eventually return as its own mirror image. We are not about to fill in all the intervening assumptions that make this conclusion plausible. Our point here is that the seemingly miraculous conclusions of relativity theory are treated with less awe when students shift away from their own spatial intuitions, which are derived from experience with concrete objects, and assume a strictly logical, propositional, deductive approach to the subject matter (see Forman, 1975). Propositional logic is only beginning to develop in adolescence.

Spatial Relations in Adulthood and the Later Years

We have discussed spatial relations in three forms: perceptual space, practical space, and representational space. There is no evidence that perceptual-space ability (shape recognition, depth perception, and so on) shows any decline with age other than that due to loss of visual acuity, which is a problem of the peripheral receptors rather than of the central functions of cognition (Birren, 1959). There does seem to be evidence, however, for decline in practical spatial abilities and representation of spatial relations.

With regard to practical space, up to the age of about 20, people improve in their ability to perceive "true vertical" even when visual frames of reference are removed. This ability is due to the person's sense of balance. In a study conducted by Comalli, Wapner, and Werner (1959), the subject was seated in a very comfortable chair. In fact, the chair was so comfortably outfitted with foam that the person didn't feel differential pressures on the right or left when the chair was tilted right or left. The experiment was conducted in a darkened room, so it became quite difficult, sitting in that chair, to determine where the "true vertical" was when the chair was tilted. The chair was tilted on silent motors and moved very slowly, so there were not even cues from the noise or the acceleration of being tilted. The subject was asked to tell the experimenter how to position a neon rod in this darkened room. The experimenter kept moving the neon rod until the subject thought that it was in a vertical position—that is, perpendicular to the floor of the room.

People younger than 20 adjusted the neon rod so it was parallel to the midline of their own body, even when they were tilted. The 20-year-olds could make the rod vertical even though it meant a departure from a visually egocentric (self-centered) vertical. Subjects beyond 60 years of age, instead, regressed to the more egocentric mode of adjusting the rod in conformity with their midline axis (Comalli, Wapner, & Werner, 1959).

Beyond the age of 50, subjects have difficulty on another task that requires monitoring body position. Szafran (1951) blindfolded his subjects and asked each of them to move his or her hand sideways 12 inches, so that it touched a post, and then move it back exactly 12 inches to the starting point. On some trials the subject was permitted to look at his or her hand after the attempt (feedback trials). These feedback trials could then be used as a guide for the subsequent trials. Trials following blindfolded trials didn't show age differences in performance. Trials following feedback trials, instead, showed less errors for subjects between 18 and 49 but not for subjects beyond age 50. The younger subjects found it easier to translate the visual feedback into kinesthetic control than did the older subjects. Here is evidence, albeit on a highly specialized task, that the older adults decline in body awareness. The body-tilt task (Comalli, Wapner, & Werner, 1959) can be interpreted in the same fashion.

Theoretically it is difficult to decide when a task is a measure of practical space or of representational space. Tasks that require the individual to conserve spatial relations in spite of object transformations (rotations, dismemberment, and so forth) probably require some intermediate representation of such relations—images, rules, or notations. The ability to handle spatial transformations does decline after middle adulthood. The reasons for this decline are not clear or, at least, are not the result of a single cause. The

block design task[2] could show a decline in the later years because of reduced eyesight, reduced demand to practice tasks of concentration, or basic
changes in the functioning of the central nervous system. Horn (1970)
makes the point that these types of spatial-visualization tasks measure fluid
intelligence—that is, the ability to mentally manipulate relations—rather
than crystallized intelligence—the knowledge of specific facts and vocabulary. As we said earlier, the decline of fluid intelligence in old age could
be the result of attitudes like greater caution and self-consciousness on
timed tests as well as of other factors not necessarily indicative of brain
dysfunction.

The ability to represent spatial relations is more than an age-related
skill. What an individual does on an everyday basis influences spatial development. Rand (1969) asked taxi drivers in Worcester, Massachusetts,
and Worcester-based airplane pilots to give verbal directions to landmarks
in the city. He discovered that the taxi drivers used a personal, uncoordi-
nated system of representation, while the pilots used an abstract, integrated
system that was useful for cities in general. One cannot say that the taxi
drivers were less experienced or less skilled in getting around Worcester.
One can say, however, that they probably would have had greater difficulty
than the pilots in learning the routes in a new town.

These are individual differences based on individual styles and
experiences—preferences expressed in particular contexts. They cannot be
interpreted as fixed abilities. What we call "intellectual decline" in old age
may also be a matter of style rather than ability. To understand the cognitive
performance of the elderly, we must spend a good deal of time looking at
the milieu and the demands made—or, more likely, not made—on elderly
people. To cite a telling example, Looft and Charles (1971) found that the
elderly do have trouble taking another person's perspective in reference to
a spatial task. However, they also found that the elderly have no such
trouble taking another person's perspective in social-communication
situations in which the subject has to describe the qualitative features of an
object not visible to the listener. Perhaps the demands for explicit communication continue to exist in old age, whereas the more esoteric tasks
of spatial rotations do not.

Causality

Like spatial relations, causal relations are fundamental to cognitive
development. Causal relations, in fact, involve relations with the added factor of movement. The substance of a causal relation is not so much the shape

---

[2]In the block design task the subject is given a drawing and is instructed to render
that drawing with mosaic tiles or blocks.

or position of objects but, rather, what makes a given object move. The position of objects is, of course, important, but so are the timing and order of movement. Which event occurred first? Was there physical contact? Like the development of spatial relations, the cognitive development of causal relations is a study of the child's increasing awareness—in this case, an awareness of the procedures by which things happen.

In his recent book *Understanding Causality*, Piaget (1974) traces the course of causality concepts from age 4 to ages 7 and 8. This book summarizes and organizes the findings of over 100 studies performed by Piaget and his associates in Geneva—studies that are related to Piaget's earlier work on infancy (Piaget, 1952b, 1954). The book concludes with a chapter relating research with children to the historical development of scientific concepts of time, space, and causality. This is a monumental work, and, for that reason, we will discuss it at length.

Causality in Infancy

The earliest forms of causal thinking occur during infancy. An infant sees a toy hanging from a string. This is a familiar object; the baby has seen it before and made it swing by touching it. He now looks at the object for a moment, then makes a deliberate swipe at it. He is not trying to grasp the hanging toy; he is trying to make it swing. It is apparent from the child's posture, gaze, and directed movement that he is anticipating an effect, an effect that he is trying to cause. The hanging toy serves as an *index*, a reminder of a past action-effect sequence. The child does more than just remember that the toy can swing; the child remembers the cause of the swinging. In this sense we say that the infant is *aware* of causes.

The important aspect of this early awareness of causes is that children learn from objects. They extract information from the physical world. We shall see later that this is only one method children use to develop concepts. Extracting information from events that occur in the physical world is called by Piaget *physical abstraction*. In the case of the swinging toy, the child makes a swipe, feels contact with the object, and sees the swing. The child is receiving feedback from the movement of his own arm and the witnessed movement of the toy. He makes a simple connection, which he will use the next time he sees the hanging toy. Yet there is not much organization to the child's behavior, not much beyond a simple connection. Children also deal with more complicated events that require much more organization of thoughts. The source of this organized thought, according to Piaget, doesn't come from looking more closely at the physical world but from reflecting on actions as a system of relations. This type of awareness Piaget terms *reflexive abstraction*, and we will have more to say about this later.

Transmission of Cause

Immediate and mediate transmission. It is not long after children learn that their hands can make objects move that they learn that one moving object can make another object, previously at rest, move. They can anticipate that, if the marble rolls into a resting marble, the resting marble will begin to move upon impact by the first one. In fact, children get much pleasure from repeatedly making such action-reaction sequences occur. The movement of one object is transmitted to another object. Since there is no object between the agent of action and the recipient of action, Piaget calls this phenomenon *immediate transmission.* Had there been two adjacent marbles resting, hit on line by a third, only the last marble would have been propelled forward. The middle marble would have remained motionless. Thus Piaget calls this second situation *mediate transmission.* One of the most interesting series of studies reported by Piaget (1974) explores the manner in which children try to explain mediate transmission and how they initially use concepts appropriate only to immediate transmissions. These studies also investigate how reflexive abstraction facilitates the development of mental operations, such as transitivity, that in turn make it possible for the child to give a correct explanation of mediate transmissions. Consider the following task, portrayed in Figure 6-4.

The child is shown a row of three marbles touching each other. A fourth marble is rolled so that it makes impact with the first in line. At that point the marble on the opposite end is propelled forward. Children are asked to explain how it is that it was the marble on the opposite end that

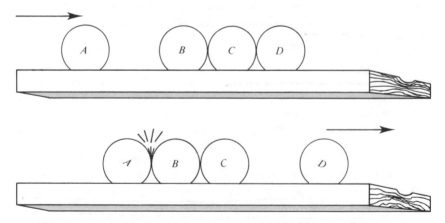

Figure 6-4. A test for the child's understanding of mediate transmission. Marble *A* is rolled in a grooved track and strikes marble *B*. Upon contact of *A* with *B*, marble *D* is propelled forward. Marbles *B* and *C* remain in place.

moved outward. Their different answers indicate the different stages children pass through in the development of the concept of causality. At stage 1a, around 4 years of age, children believe that the propelling marble, marble *A*, acts at a distance on the propelled marble, marble *D*, without any assistance from the intermediate marbles *B* and *C*. Some children at this stage even believe that marble *A* takes the place of marble *C* or that marble *A* goes behind marbles *B* and *C* and then hits marble *D*!

At stage 1b, around age 6, children imagine that each marble moves a little. The first bumps the second, the second bumps the third, and so on, until marble *D* is bumped by marble *C*. Had the marbles been spaced apart, this explanation would have been both correct and visible to the naked eye. As it were, the children's explanations were misapplications of what they did know about immediate transmission. They thought that the marbles bumped each other down the line—which is possible for immediate transmission but impossible for mediate transmission.

At stage 2, around age 7, children begin to sense that the separation of the last marble is the result of some force that passes *through* the mediate marbles. However, when questioned further, children at this stage still believe that the mediate marbles are displaced "just a little." Here the children are developing the newer concept of internal transmission while at the same time retaining the older concept of external transmission of force.

At stage 3, around age 8, the transmission of force via the mediate marble is understood as completely internal, without a change in the position of the whole marble but, instead, with an internal jolt (a vibration). The children understand that, even though the middle marbles don't change position, they must play a role in the transmission of force. This conclusion couldn't have been derived from looking more closely at the marbles; that is, it couldn't have developed from physical abstraction alone.

Transitivity. Using numerous examples like the above study, Piaget (1974) sets out to substantiate the fundamental role of object-to-object relations (causation) in the development of logical thinking (seriation, enumeration, and so on). Piaget maintains that the child's physical experience with immediate transmissions of movement nurtures the formation of the logical relation called *transitivity* (if $A = B$ and $B = C$, then $A = C$). Hitting an object now makes it fall (*A* leads to *B*). Hitting it at another time also makes it fall (*A* leads to *B* again). Soon the child anticipates that *A* will lead to *B*. She makes an *immediate inference,* an inference about the relation between two events. This she learns, as we said earlier, through physical abstraction. She has learned something general, something that she can apply to a wide range of objects such as cups, bowls, and dolls. In a sense the form of this relation has been abstracted from specific content. Once the form of the relation has been abstracted, the child can reflect on the form of the relation itself. In other words, instead of reflecting on any particular object-to-object action, she is reflecting on the form of the relation—what we call *reflexive abstraction*.

Piaget sees children's ability to reflect on the form of the relation, independently of particular content, as a shift to a new level of consciousness. Children now begin to treat certain events in the world of object-to-object relations as *necessarily* true, not just true for a few or many cases. For example, the logical operation of transitivity is attributed to the action of objects. In the case of mediate transmission of force through a row of marbles, the events at both ends of the row lead the child to make a logical conclusion about what must be happening in the middle of the row. Another example illustrates this point. Take three marbles: A (the moving marble), B (the middle one), and C (the marble that separates when A hits B). The child reasons: if force moves marble A to marble B and if force moves marble C from marble B, then it is possible that we are dealing with one force moving from A to C, not at a distance but through B.

The transitive operation is important. It prevents children from assuming that the force starts, stops, and starts again. The transitive operation makes it possible for children to consider the middle force—a force they cannot see (in movement) but that they guess is there. Of course, transitivity itself does not provide the specific explanation for mediate transmission of movement. There is nothing in the transitive operation that suggests the notion of an internal jolt, or vibration. But transitivity makes it possible for children to consider such explanations; it gives them a reason to search for an explanation that conserves the force through the "middle relation"; it prevents them from accepting the explanations of stage 1, since they violate the transitive operation; and it prevents them from believing that the stage-3 explanations are silly.

Piaget (1974) repeatedly stresses the importance of the following sequence of development. In dealing with the cause-and-effect relations between objects, children first make a physical abstraction of the form of those relations. Then they begin to reflect on the form itself (reflexive abstraction) and, in so doing, relate the form of one relation to another relation. This new type of organization between several relations takes the child into a new level of consciousness—the level of logical necessity. These mental operations are then, in turn, attributed to the actions of objects. Children can thereby understand more than what they can see, more than what they can learn by physical abstraction. We might add parenthetically that a close reading of *Understanding Causality* has great educational implications, because it stresses the importance of placing children in learning situations that require an explanation. To quote Piaget (1974),

> the child may on occasion be interested in seriating for the sake of seriating, in classifying for the sake of classifying; but, in general, it is when events or phenomena must be explained and goals attained through an organization of causes that operation will be used most [p. 17].

In another passage on the same page, Piaget explains that

> the segments of the real [world] most likely to favor the functioning of operations . . . will not be those that remain immobile or static but certainly those in which the real [object] itself is active and is transformed—in other words, wherever causality is involved.

Causal Thinking in Adulthood

Combinatorial thinking. It is a tenet of science that an effect cannot precede its cause. Yet the problems of our everyday existence often require us to discover the cause of an event when all we clearly see is the effect. Even to say of an event "This is the effect of some cause" is to go beyond the givens.

There are different levels of going beyond the givens. When a second-grade child sees a fallen tree, with wood chips lying nearby, she can probably figure out that the tree was chopped down with an axe. But it is unlikely that she is able to figure out, by combining clues, whether the person who used the axe was tall and left-handed, short and right-handed, or whatever. The adolescent, instead, has a greater ability to look at all of the clues and combine them to draw the right conclusions—the height of the notch in the tree, the angle of the axe marks, the distance of the chips from the trunk, and so on. The adolescent systematically submits the observable facts to a *system of possible causes*. In this sense, in adolescence the relation between the actual and the possible is reversed (Inhelder & Piaget, 1958). The adolescent looks at all the clues, each of which suggests a single cause, and then constructs a hypothesis that will either confirm or disconfirm the causative role of that clue. If none of the clues is confirmed individually, the adolescent has the wherewithal to systematically combine clues to test for causes that may be necessary but not sufficient. Consider the following example.

A young woman is combing her hair. As she moves her comb to the running faucet, she notices that the stream of water bends toward the comb. She wets the comb, strokes her hair again, moves the comb toward the water again, but this time the water "ignores" the comb. Is the water tired? This type of animistic thinking is quite common among preschool children. Our young woman, instead, sets out to test a series of hypotheses. She considers the various single causes: wet hair, dry hair, vigorous stroking of hair, gentle stroking of hair. She discovers that dry hair alone, while a necessary cause, is not sufficient to explain the bending of the stream of water. She must combine dry hair with vigorous stroking in order to create the effect. If she had not outlined the dimensions of the problem systematically, she may have never thought of the interaction of dry hair and vigorous stroking. The clue in this case was not the sighting of some observable feature, like wood chips at the base of a fallen tree. The clue—actually a combination of two clues—resulted from a mental operation called *combinatorial thinking* (In-helder & Piaget, 1958). It is combinatorial thinking that allows the young woman to shift from the actual observable facts to the possible and then to submit the world of physical events to a test of the possible.

The 3-year-old can anticipate that a stream of water will splash if a dish is held under it. He can do so because he has seen it happen. The significance of adolescent thinking is its deductive nature. The young woman is not anticipating events that she has seen happen in the past. She is experimentally testing events against hypotheses. The 7- or 8-year-old can experimentally test the variations of splash by changing the speed of the water, but he cannot submit his own thinking to a matrix of interacting causes. This later operation requires thinking about thinking—that is, mak-ing a complete set of propositions that may be absurd in actuality but that exist in the mind of the adolescent when single causes are combined in a matrix. Even absurd possibilities are tested by the adolescent who has faith in the procedure of trying all combinations. In this sense, the world of phys-ical events is subordinated to a mental world of possibilities. The subordina-tion of the actual to the possible is also found in the adolescent's fascination with social ideals, utopias, and romantic love.

The interesting possibility arises that the adolescents' concern with ideals and general principles makes them more likely to look at the abstract form of a set of causes. They take most any task and play around with both the immediately apparent and the less apparent possible causes. Elderly people do not necessarily use a systematic, deductive approach to questions of causation. Arenberg (1968) found that 60- to 75-year-olds do not routinely apply a deductive approach to problems that require that variables be separated and systematically tested one at a time. However, when the problems aroused their interest, these older adults did as well as younger adults. They did poorly on tasks such as finding out what makes a pendulum swing faster but put their deductive powers into full operation when asked to find which combination of ingredients made the food poisonous. The superior performance of the younger adults on the pendulum task prob-ably reflects the younger person's fascination with and general application of deductive reasoning and says less about the decline of competence in the elderly.

Animistic thinking. Even though there may be no decline in old age regarding the ability to systematically test variables, is there a change in the kinds of explanations offered for some event? Would an elderly person think, for example, that "tired tin" can cause canned food to spoil? If so, would this form of thinking be any different from that of a child who thinks that the cup fell off the shelf because it "got tired"? As we mentioned earlier, knowing what-follows-what is only part of knowing what-causes-what. In the mediate-transmission task illustrated in Figure 6-4, a 4-year-old was heard to say "The last marble was frightened by the first. That's why it moved." The attribution of life-like states to inanimate objects is called *animism*. There is evidence that elderly people think, at times, in animistic terms (Dennis & Mallinger, 1949). Several questions arise. Do all ages think animistically in certain situations? Does animistic thinking in the elderly differ from that found in childhood? That is, is animistic thinking in the elderly a regression to childhood thinking patterns? A review of the research literature by Looft and Bartz (1969) presents several possible answers.

Several studies cited in this review attest to a high percentage of college students who give animistic answers, even those students who have had courses in biology (Bell, 1954; Crannell, 1954; Crowell & Dole, 1957). Certainly neurological deterioration in old age is not a plausible explanation. The problem with most of these studies was the failure to instruct the subject to distinguish scientific definitions from metaphorical definitions. A college student, as well as an elderly adult, might say that the statement "Waves are caused by an angry sea" is true. To these subjects *angry* is no more than a metaphorical description of a sea swollen by high winds. Further interview of the students would reveal their real understanding of causation. We suspect that the attribution of vital force to inanimate objects by the child is more genuine.

The older person, state Looft and Bartz (1969), has a broader definition of animate systems. This, too, misleads the researcher. If the older person says "The sailor was eaten by the sea," he or she doesn't mean that the sea itself, in a conscious act, ground the bones of Davey Jones. It is more likely a matter of including both living and nonliving objects under the term *sea*. It is the imprecise nature of adult speech that misleads us here (Lowrie, 1954).

A third possibility is offered by Looft and Bartz (1969). The distinction between the internal source of movement characteristic of living systems and the externally induced movement characteristic of nonliving things is something that most people have just never thought about. Who can explain the difference between a leaf bending toward the sun and the water stream bending toward the comb? Our tendency to be animistic and anthropomorphic is proportionate to the amount of our prior knowledge of the event. Yet these lapses into animistic thinking are quite different from the child's simple overgeneralizations from living to nonliving things. The difference is the adult's lack of satisfaction with his or her analogy.

Summary

Both the knowledge of spatial relations and the knowledge of causal relations are basic to the formation of more specific knowledge—such as knowing how to get around in Worcester, Massachusetts, or knowing what caused the ice cream to melt. Development of basic knowledge of space and causation can be understood as an increase in conscious awareness of how we know what we know. At first, spatial relations are known in action but are not explicitly represented; therefore they are not known in general. The same can be said of causal relations. After children learn to represent in images and words key features of position and key sequences of movement, they begin to understand the system of relations as a whole—as an integrated, coordinated frame of reference.

The egocentrism of practical space and immediate causation gradually gives way to a more objectified practical knowledge. The child can make detours around obstacles and can comprehend the role of self as an agent of causation. These early objectifications of space and causation in action don't prevent the reappearance of egocentric thinking at the level of representation. Attempts to derive a set of spatial relations from another person's point of view yield to egocentric errors. Attempts to verbally describe cause-and-effect relations yield errors due to personal intuitions. Yet, just as the developing adult learns to be less egocentric about practical spatial and causal relations, he or she eventually learns to be less egocentric about representations of spatial and causal relations. There might be some regression to a more egocentric perspective in old age, but this regression is not necessarily the result of a decline in basic cognitive processes. Rather, it is more likely to be the result of a reduction in the environmental demands placed on older people to represent spatial and causal relations.

Chapter Seven

The Development
of Social Cognition

Just as we use cognition to form concepts about the physical world of space, time, and causality, we use cognition to form concepts about the social world. In order to understand ourselves and others, we must attend, remember, classify, and conserve. Some features of a social situation remain the same (are conserved) even though other features change. For example, the basic friendliness of a group is not altered when a shift toward supportive teasing takes place.

Although our concepts about the social world are different from our concepts about the physical world, the thinking process is essentially the same. After all, the same mind that learns about conservation also learns about conversation. The realization that cognitive and social development should be studied as one comprehensive system has led to an area of research called *social cognition* (see Shantz, 1975). This chapter deals with social cognition—more specifically, with the topics of self-knowledge, role taking, and moral development.

Self-knowledge continues to develop across the life span. The child begins by making a basic distinction between self and nonself. From that starting point the knowledge of self progresses through various stages, which we will discuss in detail. *Role taking,* a well-defined topic of social cognition (see Flavell, Botkin, Fry, Wright, & Jarvis, 1968), refers to the ability to assume the subjective state of another person, even when one doesn't hold that viewpoint at the moment. As you will see, role-taking competence originates from situations that in a sense are more spatial than social. The simple appreciation that the person across the table has a view of the flower arrangement on the table that is different from our own (see Chapter Six) is an elementary form of role taking. The area of *moral development* has received increasing attention by researchers in social cognition, an increase due in part to the work of Lawrence Kohlberg (1963, 1969, 1971).

A Framework for Social Cognition

How is drawing a parallel with general cognitive development going to help us understand social development better? More specifically, since social development is measured by the appropriateness of behavior in certain social situations, what does our knowledge of the person's general cognitive level tell us about the reasons for that behavior? One thing should be made clear right away. A parallel between general cognitive development and social development does not imply that smart people are more socially developed, more self-aware, and perhaps even more moral than less smart people. As a matter of fact, a more reasonable statement as a working hypothesis is that moral people are smart. (Incidentally, this statement shouldn't be confused with the statement that it is "smart" to be moral.)

There are at least two reasons why some people don't engage in higher forms of social development. Let's use moral development as an example. Some individuals, although smart enough to understand a moral problem and the principles involved in it, refuse to abide by those principles. Others, instead, are simply not smart enough to understand a moral dilemma and, therefore, never get to considering the often complex principles behind a certain action. In order to clarify this distinction between knowing-to-do and wanting-to-do, let's turn to Flavell (1974).

Flavell's Model of Social Cognition

Flavell's model of social cognition can be used as a general model for making inferences about the social world and applying such inferences. According to Flavell, any decision concerning the social world goes through four steps: existence, need, inference, and application. The person must first have some awareness of the possible *existence* of a certain social fact. The 1-year-old doesn't know yet that her internal state, such as pain or hunger, can also be the internal state of someone else. The 9-year-old, on the other hand, may not know that people sometimes behave in a certain way because they can anticipate how other people will interpret a situation. A 9-year-old, therefore, is likely to be puzzled by a newlywed's nervous rubbing at a spot of lipstick on his collar—an accident of a crowded elevator. A child who doesn't know of the existence of a certain fact of the social world—in this case, the fact that people think about other people's thoughts—will be unable to reach the appropriate conclusions in specific situations in which such awareness is relevant.

Sometimes the child may know of the existence of a social fact or phenomenon but is not aware of the *need* to consider it as a possibility. The child could understand if he thought about it, but he doesn't think about it. He does not, of his own accord, sense the need for an act of social cognition in a particular situation. Flavell's use of the term *need* in this case is similar to his use of the term *production deficiency* (Flavell, 1970). As you may recall, we mentioned production deficiency in Chapter Four in reference to children's failure to spontaneously use memory strategies that they are indeed capable of using. In production deficiency, prompting can be very useful. Similarly, when the child is not aware of the need to consider a certain social concept, some prompting may be quite helpful—"Why is the man so nervous about a stranger's lipstick mark on his collar?"

The *inference* component of Flavell's model refers to the child's ability to figure out what the other person is feeling. This requires relating the present cues (in STM) to various possibilities (in LTM). Without knowing of the existence of subjective states in others or without sensing the need to consider such states, the child cannot proceed to the inference step in social cognition. Flavell (1974) believes that the path from existence to need to inference must be walked in a progression. Once the steps of existence and need have been taken, the child brings to the task of inference all of his or her cognitive skills to guess, compare, and identify social cues in order to read a particular social situation accurately.

In the last step, *application,* the person puts his or her inference to the test of reality. Suppose that a man, sitting next to a woman who is reading a book, becomes interested in her and infers from her general demeanor that she would be receptive to a friendly "Hello! I see that you, too, are interested in Simone de Beauvoir." But this man may never dare to take the application step, and his conclusion about the woman would thus remain an idle fancy. Of course, as Flavell explains, the application of an inference may cause us to reassess such inference. In our example, if the man had gone through with the application step and the reading woman had answered his smile with an abrupt turning of the page, the man would be forced to reassess his assumption.

Figure 7-1 illustrates Flavell's model. To summarize, first the person has an awareness of the existence of a social concept—of a fact or phenomenon as a possibility of life. Then a social situation occurs in which the person senses the need to discover whether some particular social concept is relevant to that situation. As a consequence, the person engages in a process of guessing and comparing in order to make an accurate inference regarding the social concept (in our example, the subjective state of another person). That inference may or may not be applied in overt behavior—thus the dashed line between "Inference" and "Application" in Figure 7-1. If that inference is applied, the person may or may not carry out successfully

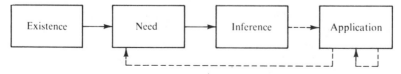

Figure 7-1. Flavell's model of social cognition.

his or her act of social thinking. If our man's "Hello!" is met by an abrupt turning of the page on the woman's part, he may remain with his same inference (she will be receptive) and make a second application. This option is represented by the short dashed arrow that feeds back into the "Application" step. Alternatively, the person who fails in his initial application can decide that he needs to reevaluate the situation. This choice is represented by a dashed arrow that feeds back into the "Need" step.

These four steps of social cognition will be useful in our review of the research on self-knowledge, role taking, and moral development across the life span. Common sense would predict that the younger the perceiver of social situations, the more likely a failure at the existence step. We do not "remind" a 2-year-old to think about ulterior motives, since a 2-year-old doesn't know what ulterior motives are. An improvement in the inference step describes the wisdom of social cognition that comes with advancing age. A life-long experience of social cognition may make older adults more sensitive to what others are feeling.

The Development of Self-Knowledge

The question "Who am I?" which haunts each of us throughout life, is rooted in the even more basic question "Am I?" Am I a single spatial entity? Do I have permanence in spite of the fact that my environment varies in its responsiveness to my efforts? We discussed these very basic forms of self-consciousness in the preceding chapter. Here we deal with the social forms of self-knowledge. When do children develop the sense of personal identity—the sense that their personalities have traits that define who they are even though the situations around them keep changing?

The self as an autonomous agent of action develops slowly, beginning with a simple distinction. Some events that the infant desires happen very often; others, quite randomly. The former, such as seeing one's own hand, are constructed as part of self. The latter, such as seeing one's mother, are constructed as not part of self. The sense of autonomy continues to develop in the child throughout the first two years of life and reaches a stage known to many parents as "the terrible 2s." By age 2, children have just become aware of the extent of their control over themselves, and they practice this newly found skill with a vengeance. The constant "No" and overall negativism of 2-year-olds are often their method of reaffirming their discovery of self.

By age 2 the child has developed a definite personality with its own styles of coping, and at 3 he or she can accept his or her own limitations without bewilderment (Murphy, 1962). This definite personality pattern, however, does not imply that the child himself or herself is aware of it. The conscious awareness of self develops through various stages, as we shall see in the pages to come.

Self-Knowledge and Cognitive Development

Alschuler and Weinstein (1976) have undertaken a promising research project to study the levels of conscious awareness that people have about themselves. This project is particularly relevant to this book because it assumes that self-knowledge is limited by the cognitive operations available to the individual. For example, a child who has difficulty integrating parts to create a pattern on any task would also find it very difficult to integrate episodes in his or her life to figure out the pattern of a personality trait.

Alschuler and Weinstein studied conscious awareness in individuals ranging in age from 7 to 68 years. The investigators asked their subjects to describe a memorable experience—including all the relevant thoughts, feelings, and actions—and analyzed their subjects' descriptions with a complex system that made it possible to identify the subjects' developmental levels. Table 7-1 shows the four levels of self-knowledge that emerged from Alschuler and Weinstein's analysis.

The parallel between the stages described by Alschuler and Weinstein and the stages of general cognitive development should be apparent. Stage 1 (elemental) is governed by mental images of physical events, sometimes out of order. In Stage 2 (situational), mental operations become more organized, more interpretive, and less bound to the surface appearance of events. By Stage 3 (patterned), events that are separated both in time and in physical appearance begin to be related and a form of "conservation of self" develops. This ability to see self-consistency no doubt involves a form of class inclusion (see Chapter Five). Statements such as "I wasn't myself" indicate an understanding of both the total "I" and that subclass of the self-concept that the speaker calls "myself." The "I" is a combination of those things the speaker calls "self" (A) and those things he or she dismisses as not part of self (A')—that is, B ("I") $= A$ ("myself") $+ A'$ ("not myself"). Stage 4 (process) requires thinking about thinking. This is similar to the stage of formal operations (see Chapter Two), which can be described as relating relations. It is not clear from Alschuler and Weinstein's report whether Stage 4 requires formal operations, but what is clear is that Stage 4 requires mental structures more complicated than those used in Stage 3.

As interesting as these results may be, we must evaluate them in the light of their source. As Ginsburg and Koslowski (1976, p. 46) state, the use of verbal descriptions doesn't tell us much about people's ability to accurately assess themselves. The fact that a person has the mental structures necessary to think about thinking doesn't mean that the person will use that competence without distortion, selective memory, denial, or defense mechanisms. And some defense mechanisms are extremely clever.

Alschuler and Weinstein's stages of self-awareness bring us back to Flavell's model of social cognition. In Flavell's scheme such stages would be represented by the existence part of social cognition. People do show an

Table 7-1. Alschuler and Weinstein's levels of self-knowledge.

Stage 1: Elemental Stage
     Subjects in this stage recount the memorable experience in a fragmented, list-like fashion. Events are incomplete and show little continuity. They are overt, external, and observable rather than subjective. There are no metasituational statements—that is, no statements that summarize several situations. The self in the story has to be inferred by the listener instead of being disclosed by the speaker. For example, "I was bit by a dog. The dog was big. It was raining. I slipped down."

Stage 2: Situational Stage
     Subjects begin to describe subjective states, but the discussion seldom goes beyond the particular situation. The various parts of the recollected experience are connected in a causal chain. There are some attempts to define the general tone of the situation, but there is still no attempt to relate the situation to other situations. The subjects stay within one time frame rather than see consistency of self across past situations. The descriptions of internal states are rather global and lacking in nuances. For example, "I was bit by a dog. I screamed when he bit me. I think I was mad and afraid. It was a rather bad day. It upset me for a long time afterward."

Stage 3: Patterned Stage
     Subjects begin to see themselves as consistent across situations. True hypotheses about self form and are tested against past experiences (for example, "I guess I must have problems with authority"). The person begins to see a pattern to his or her social behavior. The subject makes predictive statements about how he or she would probably react in a given situation, knowing what he or she knows about himself or herself. Situations are defined abstractly ("things that threaten me") rather than physically ("things that are hot"). Behavior is described dispositionally ("I have a tendency to get overly involved with members of the opposite sex") rather than overtly ("I try to kiss all the girls").

Stage 4: Process Stage
     Subjects do more than describe their personality patterns. They also have an awareness of how they deal with their internal states. Subjects can describe the process by which they control and modify their feelings and moods ("I try to make my guilt work positively by setting realistic deadlines and then feeling anxious if it looks like I'm not meeting those deadlines"). The awareness of how "self directs self" is explicit, conscious. In the previous stage generalized patterns are merely described, but there is no evidence that the self is seen as a possible agent in the change itself. In this stage the self is seen as proactive in influencing internal states ("I began to give myself permission to express my true feelings").[1]

From "Self-Knowledge Development," by A. Alschuler and G. Weinstein. An unpublished manuscript written at the School of Education, University of Massachusetts, Amherst, 1976. Reprinted by permission of the authors.

[1]This view of self-awareness in terms of stages is supported by the research of Peevers and Secord (1973) and Livesley and Bromley (1973), who identified similar stages in the verbal descriptions subjects gave of friends, someone they disliked, and themselves.

increasing awareness of the existence of various possibilities regarding their feelings and the reasons for such feelings. People also show an increase across age in the inference skills they apply to remembered events. They can interrelate more situations in order to see patterns and can differentiate external and uncontrollable events from events brought about by their own actions. In other words, maturing also means developing a sense of personal responsibility.

How do the components of Flavell's model relate to accurate self-knowledge and healthy personality adjustment? Throughout our lives, but especially in emotional situations, we need to bring to bear the existence and the inference components of our social cognition. Let's say, for example, that David is being criticized by his girlfriend, Maria. In order to benefit from a potentially negative situation, David must recognize the need to utilize his basic knowledge of his psychological goings on (existence) and make an effective application of such knowledge to better understand himself. The effectiveness of any application will depend on how open David is to what Maria is saying and on how good his intuitions are, so that subsequent applications and needs assessments can be appropriately modified (the feedback loops in Flavell's model). For example, a critical comment may cause David to flare and retaliate if he doesn't see the need to consider the existence of some potentially annoying patterns in his personality. Even if he does see the need to think about the existence of annoying patterns, he may defend himself (application) with a poor self-diagnosis, such as bringing up an irrelevant ''good point'' about himself. The process of feedback between David and Maria must be ongoing and nondefensive, so that David's initial attempts to understand Maria's criticism (application) can influence his subsequent attempts (other applications) and even the relevant personality patterns (reassessment of need).

In order to make effective use of cognition to solve social problems, one needs a strong sense of self. The relationship between self-awareness and positive self-image is more complicated than what the work of Alschuler and Weinstein indicates. We need to know whether the ability to use advanced stages of cognition in general (competence) is at all related to social adjustment and personality development (performance).

Ego Development and Cognitive Development

Ego development can be distinguished from self-knowledge. Self-knowledge, as we have discussed it, refers to the levels of awareness about self and to the mental processes (such as differentiation and interrelation) used to reach those levels. Ego development refers, instead, to the development of a positive or negative sense of self. Erikson (1963) has identified eight stages of ego development, each stage representing a polar conflict, such as basic trust versus basic mistrust, initiative versus guilt, identity versus role confusion, and ego integrity versus despair. Erikson maintains that healthy personality development depends on the successful resolution of each conflict in turn, so that there will be no residuals left that continually cause problems in relating to other people.

We are interested in two directions of influence between ego development and general cognition. One is the influence of general cognition on ego development. The other one is the influence of ego development on general cognition. With regard to the first direction of influence, we know that very bright people are not by any means immune to problems of personality adjustment. However, stereotypic statements such as "Genius is next to madness" are, to say the least, exaggerations. A more relevant issue than the correlation between intelligence and adjustment is, in our view, the way in which general cognition can be used to improve social adjustment.

Older forms of psychotherapy emphasized the uncovering of hidden desires and buried resentments through dream analysis and hypnosis. The application of the wide-awake rational mind to here-and-now problems was deemphasized. More recent forms of therapy put much more emphasis on the efficient use of cognition to solve problems of social adjustment. In fact, the humanistic movement in psychotherapy and education is based on the premise that each individual has the cognitive capacity to deal effectively with his or her personal problems (Maslow, 1968; Rogers, 1951). Awareness leads to adjustment.

Other therapeutic approaches to ego development and the establishment of a strong identity have formalized the relationship between cognition and social adjustment into an integrated whole. They have identified neurotic styles of cognition such as rigidity and overgeneralization (Shapiro, 1965) or excessive awareness of detail and inability to abstract the meaning of events (Giora, 1975). These approaches make use of agreements that resemble formal contracts between therapist and client to help the client think better. Glasser (1965) calls his approach *reality therapy* because he believes that all people with adjustment problems deny or distort the reality of the world around them. Ellis (1971) has developed an approach, which he calls *rational psychotherapy,* based on the view that emotional problems are the result of faulty conclusions and other forms of irrational thinking. Beck (1976), the originator of *cognitive therapy,* focuses on those elements in our conscious awareness that cause us problems and treats the problems as straightforward cases of misunderstanding and miscommunication. This means that problems of ego development can be treated with the same cognitive skills that are used to solve any other problem.

All these approaches share the premise that the answer to problems of social adjustment doesn't lie in the identification and resolution of repressed childhood conflicts. What the person in trouble needs to know is what he or she is currently doing that drives people away, prevents the formation of intimate relationships, or stifles creativity. These forms of therapy have demonstrated repeatedly that general cognition can be successfully applied to facilitate the development of a strong sense of self and to reduce self-defeating behaviors.

Now let's consider the other direction of influence—the influence of ego development on general cognition. How effectively can people use their cognitive abilities if they have a poor sense of self? It hardly needs to be said that a person who lacks confidence will not live up to his or her potential. What represents a richer topic of discussion is the question of how the relationship between confidence and performance changes across the life span. At least in our culture, children pass through definite cycles of emotionality as they grow from infants to adolescents—the "terrible 2s," the latency period of the grade-school years, and the storm and stress of adolescence. These emotional cycles affect the child's reasoning ability in predictable ways.

The emotional stages beyond adolescence are, instead, less predictable, since the variability in both cognitive development and ego development is tremendous. Flavell (1970) attributes the variability in cognitive development to social factors that determine one's sense of self. Marriage, parenting, retirement, and death of loved ones are frequently the source of monumental problems. The ways in which these problems are resolved affect ego development, and the level of ego development limits or frees cognition. Since social circumstances determine in large measure the success in overcoming these personal problems and since social circumstances vary considerably among individuals, there results a great deal of variability among adults in their ability to use cognition effectively. Piaget (1972) himself advises researchers to pay more attention to the social environment as an instrumental factor in cognitive development beyond late adolescence.

Nevertheless, developmental psychologists have attempted to identify the "golden years" in life—those years when one is more likely to feel good about oneself. Both popular literature (for example, Sheeny, 1974) and scientific research (Neugarten, Moore, & Lowe, 1968) have focused on this topic.

Neugarten et al. (1968) interviewed adults between the ages of 30 and 50. From such interviews it appears that middle age is seen by middle-aged people as the "command generation." Adults between 30 and 50 years of age feel that they are no longer driven by impulses and circumstances and are therefore in control of their lives. They also feel that the middle-age generation controls society—business, education, and politics. Additional research indicates that middle-aged people see themselves as being in the most productive period of their lives, when the most significant contributions to one's own career are made (Dennis, 1968). Middle age is also seen by both people in middle age and people over 50 as a period of intellectual superiority (Cameron, 1973).

How about self-concept and productivity in people over 50? The stereotype of the uninvolved, self-doubting older adult is only partially true. Dennis (1968) also found that people in scholarly careers such as writers and teachers continue to make significant contributions into their 70s. However, people in scientific and professional careers show a decline in productivity. Klein and Birren (1973) found that older adults lack confidence when faced with a challenging intellectual problem and are more susceptible to social influence. That is, when told that others their age did poorly on a particular type of problem, older subjects did less well than younger subjects who were told the same thing. Klein and Birren, however, found that the older subjects did just as well as the younger ones when both age groups were told that their contemporaries had done well on that particular type of problem.

Even though older adults show more conformity to social expectations than do younger people, they don't lack competence. The problem seems to be that older adults doubt their own assessment of their competence more than do younger adults. If this is so, couldn't these self-doubts cause older adults to gradually disengage themselves from involvement with other people and situations that challenge them beyond what they consider the limits of their competence?

Disengagement in the Later Years

With advancing years people become less concerned with the world outside and more preoccupied with themselves. Older people are less bold in taking on challenging tasks (Neugarten, 1972). Older individuals cut back their social commitments, limit the number of friends, and become less involved in civic and career activities. The social world, in turn, begins to withdraw from them. This mutual withdrawal between the older individual and society has been called *disengagement* (Henry, 1965).

Disengagement can be an adaptive mechanism in old age. Time is at one's command instead of one's being commanded by time. Material possessions become less important and lose their governing power. When success, money, career, and prestige are of no significant consequence anymore, the individual is free to be himself or herself, free to be in tune with his or her inner self and to successfully accomplish ego integrity, or the knowledge of who one really is (Erikson, 1963).

Disengagement, however, is not necessarily a good thing for the aging individual. Maddox (1963), for example, discovered that older people's morale is directly proportional to their activity in the community. Older people who are not active find it difficult to feel worthwhile; such difficulty, in turn, increases their resistance to becoming more active. Therefore, older people experience both the desire to enjoy a more leisurely life and the need to be engaged enough to feel worthwhile. In summarizing the relevant data, Havighurst, Neugarten, and Tobin (1968) advise that successful aging requires a balance between activity and disengagement. Disengagement permits the elderly to reflect on who they truly are (ego integrity) and activity confirms their sense of self. A strong sense of self and esteem for oneself can assure continued cognitive development and a fuller use of intellectual talents throughout old age.

Knowledge and attitudes about the self are only part of the broader area of social cognition. What we know of ourselves and how we regard ourselves result, in part, from how well we understand other people. If my older sister says to me "You are the best apple peeler in the family!" I can either grow in self-regard or question my sister's motives. Knowing that she has volunteered to bake 12 apple pies for the school bazaar helps me evaluate the compliment better. In the next section we discuss the development of role taking—that is, the ability to place other people's behavior in the context of their own position, purposes, and past experiences.

The Development of Role Taking

Before beginning our discussion of the development of role taking, we need to clarify two points. One is that we use the term *role* to refer to the momentary state—visual, motivational, and intentional—of another person and not to refer to a culturally defined set of behaviors, like the role of the father in the family. The other is that the development of role taking should not be confused with the socialization of the child into culturally approved roles. The development of role taking refers to the growth of the cognitive skills that are required for a child to understand other people, their emotional states, their perspectives, and the differences between these perspectives and those held by the child himself or herself. We will trace the development of role taking from the first year of life to adulthood, at least as far as current research allows.

Understanding Someone Else's Visual Experience

Social development depends in part on the person's ability to understand other people's points of view. Such ability begins with the ability to understand that the visual experience of someone else is different from our own. We cannot see another person's line of sight. To put it in simpler terms, we cannot see with someone else's eyes. We can only infer such line of sight by imagining an extension of the person's gaze until this imaginary line "meets" some object considered to be the target. If this imaginary line of sight meets a large object before it meets a small one, we infer that the small object is not visible to the other person, even though it may be visible to us.

Flavell (1974) identifies four stages of development in visual role taking. At Level 0 (1 to 2 years of age), the child

> has as yet no conception or symbolic representation of any sort of visual act or experience, with or without regard to perspective, in either self or

others. While able to anticipate that he will reencounter object X if he goes around to the other person's side of a barrier, he is still quite incapable of representing either his future or the other person's present visual experiencing of X. Internal psychological processes like seeing are simply not yet objects of cognition [Flavell, 1974, p. 94].*

This means that the Level-0 child might know that an object hidden by a screen can be found again (object permanence) but cannot compare two different points of view. He might know that the object is behind a screen but cannot consider whether a second person can see the object from his or her side of the screen. The child at Level 0 would not understand the adult's question "Can I see the toy?" To understand this question, the child would have to know that seeing depends on line of sight.

Flavell (1977) describes the Level-1 child (2 to 4 years of age) as follows:

> The . . . Level 1 child has acquired the very fundamental and important insight that another person need not always see the same object that he himself currently sees. For instance, he is likely to realize that, if a picture of an object is held vertically so that the picture's face is towards him and its back towards another person seated opposite him, he sees the depicted object but the other person does not. Similarly, he probably would be aware that, if he placed an object on the other person's side of an upright opaque screen, the other person would see it even though he himself no longer could. What he fails as yet to represent, however, is the Level 2 idea that an object which is currently seen by both is seen differently from different spatial perspectives. What is addressed at Level 1 is the global, all-or-none question of *whether* someone does or does not see something; *how* that something looks from here versus there, assuming that it is visible from both positions, is probably not yet a meaningful question. The Level 1 child thinks about viewing objects according to this theory, but not yet about views of objects [p. 126].†

At Level 1 the child can answer the question "Can I see the object that you see?" (given that a screen hides either the child's or the adult's view) but cannot answer the question "What parts of the toy do I see?" (given that the toy is visible to both the child and the adult). To understand the second question, the child would have to know that what the adult sees of an object is not necessarily what the child himself sees.

At Level 2 (beyond age 4) the child

> can represent the fact not only that he and the other see things but also that they have particular, position-determined views (perspectives) of the things

---

*This and all other quotations from this source are from "The Development of Inferences about Others," by J. H. Flavell. In T. Mischel (Ed.), *Understanding Other Persons.* Copyright 1974 by Blackwell and Mott. Reprinted by permission.

†From *Cognitive Development,* by J. H. Flavell. Copyright 1977 by Prentice-Hall, Inc., Englewood Cliffs, N. J. Reprinted by permission.

they see. Unlike the Level 1 child, he can represent differences in visual experience between himself and the other even when exactly the same objects are visible to both and can thus grasp what for the younger child would presumably be a mind-boggling possibility: a self-other difference in visual experience embedded in a self-other similarity in visual experience [Flavell, 1974, p. 96].

Flavell relates the progression from Level 1 to Level 2 to his own model of social cognition. At Level 1 the child has discovered the existence of the other's view but has not yet brought to bear a system of inference making that would permit him to know exactly how that view appears to the other person. These inference processes are more active at Level 2.

Flavell (1974) speculates on the existence of a third level and regrets the absence of relevant research. Level 3 goes beyond the particular perspective of objects. At this level the child would be able to decide which one of two objects appears larger to a person sitting across the table. The emphasis here is on appearance as opposed to reality. That is, two objects may objectively be the same height, but the one farther away appears smaller, mainly because the retinal image of the farther object is smaller than that of the nearer object. The Level-3 child would have to appreciate that (1) the object that is nearer to himself is the object that is farther away from the person sitting across the table and (2) the object that is nearer to himself looks bigger than the other one to himself but smaller than the other one to the other person. This means that the child would have to think about the size of the other person's retinal image—that is, the apparent size of nearer objects. Since thinking about the size of the retinal image, as opposed to real size, is difficult even from an egocentric point of view (Flavell, 1963, pp. 355–356), such thinking from someone else's point of view would be difficult indeed. Flavell suggests that failure at a Level-3 task might be rooted in a problem of existence—that is, the child may not know that a retinal image exists. Before the child can appreciate the Level-3 problem, he must know that the real size of an object is much larger than the size of its image on the retina.

Understanding Subjective States

As children grow in experience and ability, their awareness of others includes more subjective attributes, such as other people's thoughts and intentions. Selman and Byrne (1974) have identified five stages in the development of this more subjective form of role taking. They told children a story about a little girl named Holly. Holly had promised her father not to climb trees. But one day Holly was faced with the dilemma between keeping her promise and saving a kitten who was trapped on a tree and might fall any time. The children in the Selman and Byrne study were asked to think about how Holly felt as she decided what to do. The following are these researchers' findings.

Level-0 children (4 to 6 years) can understand that another person may have preferences and subjective states different from their own but don't have the inferential skills necessary to figure out what those subjective states may be. Level-0 children will assume that everyone in the story about Holly automatically knows how everyone else feels and thinks. Even though Level-0 children acknowledge that each person can have different feelings, they are unable to conceptualize other people as thinking and feeling beings with thoughts and feelings of their own.

At Level 1 (6 to 8 years), called *subjective role taking,* children recognize that others have individual cognitive perspectives (subjectivity). They also begin to understand that people have personal reasons for their actions, reasons that often are not apparent to outside observers. Therefore, Level-1 children understand that Holly's friends will be perplexed by Holly's reluctance to climb the tree and save the kitten, since they don't know of Holly's promise to her father.

At Level 2 (8 to 10 years), called *self-reflective role taking,* children can think not only that others have their own cognitive perspectives but also that they can make inferences about other people's perspectives. Furthermore, Level-2 children realize that they themselves (and their thoughts and feelings) can be the objects of other people's perspectives. Therefore, at this level children understand that Holly can think about her father's thinking about her dilemma and about her father's probable understanding of her breach of promise. The Level-2 child realizes that he or she (Holly in the story) can have thoughts that are themselves the object of another person's thoughts (Holly's father's thoughts). This level of reasoning is more than thinking about the thoughts of others. It is thinking about other people's thinking about one's own thinking.

What could Level 3 be? At Level 3 (10 years and older), called the *mutual role taking,* the child begins to think about two people's points of view simultaneously. To identify Level-3 children, Selman and Byrne (1974) asked "If Holly and her father discussed this situation, what might they decide together? Why?" The Level-3 child can assume the perspective of a third person even when he or she is one of the two participants. The child can look at the two-person interaction as an interaction, not just as a succession of one-way relations as in Level 2. Neither self nor other is given first-person priority—for example, "They both understand how the other might have been upset." The preadolescent at Level 3 has constructed a qualitatively distinct third-person view that includes the reciprocal first-person perspectives of Level 2. At Level 2 the child understands that both parties have first-person views of the other's thinking about self, but these views are not coordinated into a third-person view of the interaction. The Level 3 child, instead, has constructed the concept of a mutuality of perspectives.

Selman (1976) has identified yet another level of subjective perspective taking. Some years beyond Level 3 the adolescent, now capable of formal-operational thinking, can consider the perspective of people in general, not just the perspective of two particular people involved in a particular situation. This perspective is a group, or societal, perspective. The societal perspective is more than the sum of many third-person views of particular pairs of people in given social situations, like Holly and her father. The societal perspective is a type of perspective held by many—what might be called multiple third-person perspective. The adolescent at this stage can compare various types of ideologies and belief systems—that is, different rationales for moral behavior and different religious perspectives. The Level-4 adolescent can appreciate that everyone (at least everyone the Level-4 adolescent considers) will interpret a given social interaction in a particular way. In other words, Level-4 adolescents become increasingly less egocentric about their own third-person perspective. Their third-person perspective is shared by "everyone." What Level-4 adolescents lack is an awareness that these group perspectives are relative to the culture in which they themselves have been socialized. We might say that such adolescents are no longer egocentric about their third-person perspective but are sociocentric.

Beyond Level 4, somewhere in young adulthood, the person gains cultural consciousness and appreciates that even societal perspectives are relative to one particular culture. Different cultures may interpret the same social interaction in basically different ways. This Level-5 awareness enables the young adult to overcome prejudice and confusion when he or she is faced with behaviors on the part of other groups that would be abhorrent, frivolous, or inexplicable if considered from the narrow perspective of one's "home culture." The Level-5 young adult does not immediately assume that these groups are barbarian, uninformed, or silly. He or she tries to deduce the group action from the cultural values of that society, working backward from the specific actions in a variety of situations to the general cultural value. This form of thinking, which is both inductive and deductive, enables the young adult to sense the *need* to engage his or her *inferential* processes, because he or she knows of the *existence* of broad cultural values that may be different from the values held by one's own culture.

Role Taking and Aging

Does role taking develop even further along these lines beyond middle adulthood? The answer is probably no. The process seems to reverse itself, and the older adult finds it difficult to see another person's point of view. Just take as an example the elderly driver who slowly emerges from a side street and proceeds directly ahead of speeding traffic. Does he fail to think about the other drivers' fields of vision and ability to brake? Or does he think about them but assume that (a) others shouldn't be going so fast anyway and/or (b) he's got plenty of time to slow down? Either way, our fictitious senior driver is thinking egocentrically.

As our example indicates, the older person's egocentricity can take one of two forms. The person may either fail to take another's point of view or refuse to take it. In Flavell's model of social cognition the first form represents a failure to see the need for role taking. It is not reasonable, however, to conclude that a 70-year-old doesn't know of the existence of other points of view. The second form represents a failure in the application of role-taking inferences to a particular situation.

Older people, as we mentioned earlier, do disengage from social activities and emotional involvement. This means that they become more egocentric, less concerned with the subjective states of other people. It is not that the elderly cannot take another person's perspective. If the situation demands it, they can, as we saw in Chapter Six in our discussion of spatial relations. You may recall that in the course of such discussion we cited a study by Looft and Charles (1971) indicating that the elderly have no trouble taking another person's perspective in social-communication situations in which they have to describe the qualitative features of an object not visible to the listener. This suggests that older persons, in their self-preoccupation, fail to see the need, rather than to know the existence, of roles.

In the second form of egocentricity the person refuses to take someone else's perspective. It would seem likely that the older person, because of a life-long experience, would be inclined to remain benignly tolerant of changing values and points of view. But this doesn't appear to be true, at least for the older adults interviewed by Neugarten, Moore, and Lowe (1968). These researchers' data indicate that, as people age, they show a greater convergence between personal opinions and opinions ascribed to others. That is, older adults tend to assume that everyone thinks just as they do. In the Neugarten et al. study, the elderly were the least tolerant of the three generations that these researchers interviewed. People beyond 60 seem to be more opinionated and more vehement about what defines appropriate social behavior. Perhaps, as a result of feeling the discrimination of a youth-oriented culture, the elderly develop an in-group defense against alternative points of view. In Flavell's model this attitude represents a refusal to make an *application* of social cognition in spite of the fact that one has full awareness of the *need*. The awareness of the *need* could be what threatens the elderly and intensifies their rigidity.

We must temper these speculations with Kalish's (1975) warning that "individual differences among the elderly seem so great that trends in personality development and change are very difficult to discern" (p. 68). The tolerance of the elderly individual will ultimately depend on an interaction between long-established personality traits and the particular social situations in which the person finds himself or herself. Yet the fact remains that our culture, for the reasons we have repeatedly discussed, makes it difficult for the elderly person to remain open to alternative points of view.

Modification of Role-Taking Skills

Role-taking skills develop across age as the child confronts social conflicts that occur naturally. Some studies have manipulated the social environment in various ways to facilitate the development of role taking and to test the effects of increased role taking on socially approved behavior. George Spivack and Myrna Shure of the Hahnemann Community Mental Health Center in Philadelphia have been developing methods for improving the social adjustment of young children since 1969. We will briefly summarize their approach as it appears in their book *Social Adjustment of Young Children: A Cognitive Approach to Solving Real-Life Problems* (1974).

Over a period of 46 days preschool children are taught the basic concepts of *different, some,* and *all.* They are also taught how to identify emotions, how to see alternative solutions to social problems, how to infer the probable consequences of behavior, and how to relate solutions to consequences. The children actively listen to a ''script'' that the teacher uses as a guideline to provoke questions and answers from them. Here is an example of one day's lesson, which takes about 20 minutes to complete.

Solutions and Consequences Pairing

Day 43

(A girl on a bike wants a boy on a wagon to get out of her way. Use the picture of a girl and boy riding in a playground from the My Community set.)

The problem today is: This girl on the bike (point) wants this boy (point) on the wagon to get out of her way.

What is the problem? What does the girl want the boy to do? (Children repeat the problem.)

Today we're going to play our game in a new way. I'm going to ask you for one idea. I'm going to write it over here. (Draw a line down the middle of the board and point dramatically to the left side of the line.)

OK. Who has an idea of what this girl (point) can do so this (point) boy will get out of the way?

(After one solution has been offered, say:) OK. Now listen carefully. This is a hard question. If (repeat the solution), then what MIGHT happen next? (If a consequence is not offered, follow with the remaining questions, such as:) What might the boy do (say) if _____? (As soon as one consequence is offered, say:) OK, that might happen. I'm going to put all the things that might happen over here. (Point dramatically to the right side of the line.) . . .

(Repeat this line of questioning, always alternating solution and consequence, intermittently asking:) Is that a good idea? Why is that a good idea? (Some questions should be asked for nonforceful (''ask him'') as well as forceful (''hit him'') solutions) [pp. 189–190].*

In these activities the children are taught how to think of a large number of alternative solutions and consequences. Spivack and Shure (1974) reason that this approach is an improvement over that of telling the child directly why a certain behavior is not socially appropriate. When the child is told, for example, "If you play loudly, the other children cannot hear the story," it is the teacher who has done the thinking about consequences, not the child. Spivack and Shure report that these activities brought about not only improvement in role taking but also reduction in antisocial behavior.

Chandler (1973) trained delinquent adolescents in role taking by using skits in which the adolescents acted out social episodes. Each adolescent played several roles to improve his or her awareness of how each character in the skit must have felt. The skits were filmed and later viewed. After ten weeks of training, Chandler found that these adolescents showed improvement in their role-taking skills on a general test. Furthermore, when compared to control groups who simply made films without acting in them, these adolescents had approximately 50% fewer run-ins with the law over the year and a half following role-taking training. Chandler concludes that the increase in role-taking skills led to a decrease in delinquent behavior. Both the study by Spivack and Shure (1974) and that by Chandler (1973) sound an optimistic note: better thinking can lead to better behavior. Neither training technique was doctrinaire or authoritarian. The individual was taught how to consider another person's point of view, and the ultimate decision regarding how to behave was his or her own.

The Development of Moral Judgment

What elements does a person take into consideration to decide whether an act is moral or immoral? Piaget (1965) asked children to judge whether a little boy in a story should be punished or not for something he had done. In this early work Piaget found that young children were concerned almost exclusively with the amount of damage the little boy had done, while older children took into consideration the little boy's intentions. To the older children breaking a dozen cups accidentally was not as reprehensible as breaking one cup with malice and forethought. This developmental shift represents a change from focus on appearances to focus on the meaning of an act (not unlike the shift that occurs in conservation tasks discussed in Chapter Five).

Kohlberg's Stages

Lawrence Kohlberg has greatly extended Piaget's early work on the development of moral judgment. The work of Piaget and Kohlberg is relevant to the study of cognitive development because both men are interested in the reasoning behind children's moral judgment. Neither is primarily concerned with resistance to temptation or other moral behavior per se.

Kohlberg (1971) conducted a study of the reasons people give to justify their answers to moral dilemmas. His conclusion was that a person must have attained a more advanced level of cognitive development—say, concrete operations—in order to engage in more advanced forms of moral reasoning. After discussing Kohlberg's stages of moral development, summarized in Table 7-2, we shall return to the relationship between moral judgment and moral behavior and between moral reasoning and general cognition.

Consider the following dilemma. Imagine that you wake up one morning to find yourself in a hospital bed, attached by tubes to another patient. A medical team informs you that the other patient is a famous violinist and that an extensive search has been conducted to find a compatible blood type and chemistry. It has been found that you are the only one who can save the life of the violinist. The two of you must remain attached to each other for nine months in order to give the violinist's body relief from the disease he suffers from. After nine months you may be disconnected, and both of you may resume your normal lives. What would you do? Would you ask to be disconnected, or would you sustain this other person's life for nine months? Here indeed is a dilemma. If you were asked for an answer in a Kohlberg-type interview, you would also be asked to explain the rationale for your decision. Since you have only two choices, your answer per se would not be very revealing. It is the reason behind your decision that makes your answer meaningful and indicates your level of moral maturity.

Assume that your answer to the above dilemma is "It would be wrong to disconnect the tubes, because the doctors know what they are doing." This answer falls somewhere within *conventional* morality (Stage 3 or 4). If your answer is, instead, "It was wrong for the doctors to perform the operation without my permission. But, even so, the life of another person is worth nine months of inconvenience for me," you are showing that you are at the *principled* level of moral development. Further questioning could help the interviewer decide whether you are closer to Stage 5 or to Stage 6. Comments like "Well, if I were in the same situation, I wouldn't want the donor to unplug my life!" might place you closer to Level 5. Questions like "What if it were a condemned criminal rather than a famous violinist?" would help distinguish a lower from a higher stage. And so would questions such as "What if he had to remain attached to me for five years?" If you change your decision on the basis of the specifics of who and how long, the interviewer would probably conclude that your morality is not principled.

What makes one stage more advanced than another? Kohlberg didn't base his definitions on age. If he had done so—that is, if he had treated the answers from older people as more advanced than those from younger people—he would have been caught in a circular argument: older

Table 7-2. Kohlberg's stages of moral development.

Preconventional level

At this level the child is responsive to cultural rules and labels of good and bad or right and wrong but interprets these labels in terms of the physical or hedonistic consequences of the action (punishment, reward, or exchange of favors) or in terms of the physical powers of those who enunciate the rules and labels. This level is divided into the following two stages.

Stage 1: Punishment and obedience orientation. The physical consequences of the action determine its goodness or badness, regardless of the human meaning or value of these consequences. Avoidance of punishment and unquestioning deference to power are values in their own right, not in terms of respect for an underlying moral order supported by punishment and authority (the latter being Stage 4).

Stage 2: Instrumental-relativist orientation. Right action consists of that which instrumentally satisfies one's own needs and occasionally the needs of others. Human relations are viewed in terms similar to those of the marketplace. Elements of fairness, reciprocity, and equal sharing are present, but they are always interpreted in a physical, pragmatic way. Reciprocity is a matter of "You scratch my back, and I'll scratch yours," not of loyalty, gratitude, or justice.

Conventional level

At this level maintaining the expectations of the individual's family, group or nation is perceived as valuable in its own right, regardless of immediate and obvious consequences. The attitude is not only one of conformity to personal expectations and social order but one of loyalty. The individual actively maintains, supports, and justifies the order and identifies with the persons or group involved in it. This level includes the following stages.

Stage 3: Interpersonal concordance, or "good-boy/nice-girl" orientation. Good behavior is that which pleases or helps others and is approved by them. There is much conformity to stereotypical images of what is majority, or "natural," behavior. The morality of behavior is frequently judged by its intention. "He means well" becomes important for the first time. One earns approval by being "nice."

Stage 4: "Law and order" orientation. The orientation is toward authority, fixed rules, and the maintenance of the social order. Right behavior consists of doing one's duty, showing respect for authority, and maintaining the given social order for its own sake.

Postconventional, autonomous, or principled level

At this level there is a clear effort to define moral values and principles that have validity and application apart from the authority of the groups or persons holding these principles and apart from the individual's own identification with these groups. This level consists of the following two stages.

Stage 5: Social-contract, legalistic orientation (generally with utilitarian overtones). Right action tends to be defined in terms of general individual rights and of standards that have been critically examined and agreed upon by the whole society. There is a clear awareness of the relativism of personal values and opinions and a corresponding emphasis on procedural rules for reaching consensus. Aside from what is constitutionally and democratically agreed upon, the right is a matter of personal values and opinions. The result is an emphasis on the "legal point of view," but with an awareness of the possibility of changing the law in terms of rational considerations of social utility (rather than freezing it in terms of the "law and order" of Stage 4). Outside the legal realm, free agreement and contract are the binding elements of obligation. This is the "official" morality of democratic government and the U. S. Constitution.

Table 7-2 continued

Stage 6: Orientation of universal ethical principles. Right is defined by the decision of conscience in accordance with self-chosen ethical principles appealing to logical comprehensiveness, universality, and consistency. These principles are abstract moral guidelines (such as the golden rule and the categorical imperative); they are not concrete moral rules like the Ten Commandments. At heart, these are universal principles of justice, of the reciprocity and equality of human rights, and of respect for the dignity of human beings as individual persons.

Adapted from "From Is to Ought: How to Commit the Naturalistic Fallacy and Get Away with It in the Study of Moral Development," by L. Kohlberg. In T. Mischel (Ed.), *Cognitive Development and Epistemology.* Copyright 1971 by Academic Press. Reprinted by permission.

people are more advanced in moral judgment because they are older! Instead, Kohlberg selected a general range of answers and then ordered them in a logical sequence. He started with certain fundamental principles of morality and decided, without looking at the ages of his subjects, what would be stages of increased complexity and increased evidence of social consciousness. For example, Kohlberg started with the premise that morality is fundamentally the respect for the dignity of the individual, the valuing of life over property, the conviction that the individual has a right to pursue happiness, and the belief in the equality of all persons.

These fundamental principles are themselves givens. For Kohlberg's purposes, it would have been inappropriate to state that, since older people seldom adhere to these principles, these principles cannot be the highest forms of morality. Remember, to break the circularity of the argument, Kohlberg needed to assess the level of each stage independently of age and actual frequency of occurrence. Once he had defined the essence of the highest form of morality, then it was a simple matter to define a sequence of stages that, in steps, approximate this highest form—from preconventional morality, to conventional morality, and then to the highest form of postconventional morality.

While we might grant that Kohlberg's sequence has a logical consistency and that each stage is *theoretically* easier to understand than each following stage, we must ask how his conception is related to the way people *actually* think. For example, Rest, Turiel, and Kohlberg (1969) found that adolescents were not able to paraphrase a moral statement based on reasoning beyond their own stage. In other words, they couldn't understand someone else's more advanced form of moral reasoning. In a related study, Rest, Cooper, Coder, Masonz, and Anderson (1974) found that, the more advanced the young adult is in age (high school, college, graduate school) and in general intelligence, the more advanced he or she is in moral reasoning. These studies indicate that the moral stages defined by Kohlberg are another example of general cognitive development. They are more than an arbitrary sequence of rules that people learn at various times in their lives.

This is a most important point. Moral development could be the rather straightforward result of imitating different peer groups at different times. Perhaps children learn to use preconventional moral reasoning when they are young because that is what they hear most often from slightly older siblings. Perhaps adolescents give conventional-morality answers after they enter college because that is what they read in history and political-science textbooks. Give the growing individual a different set of experiences, and, according to this view of social imitation, the sequence of moral stages will be correspondingly different. Kohlberg denies that moral development is a straightforward case of social learning. He argues against the social-learning theory on two grounds: (a) his stages are increasingly complex both logically and empirically, and (b) they are ordered in the same sequence, regardless of particular cultural experiences. With regard to the first point, there is no plausible reason why the child would be exposed only to, say, preconventional morality at a young age. It is more plausible that he or she is exposed to the entire range of moral judgments but cannot understand the higher forms.

With regard to the second point, some cross-cultural data support Kohlberg's assumption that these stages are not the straightforward results of particular cultural experiences (White, 1975). In places as widely different as Zambia, the United States, Japan, England, and Hong Kong, the stages were found to be invariant in their sequence (Grimley, 1974). Even though the subjects in this study came from a variety of cultural, religious, and economic traditions, they still passed through Kohlberg's stages in the same sequence, with differences only in the rate at which they made the passage. Since these studies across different cultures used a cross-sectional method of data collection, they should be regarded as preliminary support. More definitive support can come only from longitudinal data.

Moral Judgment and Moral Behavior

What is the relationship between knowing and doing? We all are familiar with statements such as "I knew I shouldn't, but I couldn't help myself," or "It was just too important not to cheat." Kohlberg asks us to consider the proposition that moral reasoning is a prerequisite of moral action. This doesn't mean that moral reasoning invariably leads to moral behavior, but it does mean that the morality of an act can be identified only in light of a person's reasons for engaging in the act. The police officer may save a drowning man either for fear of losing his job as a police officer or for holding human life sacred. That is, an act is not intrinsically noble or highly moral. Nor can the emotional reactions to an action be an index of the morality of that action. A trained assassin could feel guilty for missing his mark; a drunken driver could feel guilty for hitting a pedestrian. Morality is a matter of proper reasons, not just proper behavior.

There is some research evidence that people who engage in proper behavior have a matching level of moral judgment; that is, their understanding of morality influences them to act in certain ways. For example, Rubin and Schneider (1973) found that 7-year-olds who showed altruistic behavior scored higher on moral-judgment tasks than subjects who didn't behave altruistically. Haan, Smith, and Block (1968) found more Stage-5 and Stage-6 scores among Berkeley students protesting denial of personal rights than among students who did not protest. (Of course, some of the nonprotesters were also at Stages 5 and 6.) In summary, a sense of moral conscience more often than not leads to moral action, but not invariably so. Furthermore, some protesters were in the lower stages of conventional morality, indicating once again that action per se cannot be treated as intrinsically highly moral.

This last point seems to be borne out frequently in research. For example, Podd (1972) found that different college students had different reasons for refusing to administer electrical shock to a confederate. The students who scored at the preconventional level of moral judgment stopped "shocking" the confederate because "he is getting angry at me." The students who scored at the postconventional level of moral judgment stopped "shocking" the confederate because "I don't think he should endure more shock." Similar behavior can be justified on different grounds, some selfish and others principled.

But don't miss the point that there *is* a relationship between reasoning in paper-and-pencil tasks such as hearing moral dilemmas and reasoning in real-life situations such as administering shock to another human being. That is, the reasons we give for the action we would take in a hypothetical dilemma are the reasons we give when we actually face the dilemma. Kohlberg proposes that this is the most important relationship between judgment and action, since action alone cannot be treated as intrinsically highly moral. This is another way of saying that moral development is necessarily a case of general cognitive development, since morality is necessarily a case of knowing why one behaves in a particular way.

Regression in Moral Judgment

Is the course of moral development a continuous progression all the way to the elder years, when wisdom and tolerance abide? Perhaps we all secretly look toward our later years as a time when we have reconciled most of life's contradictions and understand the unity of a world order. There is some evidence that these wishes may be based on romantic stereotypes of the venerable elder—evidence, however, that can itself be challenged.

Bielby and Papalia (1975) found that moral reasoning peaks in middle age (30 to 49 years) and then declines significantly after age 50. The peak level is not so high itself—only around Stage 4, still at the conventional level of moral reasoning. The level of moral reasoning for those past 50 falls to the pragmatic reasons typical of Stages 2 and 3. Bielby and Papalia (1975) conclude that older adults treat moral dilemmas in a very personal manner, probably because, in their immense experience, they have had to face similar dilemmas. By taking such a personal and often egocentric stance toward moral dilemmas, they have difficulty abstracting the more general, broader principles of postconventional morality. We can guess that their answers might be attempts to justify their own past actions about which they feel defensive. The untested-in-life adolescent and young adult probably find it easier to give reasons that make appeal to ideals higher than personal concerns.

The "decline" that Bielby and Papalia (1975) identified in their cross-sectional data may, on the other hand, be a false "decline." That is, the 60-year-olds of today may have peaked in their middle years at a stage lower than that of the 30-year-olds of today. Here, too, we must point out that generational differences in moral judgment—for example, differences in the importance assigned to authority—may be the source of what mistakenly appears to be a "decline" in moral reasoning. There is no doubt that, for those who have lived through World War II, the concepts of authority, duty, and law and order play a greater role in influencing moral judgment than is true for postwar generations.

This means that, in evaluating data pointing at what may look like regression in the elderly's moral judgment, we must keep in mind the historical and social contexts of different generations that may deeply affect moral orientations. Keniston (1969), for example, proposes that the adolescents of today are more likely than their counterparts of the past to reach postconventional morality because of changes in the historical and social contexts in which they live. Such changes as the postponement of marriage and employment, the confrontation with alternative moral viewpoints, and the discovery of corruption in older people who hold to a conventional morality cause today's youth to search for a different form of morality. Past generations simply didn't have a chance to make a reflective study of conventional morality. Through marriage, employment, or service they had to buy into conventional morality at an early age, thereby foreclosing further analysis. Keniston (1969) concludes that there is a real regression between the ages of 16 and 20 but that this regression is temporary. As is true in many areas of development, periods of regression appear just before a jump to a higher and more integrated stage of development.

The dynamics of this temporary regression are interesting, albeit somewhat speculative. Apparently, as individuals at the conventional level become aware of postconventional principles, they reflect back on their own lower forms of reasoning and feel some shame or guilt. In an attempt to justify their currently held beliefs, they overcompensate. They regress to a preconventional morality as if judgments based on such morality were somehow more acceptable than those based on conventional morality (in which, they now realize, they don't fully believe). The frustration leads to a temporary regression, not unlike the regression of a parent who, after trying in vain to reason with a child, resorts in frustration to "Well, just because I say so" (preconventional level) when the child keeps questioning the reasons for a rule of conduct. These forms of regression are quite possibly an important source of moral development and, indeed, of development in general, as we saw in Chapter Five with regard to the use of conflict in conservation training (Inhelder, Sinclair, & Bovet, 1974).

Moral Education

If the social context influences moral reasoning, as Keniston (1969) proposes, it stands to reason that schools, too, have an influence on children's moral judgment. How does this influence occur? Perhaps you have read Benjamin Franklin's *Autobiography*, in which he describes how he became a virtuous man. Each week he took a different virtue, such as honesty or thrift, and practiced it to perfection. After the first week he took another virtue and concentrated on it, adding it to his already perfected first virtue. At the end of 12 weeks he was, by self-ordination, a perfectly virtuous man.

Traditionally, schools have taken an approach similar to Franklin's in teaching moral education. The unformed elementary school student is taught the virtues of honesty, thrift, and so on through examples, morality plays, and even spelling tests ("Spell the word *lazy* as in 'Herbie wasn't paid because he was lazy'"). Kohlberg (1970) calls this direct teaching of morals the "bag of virtues," or "Boy Scout," approach and disagrees with it for several reasons.

First, this approach assumes that the current virtues of the dominant class are worthy of being taught directly. Kohlberg (1970), instead, prefers to teach moral reasoning rather than particular virtues. Second, the "bag of virtues" approach encourages the child to fixate at the conventional stage of moral reasoning, since the virtues are accepted on the basis of the teacher's authority. Kohlberg prefers a method of conflict inducement in which the child's current stage of thinking is pitted against a slightly higher stage of thinking. The conflict between different levels gradually causes the child to differentiate moral principles from simple rules of conduct. The child comes to understand that there are exceptions to rules of conduct but there are no exceptions to moral principles. That is, at some point the child understands that the rule "Thou shalt not kill" allows for exceptions, while the principle "Thou shalt prevent injustice" does not.

By exposing children to filmstrips presenting a graded series of moral dilemmas, Kohlberg (1970) encourages his subjects to think through whether it is all right to steal a circus ticket, kill an animal, and other situations that require a moral decision. Children at Stage 2 of moral reasoning are challenged by questions that present Stage-3 alternatives; children at Stage-3, with Stage-4 alternatives; and so forth. The emphasis is always on the student's reasons for a certain action. This approach emphasizes Kohlberg's view that moral development is a cognitive process and not simply the process of shaping one's conduct toward virtuous action. It is this emphasis on cognition that represents the basic difference between Kohlberg and the Skinnerian proponents of programmed instruction and between Kohlberg and developmental theorists, such as Bijou and Baer, who see development as the increase of one's effectiveness in obtaining social rewards.

Clearly Kohlberg advocates the teaching of ideals—what he calls "real knowledge of the good" (Kohlberg, 1970). What is the ultimate possible level in Kohlberg's approach? Could there be a Stage 7, beyond that of postconventional morality? Kohlberg (1973) doesn't provide us with data but tells us what such a stage might be. If Stage 6 is an appeal to a universal humanistic perspective, Stage 7 is an appeal to a cosmic perspective. One cannot answer the fundamental question of why be moral by using Stage-6 thinking. Kohlberg points out that the ultimate answer to this question involves the even more basic question of why live and the parallel question of how to face death. These questions regarding the meaning of life are basically religious questions that transcend questions of justice alone. They cannot be answered—as rules of conduct can be proven—by their practical consequences (see Gibbs, 1977). Perhaps those individuals who willingly give their lives to affirm a principle in which they believe have reached a cosmic perspective and have identified with the purpose of the universe rather than with human justice alone. Kohlberg acknowledges that teaching these higher forms of consciousness is a very difficult task—a task that is certainly beyond our current educational practices.

Critique of Kohlberg

Kohlberg's critics call him to task on several major points. One is Kohlberg's assumption that his stages of moral reasoning transcend cultural boundaries—that they are universal. Another is his lack of emphasis on social learning. Are these legitimate criticisms?

At the 1976 meeting of the Northeastern Psychological Association, one of Kohlberg's critics pointed out that in India human life is not valued over property, since an individual's life is seen simply as a step in the reincarnation process while property exists but once. Therefore, an Indian may see the killing for property as not wrong (preconventional thinking in Kohlberg's system). Had Kohlberg taken the chance to reply to his critic, he might have said that even in this case the moral principal still holds. Justice would still be upheld, since the killing wouldn't actually be "terminal" in the belief system of the Hindu. Despite the hypothetical nature of both sides of this argument, the overarching point is that Kohlberg's view of justice can account for great cultural diversity.

The second criticism comes primarily from Alston (1971) and Peters (1974). Alston maintains that Kohlberg has overstated the role of thinking in moral development and downplayed the role of social learning and emotion. Peters' critique, instead, starts with the premise that we all have certain "passions": a passion for logical consistency, clarity, and order and an abhorrence of the arbitrary. These passions can be learned from one's culture, particularly Western culture. The broader implication here is that these passions, which are fundamental to Kohlberg's theory, may themselves be the arbitrary teachings of our culture.

Kohlberg, in line with Piaget, retorts that our abhorrence of inconsistency and arbitrariness is not learned. The development of our system of moral beliefs, when given the proper chance to become fully actualized, is like the development of any other living, fully integrated system. The rules of the system and those elements in it that create tension, such as inconsistency, are not learned from the social milieu. They are intrinsic to the system, or, as we stated in our discussions of Piaget, they are endogenous to the system. While it is definitely true that we are disturbed by the discovery of inconsistency, Kohlberg does not believe that this perturbation is learned. Our conclusion is simply that, even if Kohlberg is correct, his theory is almost impossible to prove.

Summary

Knowledge about ourselves and others as social beings often requires complex forms of thinking. This chapter has discussed the relationship between social knowledge and general cognition in three areas: self-knowledge, role taking, and moral judgment. Our discussion has relied in several places on Flavell's general model of social cognition. This model makes critical distinctions between knowing that some social phenomenon, like prejudice, exists; knowing that the phenomenon needs to be considered; knowing how to infer whether the phenomenon is true; and actually putting that inference to a reality test.

Two types of self-knowledge develop as general cognition changes. The manner in which we describe ourselves (self-knowledge) proceeds through definite stages, beginning with a rather superficial description and arriving at psychological statements about patterns of feelings and personality. Also, the attitudes we have about ourselves change across the life span (ego development). These attitudes about self are affected by general forms of cognition, and they themselves affect general forms of cognition. However, there is no assurance that, as we develop in intellectual competence, we necessarily acquire a more positive self-concept. Ego development, while related to general cognitive development, depends on other factors, such as social environment, as well. Therefore, any statement to the effect that older people are withdrawn or disengaged from their social environment needs to be qualified. In itself it says very little, since these characteristics don't necessarily mean that older people have a low self-concept. They may mean, instead, that the elderly are more self-confident than younger people and are therefore more selective in their choices of friends and social contacts.

The ability to take the role of another person changes as cognitive ability increases. Early forms of role taking can be found in the child's ability to figure out another person's line of sight. At this stage taking another person's point of view literally means knowing what someone else sees from a position that is different from our own. From early childhood onward, children make progress in understanding another person's point of view—that is, how another person may feel in a given situation. Such understanding begins with the simple knowledge that others have feelings that are different from our own and arrives at the complex knowledge that our own culture has attitudes that are different from those of other cultures.

Does social awareness regress to a narrower and more egocentric position as one gets old? Two points were made with regard to this question. (1) Even if the elderly appear less aware of views that are different from their own, this lack of awareness could be a matter of choice rather than a matter of reduced social competence. (2) The question points to the danger of stereotyping elderly people. Broad statements about "the elderly" are likely to be misleading, since older people are as diverse in their social awareness as are middle-aged adults.

With regard to the modification of role taking, the studies of Spivack and Shure and of Chandler indicate that, in children and adolescents, changes in the ability to understand other people's points of view bring about an improvement in social behavior. Thus the claim that good thinking leads to improved behavior has some preliminary support.

General cognitive development can also explain the development of moral judgment. Kohlberg has identified six stages of moral development, each requiring a general form of cognition that is more complex than that required at the preceding stage. Kohlberg's theory implies that a person needs more than exposure to a highly moral peer group in order to develop moral judgment. Thus, it also implies that children should be taught how to think about moral dilemmas rather than be taught moral principles. Kohlberg has been criticized for his reliance on levels of cognitive sophistication. Some feel that a person's stages of moral development are the simple products of changes in the social demands put on that person as he or she grows older. However, if cross-cultural research shows that Kohlberg's stages appear in the same order, regardless of differences in the social demands among the cultures under study, then the reliance on increasing cognitive sophistication will appear warranted. Some cross-cultural research already supports the invariance of Kohlberg's stages; but more research needs to be done.

Epilogue

We hope that you will close this book with the feeling that it has led you to some valuable general conclusions. To help you formulate such conclusions clearly and economically, we offer in this Epilogue a brief review of the major points we have covered at length in the course of our preceding discussions.

Thinking—or, to be more precise, cognition—is a complex process that we need to study in detail in order to understand ourselves and others. Whether we believe that cognition develops by steps or whether we believe that it develops by stages depends on how we define cognition itself. If we define cognition as a single set of basic operations that hold true across the life span, we will see cognitive development as a series of steps representing increasingly efficient, but not basically different, mental skills. If, instead, we define cognition as a series of basic operations that change across the life span, we will see cognitive development as a series of stages, each representing a complete reworking of the previous ones. Werner, Piaget, and, to a degree, Bruner treat cognitive development as a series of changes in basic mental operations. Gagné, Bijou and Baer, and, to some extent, Klahr and Wallace treat cognitive development as an increase in the efficient use of the cognitive processes available in early childhood.

The choice one makes between these alternative views has broad implications. Each of the preceding chapters reflects its importance and implications. In the chapter on information processes we asked how memory and attention change over the years. Do they improve, as Piaget suggests, because of the general methods we use to remember and attend change? Or do they remain essentially the same, because the methods we use do not change, and simply get more efficient, like a well-exercised muscle? (You no doubt noted our bias for the first alternative.) Flavell's work suggests that a great deal of reasoning is involved in most memory tasks. Therefore, the stages by which memory improves should parallel those by which reasoning in general improves. The same can be said for attention.

In the chapter on logical operations the distinction between steps and stages was most emphatic. The concrete operations of classification and seriation are qualitatively different from the exclusively verbal logic of proportionality and correlation in the stage of formal operations. Preoperational children's dependence on spatial whole/part relations—a form of graphic representation—makes classification problems difficult for them. Once the concrete-operational child can use verbal representations (albeit representations of tangible objects only), he or she can solve problems of class inclusion. This is a new and higher level of consciousness and is, in turn, followed by the still higher level of formal operations, in which verbal representations can stand for other verbal representations.

Certain changes within stages are better described as steplike changes. Some studies report that children become more efficient, as time goes on, in figuring out what a set of task instructions means, what they should attend to, and what they should deliberately commit to memory for later use. In fact, the decline of performance in old age is probably best understood as a temporary loss of test-taking skills. In most cases such decline is not due to regression to a previous stage; rather, it is the outcome of the person's having forgotten how to use information efficiently or being unable to tell which piece of information is relevant to the task at hand. Usually a refresher course on the type of task in question or a modification in the content of the task results in a marked improvement in the older person's test performance.

The distinction between development by steps and development by stages was emphasized again in the chapter on space and causality. Spatial concepts develop as a result of achieving higher levels of consciousness— from seeing shapes to finding hidden objects and to drawing and describing spatial relations. To say that spatial concepts develop by steps implies a very narrow view of cognitive development. It is the very way of thinking about space that changes, not just the technical capacity to draw with greater skill. The same comments can be made with regard to causality. What changes is the way of thinking about causality. At first causality is a simple pairing of movements. Then come the awareness that some causal relationships cannot be physically observed in overt movement and the realization that causality must be inferred from those elements that we hold inviolate about physical objects. It is meaningless to say that the adolescent's ability to draw a deductive inference is just a step up from the young child's close observation of physical events. The change from observing to knowing is a stage advance, not a steplike progression.

The chapter on social cognition, too, emphasized the stage view of development. Changes in the areas of self-knowledge, role taking, and moral development indicate that the child has reached a new level of consciousness and is capable of new mental operations that make it possible to rework and reorganize all that he or she knew before. The insights about the self spring from a new ability to see patterns across diverse experiences and to infer one's own hidden motives that cannot be directly known. We grow to understand ourselves not just by remembering an ever-increasing number of facts about our personal life but also by using different cognitive operations to deal with those facts. The same is true of our growth in understanding other people's points of view and in deciding what constitutes a moral act.

Since so few theories and so few research projects deal with stage changes beyond early adulthood, how can a text on cognitive development across the life span rely so heavily on stage theory? The answer is quite simple. Texts attempting to cover cognitive development over the life span are premature. There simply aren't enough data. We have given you in this book what there is to give. The paucity of literature for the middle years— that is, the hiatus between accounts of development up to early adulthood and accounts of development beyond late adulthood—reflects the current state of the field. A comprehensive, birth-to-death theory of cognitive development may emerge as the result of one of two things—or both. Theorists like Bijou, Baer, Klahr, and Wallace may undertake to write a comprehensive step theory of quantitative changes across the life span. Alternatively, researchers following the models of Werner and Piaget may continue to probe further for stage changes beyond early adulthood (such as those that seem to characterize the metaformal operational stage). Both of these endeavors would have their weaknesses. One would be too cumbersome, too specific, and perhaps boring. The other would be forced, true only for a few individuals, and therefore of limited usefulness.

Of course, both of these "alternatives" may occur, perhaps even at the same time. But it is more likely that a third alternative will develop. Those interested in the step-by-step approach will apply their methods of research to fill in the apparent gaps between stages. These research projects should give us more information about how an individual makes the transition from one stage to the next. Once these growth processes are understood better, we won't need to define development solely in terms of stage characteristics such as concrete operations or formal operations. And once the psychologists know what individuals do to improve the quality of their lives, they will be in a better position to help those who run amok—be they young children, adolescents, young adults, middle-aged people, or old men and women. They will be in a better position, we might add, so long as people who provide human services ask themselves "How conscious am I of the reasoning I use to draw conclusions about what this person needs?"

References

Alschuler, A., & Weinstein, G. *Self-knowledge development.* Unpublished manuscript, School of Education, University of Massachusetts, Amherst, 1976.

Alston, W. P. Comments on Kohlberg's "From is to ought." In T. Mischel (Ed.), *Cognitive development and epistemology.* New York: Academic Press, 1971.

Altemeyer, R. A., Fulton, D., & Berney, K. M. Long-term memory improvement: Confirmation of a finding by Piaget. *Child Development,* 1969, *40,* 845–857.

Anders, T. R., & Fozard, J. L. Effects of age upon retrieval from primary and secondary memory. *Developmental Psychology,* 1973, *9,* 411–416.

Appel, L. F., Cooper, R. G., McCarrell, B., Sims-Knight, J., Yussen, S. R., & Flavell, J. H. The development of the distinction between perceiving and memorizing. *Child Development,* 1972, *43,* 1365–1381.

Arenberg, D. Concept problem solving in young and old adults. *Journal of Gerontology,* 1968, *23,* 279–282.

Arenberg, D. Cognition and aging: Verbal learning, memory, and problem solving. In C. Eisdorfer & M. P. Lawton (Eds.), *The psychology of adult development and aging.* Washington, D. C.: American Psychological Association, 1973.

Arlin, P. K. Cognitive development: A fifth stage? *Developmental Psychology,* 1975, *2,* 602–606.

Baldwin, A. L. *Theories of child development.* New York: Wiley, 1967.

Ball, W., & Tronick, E. Infant responses to impending collision: Optical and real. *Science,* 1971, *171,* 818–820.

Baltes, P. B., & Schaie, K. W. The myth of the twilight years. *Psychology Today,* 1974, *7,* 35–40.

Baltes, P. B., & Schaie, K. W. On the plasticity of intelligence in adulthood and old age. *American Psychologist,* 1976, *31,* 720–725.

Basowitz, H., & Korchin, S. J. Age differences in the perception of closure. *Journal of Abnormal and Social Psychology,* 1957, *54,* 93–97.

Bearison, D. J. Role of measurement operations in the acquisition of conservation. *Developmental Psychology,* 1969, *1,* 653–660.

Beck, A. T. *Cognitive therapy and the emotional disorders.* New York: International Universities Press, 1976.

Beilin, H. Learning and operational convergence in logical thought development. *Journal of Experimental Child Psychology,* 1965, *2,* 317–339.

Bell, C. R. Additional data on animistic thinking. *Scientific Monthly*, 1954, *79*, 67–69.

Belmont, J. Perceptual short-term memory in children, retardates, and adults. *Journal of Experimental Child Psychology*, 1967, *5*, 114–122.

Belmont, J. Relations of age and intelligence to short-term color memory. *Child Development*, 1973, *43*, 19–29.

Belmont, J., & Butterfield, E. *Tailoring rehearsal to meet recall requirements: Some developmental observations.* Paper presented at the biennial convention of the Society for Research in Child Development, Minneapolis, 1971.

Berndt, T. J., & Wood, D. J. The development of time concepts through conflict based on a primitive duration capacity. *Child Development*, 1974, *45*, 825–828.

Bertalanffy, L., von. *General systems theory.* New York: Braziller, 1968.

Bielby, D. D. V., & Papalia, D. E. Moral development and perceptual role-taking egocentrism: Their development and interrelationship across the life span. *International Journal of Aging and Human Development*, 1975, *6*(4), 293–308.

Bijou, S. W. Development in the preschool years: A functional analysis. *American Psychologist*, 1975, *30*, 829–837.

Bijou, S. W., & Baer, D. M. *Child development. Volume 1: A systematic and empirical theory.* New York: Appleton-Century-Crofts, 1961.

Bijou, S. W., & Baer, D. M. *Child development. Volume 2: The universal stage of infancy.* New York: Appleton-Century-Crofts, 1965.

Billow, R. M. A cognitive-developmental study of metaphor comprehension. *Developmental Psychology*, 1975, *11*(4), 415–423.

Birren, J. E. *Handbook of aging and the individual: Psychological and biological aspects.* Chicago: University of Chicago Press, 1959.

Botwinick, J., & Storandt, M. *Memory, related functions and age.* Springfield, Ill.: Charles C Thomas, 1974.

Bourne, L. E., Jr. *Human conceptual behavior.* Boston: Allyn & Bacon, 1966.

Bovet, M. Piaget's theory of cognitive development and individual differences. In B. Inhelder & H. H. Chipman (Eds.), *Piaget and his school: A reader in developmental psychology.* New York: Springer-Verlag, 1976.

Bower, T. G. R. Discrimination of depth in premotor infants. *Psychonomic Science*, 1964, *1*, 368.

Bower, T. G. R. *Development in infancy.* San Francisco: W. H. Freeman, 1974.

Brainerd, C. J. The long-term memory improvement effect: Memory improvement or concept development? In J. M. Scandura, J. H. Durnin, & W. H. Wulfeck II (Eds.), *Proceedings of the Fifth Annual Interdisciplinary Conference on Structural Learning*, Philadelphia, 1974. (a)

Brainerd, C. J. Training and transfer of transitivity, conservation, and class inclusion of length. *Child Development*, 1974, *45*, 324–334. (b)

Brainerd, C. J., & Allen, T. W. Experimental inductions of the conservation of "first-order" quantitative invariants. *Psychological Bulletin*, 1971, *75*, 128–144.

Broadbent, D. E., & Heron, A. Effects of a subsidiary task on performance involving immediate memory by younger and older men. *British Journal of Psychology*, 1962, *53*, 189–198.

Bronfenbrenner, U. Toward an experimental ecology of human behavior. *American Psychologist*, 1977, *32*(7), 513–531.

Brown, G., & Muller, D. Studies in the construction of formal operational structures. In S. Modgil & C. Modgil (Eds.), *Piagetian research: Compilation and commentary* (Vol. 3). Windsor, U.K.: NFER Publishing Company, 1976.

Bruner, J. S. *Processes of cognitive growth: Infancy* (Vol. 3, Heinz Werner Lecture Series). Worcester, Mass.: Clark University Press with Barre Publishers, 1969.

Bruner, J. S. *Beyond the information given* (J. M. Anglin, Ed.). New York: Norton, 1973.

Bruner, J. S., Olver, R. R., & Greenfield, P. M. *Studies in cognitive growth.* New York: Wiley, 1966.

Bryant, P. *Perception and understanding in young children: An experimental approach.* New York: Basic Books, 1974.

Bryant, P., & Trabasso, T. Transitive inferences and memory in young children. *Nature,* 1971, *232,* 456–458.

Buck-Morss, S. Socio-economic bias in Piaget's theory and its implications for cross-cultural studies. *Human Development,* 1975, *18,* 35–49.

Cameron, P. Which generation is believed to be intellectually superior and which generation believes itself intellectually superior. *International Journal of Aging and Human Development,* 1973, *4,* 257–270.

Canestrari, R. E., Jr. Paced and self-paced learning in young and elderly adults. *Journal of Gerontology,* 1963, *18,* 165–168.

Chandler, M. J. Egocentrism and antisocial behavior: The assessment and training of social perspective-taking skills. *Developmental Psychology,* 1973, *9,* 326–332.

Chiapetta, E. A review of Piagetian studies relevant to science instruction at the secondary and college level. *Science Education,* 1976, *60,* 253–261.

Chiseri, M. Amenability to incorrect hypotheses in the extinction of conservation of weight in college students. *Merrill-Palmer Quarterly,* 1975, *21,* 139–143.

Clark, H. H. Space, time, semantics, and the child. In T. E. Moore (Ed.), *Cognitive development and the acquisition of language.* New York: Academic Press, 1973.

Cohen, G. Hemispheric differences in serial versus parallel learning. *Journal of Experimental Psychology,* 1973, *97,* 349–356.

Cole, F., Frankel, F., & Sharp, D. Development of free-recall learning in children. *Developmental Psychology,* 1971, *4,* 109–123.

Comalli, P. E., Jr. Life-span changes in visual perception. In L. R. Goulet & P. B. Baltes (Eds.), *Life-span developmental psychology: Research and theory.* New York: Academic Press, 1970.

Comalli, P. E., Jr., Wapner, S., & Werner, H. Perception of verticality in middle and old age. *Journal of Psychology,* 1959, *47,* 259–266.

Connolly, K., & Bruner, J. S. (Eds.). *The growth of competence.* New York: Academic Press, 1974.

Corsini, D. A., & Berg, A. J. Intertask correspondence in the five to seven shift: Transposition, cue interference and spatial memory. *Child Development,* 1973, *44,* 467–475.

Crannell, C. N. Responses of college students to a questionnaire on animistic thinking. *Scientific Monthly,* 1954, *78,* 54–56.

Crowell, D. H., & Dole, A. A. Animism and college students. *Journal of Educational Research,* 1957, *50,* 391–395.

Denner, B., & Cashden, S. Sensory processing and the recognition of form in nursery school children. *British Journal of Psychology,* 1967, *58,* 101–104.

Denney, N. Classification abilities in the elderly. *Journal of Gerontology,* 1974, *29,* 309–314.

Denney, N., & Denney, D. Modeling effects on the questioning strategies of the elderly. *Developmental Psychology,* 1974, *10,* 458.

Dennis, W. Creative productivity between the ages of 20 and 80 years. In B. Neugarten (Ed.), *Middle age and aging.* Chicago: University of Chicago Press, 1968.

Dennis, W., & Mallinger, B. Animism and related tendencies in senescence. *Journal of Gerontology,* 1949, *4,* 218–221.

De Vries, R. Constancy of generic identity in the years three to six. *Monographs of the Society for Research in Child Development,* 1969, *34* (3, Serial No. 127).

Dewey, J. *Democracy and education.* New York: Macmillan, 1916.

Edwards, P. (Ed.). *The encyclopedia of philosophy* (Vol. 3). New York: Macmillan, 1967, pp. 305–324.

Eisdorfer, C. Verbal learning and response time in the aged. *Journal of Genetic Psychology,* 1965, *107,* 15–22.

Elkind, D. *Child development and education: A Piagetian perspective.* New York: Oxford University Press, 1976.

Ellis, A. *Growth through reason: Verbatim cases in rational-emotive psychotherapy.* Palo Alto: Science and Behavior Books, 1971.

Erikson, E. H. *Childhood and society* (2nd ed.). New York: Norton, 1963.

Fakouri, M. Cognitive development in adulthood: A fifth stage? *Developmental Psychology,* 1976, *12,* 472.

Fantz, R. L. The origin of form perception. *Scientific American,* 1961, *204,* 66–72.

Field, D. Long-term effects of conservation training with ESN children. *Journal of Special Education,* 1974, *8*(3), 237–245.

Fillmore, C. J. Types of lexical information. In D. D. Steinberg & L. R. Jakobovitz (Eds.), *Semantics: An interdisciplinary reader in philosophy, linguistics, and psychology.* Cambridge, U.K.: Cambridge University Press, 1971.

Flavell, J. H. *The developmental psychology of Jean Piaget.* Princeton, N. J.: Van Nostrand, 1963.

Flavell, J. H. Developmental studies of mediated memory. In H. W. Reese & L. P. Lipsitt (Eds.), *Advances in child development and behavior* (Vol. 5). New York: Academic Press, 1970.

Flavell, J. H. The development of inferences about others. In T. Mischel (Ed.), *Understanding other persons.* Oxford, U. K.: Blackwell & Mott, 1974.

Flavell, J. H. *Cognitive development.* Englewood Cliffs, N. J.: Prentice-Hall, 1977.

Flavell, J. H., Beach, D. H., & Chinsky, J. M. Spontaneous verbal rehearsal in a memory task as a function of age. *Child Development,* 1966, *37,* 283–299.

Flavell, J. H., Botkin, P. T., Fry, C. L., Wright, J. W., & Jarvis, P. E. *The development of role-taking and communication skills in children.* New York: Wiley, 1968.

Forman, G. E. On the components of spatial representation. In J. Eliot & N. J. Salkind (Eds.), *Children's spatial development.* Springfield, Ill.: Charles C Thomas, 1975.

Forman, G. E., & Kuschner, D. S. *The child's construction of knowledge: Piaget for teaching children.* Monterey, Calif.: Brooks/Cole, 1977.

Forman, G. E., Kuschner, D. S., & Dempsey, J. Visual decentration: From stereometric points to planeometric forms. *Perceptual and Motor Skills,* 1975, *41,* 343–352. (a)

Forman, G. E., Kuschner, D. S., & Dempsey, J. *Transformations in the manipulations and productions performed with geometric objects: An early system of logic in young children* (Final report). Washington, D. C.: National Institute of Education, 1975. (Grant NE-G-00-3-0051) (b)

Forman, G. E., Laughlin, F., & Sweeney, M. The development of jigsaw-puzzle solving in preschool children: An information-processing approach. *DARCEE Papers and Reports* (Kennedy Center for Research, George Peabody College for Teachers), 1971, *5*(Whole No. 8).

Fuller, R. B. *Synergetics: Explorations in the geometry of thinking.* New York: Macmillan, 1975.

Furth, H. G. *Piaget and knowledge: Theoretical foundations.* Englewood Cliffs, N. J.: Prentice-Hall, 1972.

Furth, H., Milgram, N. A. Labeling and grouping effects in the recall of pictures by children. *Child Development,* 1973, *44,* 511–518.

Gagné, R. M. Contributions of learning to human development. *Psychological Review,* 1968, *75*(3), 177–190.

Gagné, R. M. *The conditions of learning* (2nd ed.). New York: Holt, Rinehart & Winston, 1970.

Garber, E., Simmons, H., & Robinson, P. *The effect of task parameters on surface conservation in the elderly.* Unpublished manuscript, Cornell University, 1974.

Gardner, M. *The ambidextrous universe: Left, right, and the fall of parity.* New York: Basic Books, 1969.

Gelman, R. Conservation acquisition: A problem of learning to attend to relevant attributes. *Journal of Experimental Child Psychology,* 1969, *7,* 167–187.

Gibbs, J. Kohlberg's stages of moral judgment: A constructive critique. *Harvard Educational Review,* 1977, *47,* 43–61.

Ginsburg, H., & Koslowski, B. Cognitive development. *Annual Review of Psychology,* 1976, *27,* 29–61.

Ginsburg, H., & Opper, S. *Piaget's theory of intellectual development: An introduction.* Englewood Cliffs, N. J.: Prentice-Hall, 1969.

Giora, Z. *Psychopathology: A cognitive view.* New York: Gardner Press, 1975.

Girgus, J. S., & Hochberg, J. Age differences in sequential form recognition. *Psychonomic Science,* 1970, *21,* 211–212.

Glasser, W. *Reality therapy: A new approach to psychiatry.* New York: Harper & Row, 1965.

Gödel, K. Consistency of the continuum hypothesis. *Annals of Mathematical Studies* (No. 3). Princeton, N. J.: Princeton University Press, 1940.

Gollin, E. S., Moody, M., & Schadler, M. Relational learning of a size concept. *Developmental Psychology,* 1974, *10*(1), 101–107.

Goulet, L. R. The interface of acquisition: Models and methods for studying the active, developing organism. In J. R. Nesselroade & H. W. Reese (Eds.), *Life-span developmental psychology: Methodological issues.* New York: Academic Press, 1973.

Gratch, G. Recent studies based on Piaget's view of object concept development. In L. B. Cohen & P. Salapatek (Eds.), *Infant perception: From sensation to cognition.* New York: Academic Press, 1975.

Greenfield, P. M., & Schneider, L. Building a tree structure: The development of hierarchical complexity and interrupted strategies in children's construction activity. *Developmental Psychology,* 1977, *13,* 229–313.

Grimley, L. K. A cross-cultural study of moral development. *Dissertation Abstracts International,* 1974, *34*(7), 3613A–4477A (3988A).

Haan, N., Smith, M. B., & Block, J. Moral reasoning of young adults: Political-social behaviour, family background, and personality correlates. *Journal of Personality and Social Psychology,* 1968, *10*(3), 183–201.

Halford, G. S., & Fullerton, T. J. A discrimination task which induces conservation of number. *Child Development,* 1970, *41,* 205–213.

Harris, D. B. Problems in formulating a scientific concept of development. In D. B. Harris (Ed.), *The concept of development.* Minneapolis: University of Minnesota Press, 1957.

Havighurst, R. J., Neugarten, B. L., & Tobin, S. S. Disengagement and patterns of aging. In B. L. Neugarten (Ed.), *Middle age and aging.* Chicago: University of Chicago Press, 1968.

Henry, W. E. Engagement and disengagement: Toward a theory of adult development. In R. Kastenbaum (Ed.), *Psychobiology of aging.* New York: Springer, 1965.

Heron, A. Immediate memory in dealing with and without simple rehearsal. *Quarterly Journal of Experimental Psychology*, 1962, *14*, 94–103.

Hilgard, E. R., & Bower, G. H. *Theories of learning* (4th ed.). New York: Appleton-Century-Crofts, 1974.

Hill, S. A. A study of the logical abilities of children (Doctoral dissertation, Stanford University, 1961). *Dissertation Abstracts*, 1961, *21*, 3359. (University Microfilms No. 61-1229)

Hooper, R., & Sheehan, N. Logical concept attainment during aging years: Issues in the neoPiagetian research literature. In W. Overton, H. Furth, & J. Gallage (Eds.), *Yearbook of developmental epistemology* (Vol. 1). New York: Plenum, 1976.

Horn, J. L. Organization of abilities and the development of intelligence. *Psychological Review*, 1968, *75*, 242–259.

Horn, J. L. Organization of data on life-span development of human abilities. In L. R. Goulet & P. B. Baltes (Eds.), *Life-span developmental psychology: Research and theory* (Vol. 1). New York: Academic Press, 1970.

Hornblum, J., & Overton, W. *Area and volume conservation among the elderly: Assessment and training.* Paper presented at the biennial meeting of the Society for Research in Child Development, Denver, 1975.

Hulicka, I. M., & Weiss, R. L. Age difference in retention as a function of learning. *Journal of Consulting Psychology*, 1965, *29*, 120–129.

Hultsch, D. Learning to learn in adulthood. *Journal of Gerontology*, 1974, *29*, 302–308.

Inhelder, B., & Piaget, J. *The growth of logical thinking from childhood to adolescence.* London: Routledge & Kegan Paul, 1958.

Inhelder, B., & Piaget, J. *The early growth of logic in the child.* New York: Norton, 1964.

Inhelder, B., Sinclair, H., & Bovet, M. *Learning and the development of cognition.* Cambridge, Mass.: Harvard University Press, 1974.

Jackson, J. P. Development of visual and tactual processing of sequentially presented shapes. *Developmental Psychology*, 1973, *8*, 46–50.

James, W. *Talks to teachers on psychology.* New York: Holt, 1899.

Kagan, J. Impulsive and reflective child: Significance of conceptual tempo. In J. D. Krumboltz (Ed.), *Learning and the educational process.* Chicago: Rand-McNally, 1965.

Kagan, J., & Lewis, M. Studies of attention in the human infant. *Merrill-Palmer Quarterly*, 1965, *11*, 95–127.

Kalish, R. A. *Late adulthood: Perspectives on human development.* Monterey, Calif.: Brooks/Cole, 1975.

Kamin, L. J. Differential changes in mental abilities in old age. *Journal of Gerontology*, 1957, *12*, 66–70.

Kaplan, A. *The conduct of inquiry: Methodology for behavioral science.* San Francisco: Chandler, 1964.

Keeney, T. J., Cannizzo, S. R., & Flavell, J. H. Spontaneous and induced verbal rehearsal in a recall task. *Child Development*, 1967, *38*, 953–966.

Kendler, T. S., & Kendler, H. H. Reversal and nonreversal shifts in kindergarten children. *Journal of Experimental Psychology*, 1959, *58*, 56–60.

Keniston, K. Moral development, youthful activism and modern society. *Youth and Society*, 1969, *1*, 110–127.

Kennedy, J. M. A preliminary proposal about a Piagetian stage that might follow the formal operations stage. In J. M. Scandura, J. H. Durnin, & W. H. Wulfeck II (Eds.), *Proceedings of the Fifth Annual Interdisciplinary Conference on Structural Learning*, Philadelphia, 1974.

Kingsley, R. C., & Hall, V. C. Training conservation through the use of learning sets. *Child Development,* 1967, *38,* 1111–1126.

Kinsbourne, M. Age effects on letter span related to rate and sequential dependency. *Journal of Gerontology,* 1973, *28,* 317–319.

Klahr, D., & Wallace, J. G. *Cognitive development: An information-processing view.* Hillsdale, N. J.: Erlbaum, 1976.

Klein, R., & Birren, J. Age, perceived self-competence and conformity: A partial explanation. *Proceedings of the 81st Annual Convention of the American Psychological Association,* 1973, *8,* 778–779.

Knowles, M. S. *The modern practice of adult education.* New York: Association Press, 1976.

Kobasigawa, A. Utilization of retrieval cues by children in recall. *Child Development,* 1974, *45,* 127–134.

Koestler, A. *The ghost in the machine.* New York: Macmillan, 1967.

Kohlberg, L. Moral development and identification. In H. Stevenson (Ed.), *Child psychology: 62nd yearbook of the National Society for the Study of Education.* Chicago: University of Chicago Press, 1963.

Kohlberg, L. Stage and sequence: The cognitive-developmental approach to socialization. In D. Goslind (Ed.), *Handbook of socialization: Theory and research.* New York: Rand-McNally, 1969.

Kohlberg, L. Education for justice: A modern statement of the Platonic view. In N. F. Sizer & T. R. Sizer (Eds.), *Moral education: Five lectures.* Cambridge, Mass.: Harvard University Press, 1970.

Kohlberg, L. From is to ought: How to commit the naturalistic fallacy and get away with it in the study of moral development. In T. Mischel (Ed.), *Cognitive development and epistemology.* New York: Academic Press, 1971.

Kohlberg, L. Continuities in childhood and adult moral development revisited. In P. B. Baltes & K. W. Schaie (Eds.), *Life-span developmental psychology: Personality and socialization.* New York: Academic Press, 1973.

Kohnstamm, G. A. *Teaching children to solve a Piagetian problem of class inclusion.* Uitgeverij, Netherlands: Mouton, 1967.

Langer, J. Werner's comparative organismic theory. In P. H. Mussen (Ed.), *Carmichael's manual of child psychology* (3rd ed., Vol. 1). New York: Wiley, 1970.

Langford, P. E. The development of the concept of development. In S. Modgil & C. Modgil (Eds.), *Piagetian research: Compilation and commentary* (Vol. 3). Windsor, U. K.: NFER Publishing Company, 1976.

Laurendeau, M., & Pinard, A. *The development of the concept of space in the child.* New York: International Universities Press, 1970.

Levy, J. Possible basis for the evolution of lateral specialization of the human brain. *Nature,* 1972, *224,* 614–615.

Levy, J., Trevarthen, C., & Sperry, R. W. Perception of bilateral chimeric figures following hemispheric deconnexion. *Brain,* 1972, *95,* 61–78.

Lipsitt, L. P. Learning processes of newborns. *Merrill-Palmer Quarterly,* 1966, *12,* 45–71.

Livesley, W. J., & Bromley, D. B. *Person perception in childhood and adolescence.* London: Wiley, 1973.

Longobardi, E. T., & Wolff, P. A comparison of motoric and verbal responses on a Piagetian rate-time task. *Child Development,* 1973, *44,* 433–437.

Looft, W. R., & Bartz, W. H. Animism revived. *Psychological Bulletin,* 1969, *71,* 1–19.

Looft, W. R., & Charles, D. C. Egocentrism and social interaction in young and old adults. *Aging and Human Development,* 1971, *2,* 21–28.

Lovell, K., & Ogilvie, E. A study of the conservation of substance in the junior school child. *British Journal of Educational Psychology*, 1960, *30*, 109–118.

Lovell, K., & Ogilvie, E. A study of the conservation of weight in the junior school child. *British Journal of Educational Psychology*, 1961, *31*, 138–144.

Lowe, G., Ranyard, R. H., & McDonald, J. Children's estimates of proportion: Developmental and cognitive factors. In S. Modgil & C. Modgil (Eds.), *Piagetian research: Compilation and commentary* (Vol. 3). Windsor, U. K.: NFER Publishing Company, 1976.

Lowrie, D. E. Additional data on animistic thinking. *Scientific Monthly*, 1954, *79*, 69–70.

Luria, A. R. *Cognitive development: Its cultural and social foundations*. Cambridge, Mass.: Harvard University Press, 1976.

Maddox, G. L. Activity and morale: A longitudinal study of selected elderly subjects. *Social Forces*, 1963, *42*, 195–204.

Markman, E. The facilitation of part-whole comparisons by use of the collective noun "family." *Child Development*, 1973, *44*, 837–840.

Marmor, G. S. Mental rotation and number conservation: Are they related? *Developmental Psychology*, 1977, *13*, 320–325.

Maslow, A. H. *Toward a psychology of being* (2nd ed.). New York: Van Nostrand, 1968.

McKinnon, J. Earth science, density, and the college freshman. *Journal of Geological Education*, 1971, *19*, 218–220.

McLuhan, M. *Understanding media: The extensions of man*. Toronto: McGraw-Hill, 1964.

Melton, A. W. Implications of short-term memory for a general theory of memory. *Journal of Verbal Learning and Verbal Behavior*, 1963, *2*, 1–21.

Modgil, S., & Modgil, C. (Eds.). *Piagetian research: Compilation and commentary*. Windsor, U. K.: NFER Publishing Company, 1976.

Mosher, F. A., & Hornsby, J. R. On asking questions. In J. S. Bruner, R. R. Olver, & P. M. Greenfield (Eds.), *Studies in cognitive growth*. New York: Wiley, 1966.

Munsinger, H. Light detection and pattern recognition. In L. R. Goulet & P. B. Baltes (Eds.), *Life-span developmental psychology: Research and theory*. New York: Academic Press, 1970.

Murphy, L. B. *The widening world of childhood*. New York: Basic Books, 1962.

Murray, F. B. Cognitive conflict and reversibility training in the acquisition of length conservation. *Journal of Educational Psychology*, 1968, *59*(2), 82–87.

Murray, F. B. Acquisition of conservation through social participation. *Developmental Psychology*, 1972, *6*, 1–6.

Nagel, E. Determinism and development. In D. B. Harris (Ed.), *The concept of development*. Minneapolis: University of Minnesota Press, 1957.

Neimark, E. Intellectual development during adolescence. In F. D. Horowitz (Ed.), *Review of child development research*. Chicago: University of Chicago Press, 1975.

Neugarten, B. L. The awareness of middle age. In B. L. Neugarten (Ed.), *Middle age and aging*. Chicago: University of Chicago Press, 1968.

Neugarten, B. L. Personality and the aging process. *The Gerontologist*, 1972, *12*, 9–15.

Neugarten, B. L., Moore, J. W., & Lowe, J. C. Age norms, age constraints, and adult socialization. In B. L. Neugarten (Ed.), *Middle age and aging*. Chicago: University of Chicago Press, 1968.

Nolen, P. Acquisition of logical codes: Forms, content and language. In S. Modgil & C. Modgil (Eds.), *Piagetian research: Compilation and commentary* (Vol. 3). Windsor, U. K.: NFER Publishing Company, 1976.

Norcross, K. J., & Spiker, C. C. Effects of mediated association on transfer in paired-associate learning. *Journal of Experimental Psychology*, 1958, *55*, 129–134.

O'Brien, T. C. Deformation and the four-card problem. *Educational Studies in Mathematics*, 1975, *6*, 23–29.

O'Brien, T. C., Shapiro, B. J., & Reali, N. C. Logical thinking: Language and context. *Educational Studies in Mathematics*, 1971, *4*, 201–219.

Olson, D. R. On the relations between spatial and linguistic process. In J. Eliot & N. J. Salkind (Eds.), *Children's spatial development*. Springfield, Ill.: Charles C Thomas, 1975.

Overton, W., & Reese, H. Models of development: Methodological implications. In J. R. Nesselroade & H. Reese (Eds.), *Life-span developmental psychology: Methodological issues*. New York: Academic Press, 1973.

Papalia, D. E. The status of several conservation abilities across the life-span. *Human Development*, 1972, *15*, 229–243.

Papalia, D. E., & Bielby, D. D. V. Cognitive functioning in middle and old-age adults: A review of research based on Piaget's theory. *Human Development*, 1975, *18*, 424–443.

Peevers, B., & Secord, P. Developmental changes in attribution of descriptive concepts to persons. *Journal of Personality and Social Psychology*, 1973, *27*, 120–128.

Peill, E. J. *Invention and discovery of reality*. New York: Wiley, 1975.

Peters, R. S. *Psychology and ethical development*. London: Allen & Unwin, 1974.

Piaget, J. *The child's conception of number*. London: Routledge & Kegan Paul, 1952. (a)

Piaget, J. *The origins of intelligence in children*. New York: International University Press, 1952. (b)

Piaget, J. *The construction of reality in the child*. New York: Basic Books, 1954.

Piaget, J. *The moral judgment of the child*. New York: Free Press, 1965.

Piaget, J. *Six psychological studies*. New York: Vintage Books, 1967.

Piaget, J. *The mechanism of perception*. New York: Basic Books, 1969.

Piaget, J. Piaget's theory. In P. H. Mussen (Ed.), *Carmichael's manual of child psychology* (3rd ed., Vol. 1). New York: Wiley, 1970.

Piaget, J. *Insights and illusions of philosophy*. New York: World, 1971.

Piaget, J. Intellectual evolution from adolescence to adulthood. *Human Development*, 1972, *15*, 1–12.

Piaget, J. *Understanding causality*. New York: Norton, 1974.

Piaget, J., & Inhelder, B. *The psychology of the child*. New York: Basic Books, 1969.

Piaget, J., & Inhelder, B. *Mental imagery in the child*. New York: Basic Books, 1971.

Piaget, J., & Inhelder, B. *Memory and intelligence*. New York: Basic Books, 1973.

Podd, M. H. Ego identity status and morality: The relationship between two developmental constructs. *Developmental Psychology*, 1972, *6*, 497–507.

Pufall, P. B. Induction of linear-order concepts: A comparison of three training techniques. *Child Development*, 1973, *44*, 642–645.

Rabbitt, P. M. Age and discrimination between complex stimuli. In A. T. Welford & J. E. Birren (Eds.), *Behavior, aging, and the nervous system*. Springfield, Ill.: Charles C Thomas, 1965.

Rajalakshmi, R., & Reeves, M. Changes in tachistoscopic form perception as a function of age and intellectual status. *Journal of Gerontology,* 1963, *19,* 270–278.

Rand, G. Some Copernican views of the city. *Architectural Forum,* 1969, *132,* 77–81.

Reese, H. W. The development of memory: Life-span perspectives. In H. W. Reese (Ed.), *Advances in child development and behavior* (Vol. 11). New York: Academic Press, 1976.

Reese, H. W., & Overton, W. F. Models of development and theories of development. In L. R. Goulet & P. B. Baltes (Eds.), *Life-span developmental psychology: Research and theory.* New York: Academic Press, 1970.

Renner, J. W., Stafford, D. G., Lawson, A. E., McKinnon, J. W., Friot, F. E., & Kellogg, D. H. *Research, teaching, and learning with the Piaget model.* Norman: University of Oklahoma Press, 1976.

Rest, J., Cooper, D., Coder, R., Masonz, J., & Anderson, D. Judging the important issues in moral dilemmas: An objective measure of development. *Developmental Psychology,* 1974, *10*(4), 491–501.

Rest, J., Turiel, E., & Kohlberg, L. Relations between level of moral judgment and preference and comprehension of the moral judgment of others. *Journal of Personality,* 1969, *37,* 225–252.

Rogers, C. R. *Client-centered therapy: Its current practice, implications, and theory.* Boston: Houghton Mifflin, 1951.

Rubin, K. H. Decentration skills in institutionalized and noninstitutionalized elderly. *Proceedings of the 81st Annual Convention of the American Psychological Association,* 1973, *8,* 759–760.

Rubin, K. H., & Schneider, F. W. The relationship between moral judgment, egocentrism, and altruistic behaviour. *Child Development,* 1973, *44,* 661–665.

Salapatek, P. H., & Kessen, W. Visual scanning of triangles by the human newborn. *Journal of Experimental Child Psychology,* 1966, *3,* 155–167.

Selman, R. L. Stages of role-taking and moral judgment as guides to social interaction. In T. Lickona (Ed.), *A handbook of moral development.* New York: Holt, Rinehart & Winston, 1976.

Selman, R. L., & Byrne, D. F. A structural-developmental analysis of levels of role taking in middle childhood. *Child Development,* 1974, *45,* 803–806.

Senn, M. J. E. Insights on the child development movement in the United States. *Monographs of the Society for Research in Child Development,* 1975, *40*(3–4, Serial No. 161).

Shantz, C. U. The development of social cognition. In E. M. Hetherington (Ed.), *Review of child development research* (Vol. 5). Chicago: University of Chicago Press, 1975.

Shapiro, B. J., & O'Brien, T. C. Logical thinking in children aged six through thirteen. *Child Development,* 1970, *41,* 823–829.

Shapiro, D. *Neurotic styles.* New York: Basic Books, 1965.

Sheeny, G. *Passages: Predictable crises of adult life.* New York: Dutton, 1976.

Shepard, J. L. Compensation and combinatorial systems in the acquisition and generalization of conservation. *Child Development,* 1974, *45,* 717–730.

Shepard, R., & Metzler, J. Mental rotation of three-dimensional objects. *Science,* 1971, *171,* 701–703.

Shipley, E. *An experimental exploration of the Piagetian class-inclusion task. Technical Report 18: The acquisition of linguistic structure.* Unpublished manuscript, University of Pennsylvania, 1971.

Siegel, L. S. Development of the concept of seriation. *Developmental Psychology,* 1972, *6*(1), 135–137.

Sigel, I. E. How intelligence tests limit understanding of intelligence. *Merrill-Palmer Quarterly*, 1963, *9*, 39–56.

Sigel, I. E., Anderson, L. M., & Shapiro, M. Categorization behavior of lower- and middle-class Negro preschool children: Differences in dealing with representation of familiar objects. *Journal of Negro Education*, Summer 1966, 218–229.

Sigel, I. E., & Olmstead, P. Modification of cognitive skills among lower-class Black children. In J. Hellmuth (Ed.), *Disadvantaged children. Volume 3: Compensatory education—A national debate.* New York: Brunner/Mazel, 1970.

Sigel, I. E., Roeper, A., & Hooper, F. H. A training procedure for acquisition of Piaget's conservation of quantity: A pilot study and its replication. *The British Journal of Educational Psychology*, 1966, *36*, 301–311.

Silverman, I. W., & Geiringer, E. Dyadic interaction and conservation induction: A test of Piaget's equilibration model. *Child Development*, 1973, *44*, 815–820.

Silverman, I. W., & Stone, J. Modifying cognitive functioning through participation in a problem solving group. *Journal of Educational Psychology*, 1972, *63*, 603–608.

Skinner, B. F. *About behaviorism.* New York: Knopf, 1974.

Slobin, D. I., & Welsh, C. A. Elicited imitation as a research tool in developmental psycholinguistics. In C. Ferguson & D. I. Slobin (Eds.), *Studies of child language development.* New York: Holt, Rinehart & Winston, 1973.

Smedslund, J. The acquisition of conservation of substance and weight in children. VI: Practice on continuous versus discontinuous material in conflict situations without external reinforcement. *Scandinavian Journal of Psychology*, 1961, *2*, 203–210.

Snelbecker, G. E. *Learning theory, instructional theory and psychoeducational design.* New York: McGraw-Hill, 1974.

Spivack, G., & Shure, M. B. *Social adjustment of young children: A cognitive approach to solving real-life problems.* San Francisco: Jossey-Bass, 1974.

Strauss, S., & Rimalt, I. Effects of organizational disequilibrium training on structural elaboration. *Developmental Psychology*, 1974, *10*, 526–533.

Szafran, J. Changes with age and with exclusion of vision in performance at an aiming task. *Quarterly Journal of Experimental Psychology*, 1951, *3*, 111–118.

Talland, G. A. Three estimates of the word span and their stability over the adult years. *Quarterly Journal of Experimental Psychology*, 1965, *17*, 301–307.

Troll, L. E. *Early and middle adulthood: The best is yet to be—maybe.* Monterey, Calif.: Brooks/Cole, 1975.

Underwood, B. J. *Experimental psychology.* New York: Appleton-Century-Crofts, 1949.

Verville, E., & Cameron, N. Age and sex differences in the perception of incomplete pictures by adults. *Journal of Genetic Psychology*, 1946, *68*, 149–157.

Vief, G., & Gonda, J. *Cognitive strategy training and intellectual performance in the elderly.* Unpublished manuscript, University of Wisconsin, 1975.

Vurpillot, E. The development of scanning strategies and their relation to visual differentiation. *Journal of Experimental Child Psychology*, 1968, *6*, 37–54.

Vygotsky, L. S. *Thought and language.* Cambridge, Mass.: M.I.T. Press, 1962.

Wallace, J. G. Some studies of perception in relation to age. *British Journal of Psychology*, 1956, *47*, 283–297.

Wallach, L., Wall, A. J., & Anderson, L. Number conservation: The role of reversibility, addition, subtraction and misleading perceptual cues. *Child Development*, 1967, *38*, 425–442.

Wallach, M. A. Research on children's thinking. In H. Stevenson (Ed.), *Child psychology: 62nd yearbook NSSE*. Chicago: University of Chicago Press, 1963.

Watson, J. B., & Rayner, R. Conditioned emotional reactions. *Journal of Experimental Psychology*, 1920, *3*, 1–14.

Watson, J. S. Memory and "contingency analysis" in infant learning. *Merrill-Palmer Quarterly*, 1967, *13*, 19–22.

Werner, H. *Comparative psychology of mental development*. New York: International Universities Press, 1948.

Werner, H., & Kaplan, B. *Symbol formation: An organismic-developmental approach to language and the expression of thought*. New York: Wiley, 1963.

Werner, H., & Kaplan, E. The acquisition of word meanings: A developmental study. *Monographs of the Society for Research in Child Development*, 1952, *15*(1, Whole No. 51).

Wertheimer, M. Psychomotor coordination of auditory and visual space at birth. *Science*, 1961, *134*, 1962.

Weston, H. C. The effect of age and illumination upon visual performance with close sights. *British Journal of Ophthalmology*, 1948, *32*, 64–65.

White, C. B. Moral development in Bahamian school children: A cross-cultural examination of Kohlberg's stages of moral reasoning. *Developmental Psychology*, 1975, *11*(4), 535–536.

White, R. W. Motivation reconsidered: The concept of competence. *Psychological Review*, 1959, *66*, 297–333.

White, S. H. Evidence for a hierarchical arrangement of learning processes. In L. P. Lipsitt & C. C. Spiker (Eds.), *Advances in child development and behavior* (Vol. 2). New York: Academic Press, 1965.

Whiteman, M., & Peisach, E. Perceptual and sensorimotor supports for conservation tasks. *Developmental Psychology*, 1970, *2*, 247–256.

Whorf, B. L. Science and linguistics. In J. B. Carroll (Ed.), *Language, thought, and reality: Selected writings of Benjamin Lee Whorf*. Cambridge, Mass.: M.I.T. Press, 1956.

Winer, G. A. An analysis of verbal facilitation of class-inclusion reasoning. *Child Development*, 1974, *45*, 224–227.

Witkin, H. A., Dyk, R. B., Faterson, H. B., Goodenough, D. R., & Karp, S. A. *Psychological differentiation*. New York: Wiley, 1962.

Wohlwill, J. F. Responses to class-inclusion questions for verbally and pictorially present items. *Child Development*, 1968, *39*, 449–465.

Yonas, A., & Pick, H. L., Jr. An approach to the study of infant space perception. In L. B. Cohen & P. Salapatek (Eds.), *Infant perception: From sensation to cognition. Volume 2: Perception of space, speech, and sound*. New York: Academic Press, 1975.

Zaporozhets, A. V., & Elkonin, D. B. (Eds.). *The psychology of preschool children*. Cambridge, Mass.: M.I.T. Press, 1971.

Zigler, E. Metatheoretical issues in developmental psychology. In M. Marx (Ed.), *Theories in contemporary psychology*. New York: Macmillan, 1963.

Zimmerman, B. J., & Rosenthal, T. L. Conserving and retaining equalities and inequalities through observation and correction. *Developmental Psychology*, 1974, *10*, 260–268.

Name Index

Subject Index